SpringerBriefs in Environment, Security, Development and Peace

Migration Studies

Volume 17

Series editor

Hans Günter Brauch

For further volumes:
http://www.springer.com/series/11825
http://www.afes-press-books.de/html/SpringerBriefs_ESDP_MiS.htm

Premjai Vungsiriphisal · Dares Chusri
Supang Chantavanich
Editors

Humanitarian Assistance for Displaced Persons from Myanmar

Royal Thai Government Policy and Donor, INGO, NGO and UN Agency Delivery

Springer

Chulalongkorn University
INSTITUTE OF ASIAN STUDIES CHULALONGKORN UNIVERSITY
Asian Research Center for Migration

Editors
Premjai Vungsiriphisal
Dares Chusri
Supang Chantavanich
Asian Research Center for Migration
Chulalongkorn University
Bangkok
Thailand

ISSN 2193-3162 ISSN 2193-3170 (electronic)
ISBN 978-3-319-02794-4 ISBN 978-3-319-02795-1 (eBook)
DOI 10.1007/978-3-319-02795-1
Springer Cham Heidelberg New York Dordrecht London

Library of Congress Control Number: 2013951794

Printed on acid-free paper

Springer is part of Springer Science+Business Media (www.springer.com)

Other Books by the Asian Research Center for Migration Chulalongkorn University Bangkok, Thailand in this Book Series Published by Springer

Yongyuth Chalamwong, Naruemon Thabchumpon and Supang Chantavanich, (Eds.): *Temporary Shelters and Surrounding Communities—Livelihood Opportunities, the Labour Market, Social Welfare and Social Security*. SpringerBriefs in Environment, Security, Development and Peace, vol. 15—Migration Studies Subseries No. 2 (Cham–Heidelberg–Dordrecht–London–New York: Springer-Verlag, 2014).

Suwattana Thadaniti and Supang Chantavanich (Eds.): *The Impact of Displaced People's Temporary Shelters on their Surrounding Environment*. SpringerBriefs in Environment, Security, Development and Peace, vol. 16—Migration Studies Subseries No. 3 (Cham–Heidelberg–Dordrecht–London–New York: Springer-Verlag, 2014).

Ben Harkins and Supang Chantavanich (Eds.) in cooperation with Nawita Direkwut and Aungkana Kamonpetch: *Resettlement of Displaced Persons on the Thai-Myanmar Border*. SpringerBriefs in Environment, Security, Development and Peace, vol. 18—Migration Studies Subseries No. 5 (Cham–Heidelberg–Dordrecht–London–New York: Springer-Verlag, 2014).

Acknowledgments

The research team for Part I of this analysis of Royal Thai Government Policy towards displaced persons from Myanmar wishes to thank the displaced persons who reside in the nine temporary shelters in Thailand. Despite the fact that they are living with an uncertain future and little hope of return to their homeland, they still show their spirit and tolerance to visitors, including several visits of the research teams of this project. We hope this study may bring some changes to their lives. Without them, this research is meaningless. Our gratitude also goes to district officers and territorial defence security corps in the study areas, officers of the Royal Thai Government, especially the Operating Centre for Displaced Persons, Foreign Affairs Division to the Interior and Provincial Administration Office, Ministry of Interior, Office of National Security Council, Ministry of Foreign Affairs, Border Affairs Department, Office of the Supreme Commander, for their everlasting support in our inquiries. Also, we would like to express our appreciation to all staff of the humanitarian organisations working in the shelters for their spirit and hard work under limitations.

Further, we have to thank the United Nations Development Programme and European Union for their support to make this research possible, and our thanks also go to Dr. Supang Chantavanich for her decision to undertake this project, and the staff of the Asian Research Centre for Migration for their support for this research.

The research team for Part II wishes to acknowledge the inputs provided by key informants, including displaced persons and local authorities from Tham Hin, Mae La and Ban Mai Nai Soi shelters, the Thai Ministry of Interior, various NGOs, WHO, EU and Bangkok-based Embassies including those of Australia, Belgium, Canada, Denmark, The Netherlands, New Zealand, Norway, Switzerland, UK and USA.

The research team would like to thank the Asian Research Centre for Migration, specifically Prof. Dr. Supang Chantavanich, the Director, for providing the opportunity for our team to engage in this project. The research team also is thankful to the European Union and the United Nations Development Programme for their management and technical support of this study.

The Co-editors would like to thank the *Springer Briefs in Environment, Security, Development and Peace*, the Language Editor Graham Bennett, the book Series and Copy Editor PD Dr. Hans Günter Brauch, to Dr. Johanna Schwarz,

Ms. Agata Oelschlaeger, Ms. Janet Sterritt of Springer's editorial office in Heidelberg, Germany and to Springer's book production team in Chennai in India.

The views and opinions expressed herein are those of the authors and do not necessarily reflect the official position of UNDP or the other organisations mentioned in this report.

Bangkok, August 2013

Premjai Vungsiriphisal
Dares Chusri
Supang Chantavanich

Contents

Abbreviations

AFPFL	Anti-Fascist Peoples League
ARC	American Refugee Committee
ASEAN	Association of South East Asian Nations
AUP	Aid to Uprooted People
BPP	Border Patrol Police Bureau
CAN	Community Agriculture and Nutrition
CBO	Community-Based Organisations
CCSDPT	Committee for Coordination of Services to Displaced Persons in Thailand
COERR	Catholic Office for Emergency Relief and Refugees
CPA	Comprehensive Plan of Action
CPB	Communist Party of Burma
CRC	Convention on the Rights of the Child
DFID	UK Department for International Development
DKBA	Democratic Karen Buddhist Army
DPA	Department of Provincial Administration
DP	Displaced Persons
EC	European Commission
ECHO	European Community Humanitarian Aid Department
FSP	Further Study Program
GHD	Good Humanitarian Donorship
IDP	Internally Displaced Person
IGOs	International Governmental Organisations
IOM	International Organisation for Migration
IRC	International Rescue Committee
KHRG	Karen Human Rights Group
KNPP	Karenni National Progressive Party
KnRC	Karenni Refugee Committee
KNU	Karen National Union
KRC	Karen Refugee Committee
KWO	Karen Women's Organisation

LAC	Legal Aid Centre
LMTC	Leadership and Management Training College
MOD	Ministry of Defence
MOE	Ministry of Education
MOF	Ministry of Finance
MOFA	Ministry of Foreign Affairs
MOI	Ministry of Interior
MOPH	Ministry of Public Health
MOSHS	Ministry of Human Security and Social Development
NGO	Non-governmental Organisation
NLD	National League for Democracy
NSC	National Security Council
OCDP	Operation Centre for Displaced Person
PAB	Provincial Admissions Board
POC	Persons of Concern
PRS	Protracted Refugee Situation
RSD	Refugee Status Determination
RTG	Royal Thai Government
SEP	Special English Program
SGBV	Sexual and Gender-Based Violence
SSA	Shan State Army
TBBC	Thailand Burma Border Consortium
TDSC	Territorial Defence Security Corps
UN	United Nations
UNDP	United Nations Development Program
UNHCR	United Nations High Commissioner for Refugees
WEAVE	Women's Education for Advancement and Empowerment
WHO	World Health Organisation
ZOA	ZuidOostAzie/Refugee Care for The Netherlands

Executive Summary: Part I

More than 1,00,000 displaced persons from Myanmar exist in nine temporary settlements on the Thai side of the border with Myanmar in a *protracted refugee situation* which has persisted for more than 25 years. The Royal Thai Government (RTG), which is not a signatory to the 1951 UN Convention on the Rights of Refugees, uses its own terminology to describe those who have fled persecution and conflict in Myanmar; hence *displaced persons* rather than refugees. There has always been some low-level flow of displaced persons into Thailand from Myanmar, mostly absorbed by local populations who often had familial and ethnic links. However, the upsurge of fighting in Myanmar after 1984, and especially following the uprising in 1988 and the ignoring of the overwhelming electoral victory of Aung San SuuKyi's National League for Democracy in 1990, led to much larger numbers of displaced persons crossing the border. The RTG finally made the decision to consolidate the large number of small, informal settlements into the nine formal settlements that now exist, eventually giving permission for non-governmental organisations (NGOs) to take on the practical administration of the settlements, and to involve UNHCR in the screening of asylum seekers.

RTG policy has been largely responsive to the displaced persons issue, rather than proactive, and it still has no formal asylum law. This has led to practical difficulties in dealing with the displaced persons, and has also enabled the RTG to maintain an apparent ambivalence to the situation in public. In particular, the RTG has maintained that the displaced persons are a national security issue, which has led to reluctance to consider certain solutions. The displaced persons issue has been made more complex by the 2 million migrant workers from Myanmar in Thailand, and by the RTG's strategic relationship with the government of Myanmar. The lack of clear and open policy on the displaced persons has meant that they are usually considered first and foremost as potential illegal immigrants; they have been given long-term sanctuary and protection from *refoulement*, but within closed settlements which have created conditions of dependence and have severely limited self-reliance in contrast to international standards on treatment of refugees.

The internal factors influencing the RTG policy include concern for security of its sovereignty, local resistance, negative public attitude and other issues that remain difficult to resolve. Externally, the relationship with Myanmar, and

Thailand's commitment to various international conventions, impact on policy towards displaced persons.

The displaced persons express relative satisfaction with the treatment they have received in Thailand, and in areas such as healthcare they have done better than some Thai communities. In other areas, such as education, income generation and access to justice, the displaced persons have faced restrictions, though the RTG has improved practice in these areas as its policy response has developed and evolved through experience and external scrutiny.

However, a permanent solution remains elusive. Of the standard *durable* approaches, resettlement has been the most successful, with over 64,000 displaced persons going to third party countries such as the USA and various countries in the EU. Resettlement was initially opposed by the RTG as representing a *pull factor* for new displaced persons, and the displaced persons themselves are divided in opinion; younger, better educated displaced persons are more positive, but others cite loss of family ties and the permanent exclusion from their homeland as being negative factors. It is also clear that resettlement has not reduced the settlement populations; resettled displaced persons have been replaced by new displaced persons. It is also for the reason of avoiding the creation of another pull factor that the RTG opposes local integration, pointing to the half million internally displaced people (IDPs) allegedly in the border areas of Myanmar who are potential displaced persons. Thai public opinion is also largely rather negative.

All stakeholders agree, however, that Myanmar is a long way from being safe for voluntary repatriation, the third of the durable solutions. Ethnic conflict continues, and the reasons for the original exodus remain. This study concludes that each solution could play some part, but none will provide a definitive solution. Instead, it is proposed that an approach puts the emphasis on the displaced persons in the long term returning to Myanmar, and gives a framework for the shorter term *self-reliance* strategies that then become clearly a part of developing displaced persons for a life in Myanmar. Repatriation remains the goal amongst displaced persons themselves, but many have lost hope that it is possible. The current study notes the potential for political change in Myanmar now, which has never been greater in the past 20 years: the release of Aung San SuuKyi, the increased dialogue between the RTG and the government of Myanmar after the admittedly flawed 2010 election, the increasingly willingness of ASEAN countries to pursue careful engagement with Myanmar. All these and other factors point to Myanmar having to open up and change. However, this study notes that this will indeed be a long-term process that requires active engagement of all international and regional actors to keep it on course. This will mean, for example, real momentum from ASEAN, and positive moves by the UN and others in development and trade with Myanmar, providing leverage on human rights with the aim of making Myanmar, or at least significant parts of it, safe for return. It will mean, ultimately, change from those in power in Myanmar; but it could be that concessions will need to come first from the international community.

It also means, the study points out, that the RTG will need to continue to reduce the restrictions on the displaced persons, for instance on freedom of movement.

Areas such as education and income generation will also need to develop; but within the *self-reliance pending repatriation and resettlement* framework. The resettlement programme will need to continue; and some local integration offered to some segments of the displaced person population by the RTG will help.

Ultimately, the study concludes that making Myanmar a safe place for return, and effectively addressing the root causes of the flow of displaced persons, is the only solution to this protracted problem that can succeed and is truly durable in nature. Life can be made more fulfilling and productive for the displaced persons in the interim; but their voluntary repatriation, when conditions are right, is the only way the problem will be definitively and satisfactorily solved.

Executive Summary: Part II

This part analyses the role of donors, international organisations and non-government organisations (NGOs) in dealing with Burmese displaced persons in Thailand. It examines the rationale behind international intervention, funding policies and organisational mandates; implementation strategies and the dynamics of cooperation among stakeholders including the Royal Thai Government (RTG); as well as the operating environment and impacts of this for effective intervention. Findings will be applied to facilitate the design of an improved strategy to implement policy and to advocate for a change in policy towards sustainable and long-term solutions for the protracted refugee situation along the Thai–Myanmar border.

Qualitative and quantitative approaches are applied in this research. A field study was conducted from June 2010 to January 2011 using a combination of key informant interviews with donor and NGO staff and RTG officials, as well as focus group discussions and structured questionnaires with 444 shelter residents at three purposively selected temporary shelters of Tham Hin, Mae La and Ban Mai Nai Soi.

This protracted refugee situation of more than 25 years has its root causes in human rights violations due to internal conflict in Myanmar between ethnic minority groups and the Myanmar government which have been ongoing with no sign of peaceful, mutual agreement since 1984. This study identifies a series of issues in the interplay of various stakeholders and makes recommendations for improved cooperation as they attempt to find durable solutions to this displaced people situation.

Responsibility for displaced persons is not borne by a single body but shared among the RTG, donors and international and other NGOs. These bodies work in differing capacities based on their own mandate, mission and policy, and it is unsurprising to find differences in approach and practice. These differences are predominately based on stakeholders' consideration of the current situation as an *emergency* or otherwise and their resultant policy approach to serving immediate basic needs versus providing opportunities for self-reliance. These gaps sometimes hinder effective cooperation between stakeholders.

Restrictive RTG policy on displaced persons is premised upon temporary asylum and eventual repatriation. The focus on preventing new influxes and restriction of movement has increased displaced persons' dependence on external assistance and limited opportunity for self-determination. The RTG should consider the current situation and explore ways to adopt international law to support displaced persons' self-reliance and provide suggestions or recommendations on the feasibility of project operations. The result of pre-screening pilot projects in four temporary shelters in 2009 should be disclosed soon to demonstrate public accountability. The Provincial Admissions Board (PAB) system should be reactivated as a priority to work more effectively in screening and determining displaced persons status so that new asylum seekers can access protection and basic needs and services, including resettlement options in a timely manner.

There is also a gap in the donor–host government relationship that may affect cooperation to deliver durable solutions. There is a lack of effective communication among donor groups themselves, between donors and RTG, and donors and NGOs prohibiting information sharing and coordination processes.

In some cases the long-term provision of support with little or no progress has created a situation of donor fatigue. Donor aid policy has been gradually shifting towards linking relief and development since 2007. The inability of donors to commit to multiyear funding and the realignment of policy from emergency aid to a developmental model yield many challenges. Some donor countries are still recovering from economic crises and trends are revealing disaster response to be the priority of humanitarian assistance. All these factors may contribute to funding shortages and also affect food security for displaced persons in temporary shelters.

Most NGO programme activities are also increasingly developmentally focused. Again, yearly funding prohibits long-term development plans and the ability to fill specific funding gaps to provide opportunities for displaced persons self-reliance. However, displaced persons are engaged in many aspects of camp and project management. Pilot projects on vocational training and agriculture are underway in most camps, though most are small scale and close monitoring and evaluation of these initiatives is necessary to ensure accountability and viability of expansion.

Donors should approach displacement holistically, in both the original and host countries and in both the emergency and development phases. Cross-border programmes should work to support people in need internally in Myanmar and prevent the movement of new asylum seekers across the Thai–Myanmar border.

UNHCR and CCSDPT have developed a 5-year strategic plan to provide direction to durable solutions for displaced persons. It is a selective strategy that tends to focus on local integration rather than a comprehensive package of solutions including resettlement, local integration and repatriation. Negotiation and dialogue to bring durable peace to Myanmar must be facilitated by the RTG through ASEAN and UNHCR through the UN General Assembly.

Agreement on policy direction must also be reached in relation to resettlement; whether to sustain or end the programme if it is seen to create pull factors or a brain-drain. If resettlement continues to be a viable and desired option, an implementation action plan and ongoing advocacy with third party countries are needed.

More channels for communication in an environment which fosters trust are necessary. UNHCR and CCSDPT should facilitate coordination, consultation and collaboration with donors and high level RTG representatives to obtain mutual agreement on development strategies for displaced persons, particularly the development of economic self-sufficiency which must be a common goal of all partners. Definition of strategies such as *local integration* will improve understanding of the nature and extent of self-reliance and interventions. Moreover, the concepts of *responsibility sharing* or *partnership principles* may create a more positive working environment, in contrast to *burden sharing* or *burden shifting*.

By drawing on themes raised by displaced persons and RTG, donor and I/NGO stakeholders in field research, this study provides practical and realistic recommendations for policy options to reach durable solution for displaced persons in temporary shelters along Thai–Myanmar border.

Part I
Analysis of the Royal Thai Government Policy Towards Displaced Persons from Myanmar

Chapter 1
Introduction

Premjai Vungsiriphisal, Graham Bennett, Chanarat Poomkacha, Waranya Jitpong and Kamonwan Reungsamran

Abstract The nature of the displaced persons issue, in particular its protracted nature, is outlined, including a brief summary of its origins. The research objectives are stated, along with key questions, and the study framework is presented. The methodology, using a mixture of quantitative and qualitative approaches, is outlined, together with an explanation of the sampling used to identify respondents to the survey. The phases of the issue, and the different approaches that have been applied, are charted, from the original establishment of the camps and provision of humanitarian aid, to the current situation where donor fatigue and the continued confinement of more than 100,000 people demands a solution.

Keywords Burmese refugees · Displaced persons · Thai refugee policy · Myanmar · Ethnic conflict · Aung San Suu Kyi · Research objectives

---

P. Vungsiriphisal (✉) · G. Bennett · C. Poomkacha · W. Jitpong · K. Reungsamran
Asian Research Center for Migration, Institute of Asian Studies, Chulalongkorn University, 3rd floor, Prachadhipok Rambhai-Barni Building, Bangkok 10330, Thailand
e-mail: premjai.v@chula.ac.th

G. Bennett
e-mail: grahambennett777@hotmail.co.uk

C. Poomkacha
e-mail: cpoomkacha@abeam.com

W. Jitpong
e-mail: wec135@hotmail.com

K. Reungsamran
e-mail: kamonwan24@yahoo.com

P. Vungsiriphisal et al. (eds.), *Humanitarian Assistance for Displaced Persons from Myanmar*, SpringerBriefs in Environment, Security, Development and Peace 17,
DOI: 10.1007/978-3-319-02795-1_1,

1.1 Statement of the Problem

The situation of Burmese asylum seekers in Thailand, or *displaced persons* as the Royal Thai Government (RTG) has termed them under its own policy, has become one of the most protracted in the world today. The reasons for the original flows of the groups largely remain; the Burmese Army continues to clash with the armed ethnic groups of the border regions, continuing to make life very difficult for the communities of Karens, Karenni, Mon, Shan and other ethnic communities, whether it be by enforcing slave labour, forced relocation or denying the conditions needed to pursue a viable economic existence. Real democracy and justice in Myanmar remain elusive.

The flow of those seeking refuge from fighting and oppression in Myanmar gathered pace in the early 1980s, and included those political activists who escaped the crackdown by the Myanmar authorities following the democracy uprising in 1988, and the result of which was ignored a widely acknowledged Aung San SuuKyi's victory of 1990 general election. The upturn in fighting in 1995 onward on the Thai–Myanmar border again led to influx of new displaced persons, and the population of the settlements reached somewhere between 100,000 with steady annual flows. In January 2011, the registered population in nine shelters was 97,956, with addition of an approximate 50,000 unregistered people who are waiting for their status to be determined.

Since the beginning, the shelters have operated a confinement policy, reflecting the RTG's concern with the security of its national sovereignty in relation to the flows of displacement from Myanmar. However, the last several years have seen a significant shift in many aspects of the policy. The RTG and UNHCR have established more formalised engagement procedures for reception, status determination, and registering of displaced persons in the camps, as well as providing a legal aid centre and permitting the execution of a large-scale third country resettlement programme. Additionally, access to education has been expanded beyond basic levels and there has been increased cooperation between governmental and humanitarian organisations to provide vocational training as well as expanded opportunities for income generating activities within the camps (Adelman 2008).

However, movement and employment for displaced persons outside of the shelters is still officially prohibited. The negative impacts of restricting the displaced persons to the shelter environment for the past two decades with limited social and livelihood opportunities have been well documented. The incidence of domestic and sexual violence (UNHCR 2005a, b, c), psychological problems, unplanned pregnancies and a variety of other social problems have occurred in the shelters. Additionally, dependency on external assistance has begun to take a toll on the displaced persons' capabilities for future self-sufficiency outside of the shelters. The attempt to increase displaced persons' self-reliance as stated in the CCSDPT/UNHCR Comprehensive Plan (CCSDPT/UNHCR 2007) has not yet seen any progress.

At the same time, the RTG has to balance the need of its own citizens for resource usage, land use, degradation of natural resources, and expenses associated with playing host to a large group of displaced persons, including national security concerns, and the personnel commitments necessary to provide safe asylum in the shelters. The current policy was formulated in a reactive process and was never intended to be implemented on more than a temporary basis which points towards the need to reassess the current situation and reformulate the policy approach with the assistance of the relevant government authorities (Sciortino/Punpuing 2009).

This study aims to analyse the current policies of the RTG towards displaced persons in order to provide empirical evidence of the factors that contribute to the formulation and development of the existing policy. The findings will serve as the groundwork for stakeholders including RTG, UNHCR, other UN agencies, humanitarian agencies and displaced persons themselves to work for the formulation of more solution-oriented policy and improvement of the current displaced persons situation.

1.2 Research Objectives, Study Framework and Study Areas

1.2.1 Research Objectives

1. Analyse the historical development of RTG policies towards displaced persons from Myanmar
2. Analyse the impact of current policies towards displaced persons from Myanmar and other stakeholders, including gender-based differences in affect
3. Determine the internal and external factors that influence the existing RTG policies towards displaced persons from Myanmar
4. Analyse the interventions by donors, NGOs, and international organisations and the RTG's policy response
5. Explore alternative policy options towards displaced persons from Myanmar which would provide a more sustainable and solutions-oriented approach including identifying obstacles to a shift in policy.

1.2.2 Study Framework

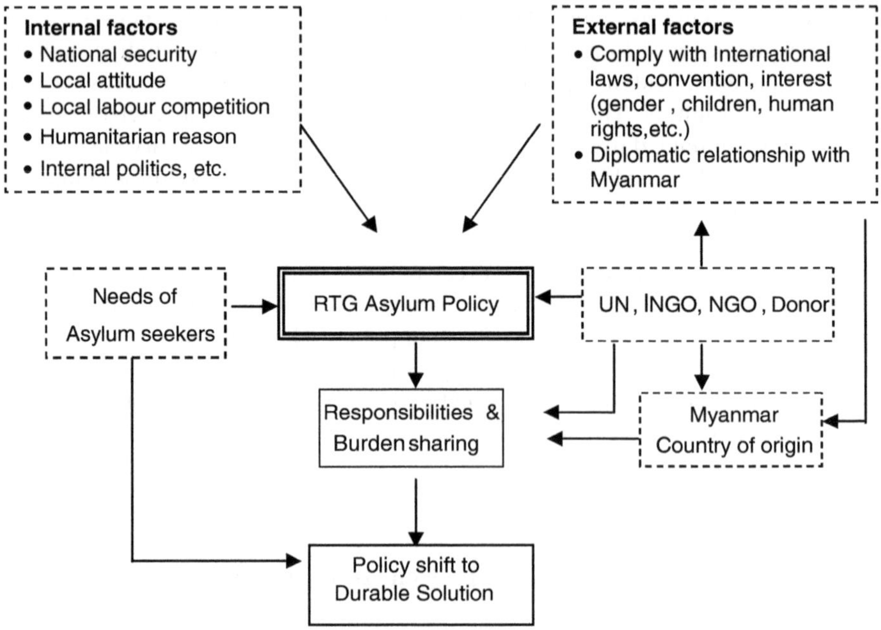

Fig. 1.1 Study framework. *Source* The Authors

1.3 Methodology

The research methodology uses several qualitative research techniques including desk review, key informant interview, focus groups interview and quantitative technique for baseline survey. The qualitative data has been collected at national and operational levels to achieve the understanding of the formulation of RTG asylum policy, constraints and its impact.

- National level—interviews with RTG Key Informants have been conducted at national levels including officers from Ministry of Interior, Ministry of Foreign Affairs, Ministry of Defence, Ministry of Education, Ministry of Human Security and Social Affairs, Ministry of Public Health, Ministry of Justice, National Security Council, staff of UN agencies.
- Operational level—interviews include district officers such as camp commanders, territorial defence security corps, local administration officers, displaced persons, staff of humanitarian organisations.

Also, along with the quantitative interview for baseline survey, several focus group discussions (FGD) with displaced persons have been conducted to gather in-depth or sensitive and additional information to the baseline survey. In order to cover all possible variation, the selection criteria for sampling included 18 years and above, gender, ethnic, religions, registered status, applicant for resettlement and non applicant, to select the respondents. The sampling size is randomly selected according to these.

To specify the samplings size, each team applied Taro Yamane formula as follows:

$$n = \frac{N}{1 + e^2 N}$$

where N = Element of population, in this study was 145,786, e = Error of sampling, in this study was 5 % or 0.05 proportion, n = sample size

$$n = \frac{145{,}786}{1 + 145{,}786(0.05)^2}$$

Sample size = 400 displaced persons for each team

The total sampling has been distributed according to the population of selected study areas. The actual sampling comes up to 444 respondents to cover some missing responses but all can be used for analysis. The sampling sizes are broken down as follows:

Temporary shelters	Sampling size
ThamHin	113
Mae La	218
Ban Mai NaiSoi	113
Total	444

The survey was carried out using a structured questionnaire in three selected areas: Ban Mai NaiSoi shelter, Muang District, Mae Hong Son Province; Mae La shelter, Thasongyang District, Tak Province; and ThamHin shelter, SuanPueng District, Rachaburi Province. These three areas were selected purposively to cover all major ethnicities, as well as the size of the shelters. The interviews were announced publicly, respondent displaced persons participated in the survey voluntary with informed consent, and identities were concealed. The sampling for baseline survey was balanced between male and female respondents. FGDs were separated by gender. Data from baseline survey and qualitative interviews have been analysed and integrated to reflect the needs of displaced persons regarding the impact of RTG policy implementation.

The 444 respondents comprised of 55.4 % female and 44.6 %. The majority 68 % were between 25–59 years, 28.38 % between 18–24 years and the rest 3.38 % over 60 years. Half of the sample was collected from Mae la, the largest shelter, the other half divided between ThamHin and Ban Mai NaiSoi shelters. The respondents comprised 68.47 % married, 27.48 % single and 4.05 % separated or widowed; 56.76 % were registered, 33.3 % non registered and 9.9 % waiting to confirm their status; 48 % were Karen/S'gaw, 18.92 % Karenni, 22.30 % Karen/Po, 4.5 % Burmese, the rest a mix of other ethnicities. The majority has stayed in the shelters between 10–20 years, 56 % were Christian, 31 % Buddhist, 9.01 % Muslim, 3.15 % animist and 0.68 % had another faith. Majority 75 % were literate, 25 % illiterate. Half of the respondents were living with 5–8 family members. Almost half 47.3 % were born in Karen state, 11.26 % from Kayah state, the rest from Kachin, Mon, Shan states born in the settlements in Thailand. Slightly over half engage in employment, income of 48.1 % are between Baht 501–1000.

References

Adelman, H. (Ed.) 2008: *Protracted Displacement in Asia* (Aldershot: Ashgate).

CCSDPT/UNHCR, 2007: *Comprehensive Plan 2007/8: A Comprehensive Plan Addressing the Needs of Displaced Persons on the Thailand/Myanmar (Burma) Border* (Bangkok: UNHCR/CCSDPT).

Sciortino, R.; Punpuing, S., 2009: *International Migration in Thailand 2009* (Bangkok: IOM).

UNHCR, 2005a: *Handbook for Planning and Implementing Development Assistance for Refugees (DAR) Programmes: Overview of Part I: Main Concepts and Issues, Module One and Two.* http://www.unhcr.org/44c4854b2.html.

UNHCR, 2005b: *Handbook for Self-reliance: Book 1—Why self-reliance?* http://www.unhcr.org/44bf3e252.html.

UNHCR, 2005c: *Refugee Status Determination Identifying who is a refugee: self study module 2* (Geneva: UNHCR). http://www.unhcr.org/43144dc52.html.

Chapter 2
Literature Review

Premjai Vungsiriphisal, Graham Bennett, Chanarat Poomkacha, Waranya Jitpong and Kamonwan Reungsamran

Abstract Key sources are reviewed, outlining both the history and development of the displaced persons issue on the Thai–Myanmar border, especially its protracted nature, and the evolution of the RTG's policy and practice towards displaced persons. The complex reasons for the RTG's ambivalence on this issue are charted, including concerns over national security and the relationship with the Myanmar government. The Literature on the standard durable solutions, resettlement, local integration and repatriation, is examined, including the application of these approaches in Thailand.

Keywords Displaced persons · Burmese refugees · Persons of concern · Local integration · Repatriation · Resettlement · Thai refugee policy · Myanmar · Refugee camps

P. Vungsiriphisal (✉) · G. Bennett · C. Poomkacha · W. Jitpong · K. Reungsamran
Asian Research Center for Migration, Institute of Asian Studies, Chulalongkorn University, 3rd floor, Prachadhipok Rambhai-Barni Building, Bangkok 10330, Thailand
e-mail: premjai.v@chula.ac.th

G. Bennett
e-mail: grahambennett777@hotmail.co.uk

C. Poomkacha
e-mail: cpoomkacha@abeam.com

W. Jitpong
e-mail: wec135@hotmail.com

K. Reungsamran
e-mail: kamonwan24@yahoo.com

P. Vungsiriphisal et al. (eds.), *Humanitarian Assistance for Displaced Persons from Myanmar*, SpringerBriefs in Environment, Security, Development and Peace 17,
DOI: 10.1007/978-3-319-02795-1_2,

2.1 Introduction

The political conflict within Myanmar has forced large-scale displacement of a broad mix of ethnic groups across the border into Thailand over two decades. Since their establishment in 1984, documented and undocumented displaced persons residing in nine temporary camps along the Thai–Myanmar border have become one of the largest protracted refugee situations in East Asia (Adelman 2008). The registered shelters population in December 2010, as documented by the UNHCR, was approximately 109,000 and there are estimated to be at least an additional 50,000 unregistered inhabitants in the camps who may or may not meet the criteria established for displaced person status (TBBC 2010a, b).

Thailand possesses a long and vital history of providing shelter to thousands of asylum seekers fleeing from conflict in their home countries. Despite the threats to national security and the challenges faced in hosting hundreds of thousands of foreign citizens, Thai policy has, for the most part, tended to follow the spirit of international humanitarian agreements on the treatment of refugees. While the Royal Thai Government (RTG) has placed concerns for the safety and security of its own citizens at the forefront of its policy, it has allowed displaced persons from Myanmar to reside in Thailand for over 25 years, with organised and effective aid services provided in cooperation with various international NGOs and donors, including UNHCR (TBBC 2004)

2.2 The Implication of the Status of Displaced Persons

Under international law, the conferring of *refugee* status carries with it important obligations for any state that is providing sanctuary. The RTG's insistence on not assigning this status to those fleeing from Myanmar is therefore critical in understanding the current situation.

The context of the broader discourse on refugees is critical to a comprehensive understanding of the RTG's policy towards displaced persons from Myanmar, since Thailand has generally viewed its national policies towards refugees as being something of a special case in the spectrum of humanitarian approaches. The definition of refugee status can be seen to be time-specific, both in terms of describing new situations, and in reflecting the perspective and mandate of the body that is defining the term. The RTG's alternative definitions used for the people fleeing from fighting and political instability from Myanmar are *Displaced Persons fleeing fighting from Myanmar* and *Person of Concern* (POC) (MOI).

Thailand has not ratified the UN convention related to refugee status. In principle, therefore, policy towards displaced persons from Myanmar is governed by national legislation. In practice, Thai policy does, in many ways, reflect and abide by the spirit of the UN convention (Muntarphorn 2004). It is also true that in a number of cases, where countries have ratified the Convention, it has not then been enacted in national law. Also, other countries that have not acceded to the refugee instruments continue to provide refuge for those fleeing persecution and respect the principle of non-refoulement, an international norm for refugee protection.

With a history of more than 30 years of receiving displaced persons onto Thai soil from armed conflicts in Indochina, the response of the RTG to the outflow of people from Myanmar has been shaped by lessons learned from past experiences. One view put forward is that, overwhelmed by refugee inflows from its politically unstable neighbouring countries for decades, reaching a peak of over 1 million Indochinese refugees within Thailand's borders, the RTG has preferred to maintain a large margin of policy discretion in managing refugee flows (Loescher/Milner 2005a, b).

As well as persons who are given refugee status according to the definition given in the 1951 UN Convention, there are other groups of people not in the convention's definition who the United Nations General Assembly and the Secretariat gave the mandate to UNHCR to assist. These are POCs, and include IDPs who are not exiled from their home country, but live effectively as refugees in their own land (Kanyabarn 1998).

In the Thai context, Caouette and Pack identified POCs such as students and other political activists who fled Myanmar following the 1988 crackdown by the government on the pro-democracy movement and who register with the UNHCR and are provided with a degree of financial support and asylum status. Most of this group consists of the approximately 10,000 who fled to the jungle after the government reprisals and who eventually found their way to Bangkok. Due to the continued resistance to the use of the term *refugee* on the part of the RTG, those who are accepted through the standard refugee status determination procedures of the UNHCR are officially termed POCs. Only those who are able to provide proof that they participated in the 1988 demonstrations and who are able to make it to Bangkok to apply in person at the UNHCR offices are eligible for POC status. However, the process can sometimes take several months during which time the applicants must generally support themselves as illegal migrant workers, and sometimes even afterwards, in order to cover daily living expenses (Caouette/Pack 2002).

The National Security Council (NSC) has its own definition, UNHCR-POC, to describe POCs who are assisted by UNHCR according to the UN Convention and any other document or decision of UNHCR and/or the UN. However, from the POC's point of view, even those who are officially recognised as having POC status are forced to live in a tenuous position of personal insecurity in Bangkok, due to the fact that they are still illegal immigrants under Thai law (Colm 2004). The Maneeloy shelter is provided as a *safe area* to these POC from Myanmar but some are refused the right to reside in the shelter or eventually continue their political activities outside the shelter. After the seizing of hostages at the Myanmar Embassy in Bangkok on 1st October 1999, and the chaotic incident in Maneeloy to show their disapproval of the shelter living conditions, their movement has been strictly restricted (Trichot 2003).

Displaced persons in Thailand have been defined as *persons who are not counted as refugees, but due to any reasons, have fled from their habitual residence but have not yet lost their nationality. Their migration into another country is considered illegal under the immigration law of that country* (Chumak/Nualsuwan 1982).

The expanded mandate UNHCR received from the United Nations General Assembly and Economic & Social Council extends assistance to include not only refugees but also displaced persons who fled from their country of nationality or habitual residence for fear of persecution from the same causes as for refugees. These include war, fighting, flooding, earthquake, drought, epidemic or any situation that results in people disorder, external aggression or occupation, foreign domination (Chatsuwan 1983).

As a sovereign state, Thailand has the right not to accede to the UN Convention on the Status of Refugees since the rights of refugees would consume considerable resources from Thailand as a host country. However, since the country has been the first asylum for displaced persons from Myanmar for almost three decades, Thailand has collaborated with humanitarian organisations and UNHCR to provide assistance and protection to these groups for many years, not on the grounds of *refugee* status, but as displaced persons. The Thai Ministry of Interior (MOI) has given the definition of displaced persons as those *who, according to the Immigration Law, illegally immigrate to the national territory due to chaos, fighting or war* (MOI).

The term *displaced persons* also covers various groups of people who have fled from the politically difficult situation in Myanmar: the group of 47,735 displaced persons who fled from Myanmar before 19th March, 1976 who have been registered and permitted to work in restricted areas in Thailand (Cabinet Resolution, March 1992); the group of 55,787 displaced persons, who fled to Thailand from fighting and political instability in Myanmar during 1984–1992, and who are registered with permanent residence in nine border provinces and permission to work; students and opposition groups of Burmese Government, who fled from Myanmar after the 1988 demonstration protest, and have been granted UNHCR POC status (Suntarachoon 1994).

Research done by The Senate Committee on Foreign Affairs in 2004 pointed out that the response of the RTG policy towards the Myanmar displaced persons is mainly a result of economic concerns. The evidence presented showed that, after the Myanmar Government closed the border, the RTG allowed ethnic insurgent forces encamped close to the border to benefit from the resources and hospital services provided for Thai people. As a consequence, the policy of the NSC emphasises resettlement to a third country and repatriation as the preferred options, forbidding local integration because of national security and economic concerns such as the problem of housing ethnic forces in Thai territory, criminal cases, epidemics and contamination and degradation of natural resources such as water and forests.

The policy of the MOI has been intercepting and pushing back the displaced persons immediately to Myanmar. Where this is not possible, then the next best option is retaining the displaced persons in the temporary shelters along the border.

In addition, the MOI also has drawn up a framework for the registration of displaced persons and humanitarian aid in cooperation with UNHCR. Displaced persons who are not eligible to access the shelters in Thailand but who are also unable to return to their home villages in Myanmar have no other option than to try to integrate into local communities and work as illegal labourers (Caouette/Pack 2002). The status of displaced persons compared to refugees is therefore crucial in the treatment of newcomers from Myanmar. Displaced persons are deemed to have fled from their habitual residence on a temporary basis; their displacement is not only from *fleeing fighting political turmoil*, but it can be from any disaster, such as floods; nationality has not changed as a result of displacement from their habitual residence; and when the circumstances that caused them to flee from their country of origin have ceased to exist, they are expected to return to the country of their former habitual residence (Kanyabarn 1998).

It is well documented that the RTG takes the view that displaced persons who are under the humanitarian aegis in Thailand are not determined as refugees. But the RTG allows them temporary stay in the country with the assistance from international organisations and NGOs, with the following restricted terms: they are allowed to stay only on a temporary basis, with the RTG facilitating and assisting them to a safe temporary shelter on humanitarian basis; they have to stay only in the provided area, which is termed a *temporary shelter*, not a refugee camp; and when the circumstances that caused them to flee have changed or ceased, then they must return to the country of their former habitual residence. The RTG will facilitate and assist them to their home country with safety and dignity (ibid 1998).

The largest portion of the forced migration flows into Thailand is made up of those classified as economic migrants rather than refugees, but differentiating between the two groups is an intrinsically problematic task. In practical fact rather than legislative definition, the push factors of political persecution and economic hardship are quite often entwined. The theoretical literature on this concept shows that what has been termed the *migration/asylum nexus* is actually closer to a continuum rather than a dichotomy (Adelman 2008).

In a survey conducted in 2006 of 1,704 nationals from Myanmar in the border provinces of Tak, Mae Hong Son and Chiang Mai, it was concluded that it was very difficult to distinguish between forced migrants and genuine labour migration, and that as many as 50 % of illegal migrant labourers in Thailand may actually deserve protection status as refugees (Sciortino/Punpuing 2009). While it is estimated that between 1 and 2 million Burmese have entered Thailand searching for work, the underlying political concerns have exerted significant influence over the scale of these flows as well. Conversely, while they may have fled Myanmar for political reasons, forced migrants may choose to remain undocumented out of fear that they will apply and be denied displaced person status (Adelman, ibid 2008).

In interviews by the Karen Human Rights Group (KHRG) with forced migrants in Thailand, while a large portion explained their motivation as seeking protection for their physical security, such as those fleeing generalised conflict, direct attacks on their home villages or persecution as possible supporters of insurgent groups, a significant subset also described their motivation as fleeing from economic hardship. There is a sizable group living displaced within Myanmar or across the border in Thailand who left their homes because exploitative SPDC policies made the pursuit of a basic livelihood in their home villages untenable. For these displaced persons, remaining in their SPDC-controlled villages in Myanmar would mean a loss of access to income generating activities, basic freedoms and other fundamental human rights. It had become nearly impossible to earn a basic livelihood in Myanmar.

While the push factors of political oppression, exploitation, armed conflict and livelihood deprivations have already been discussed, it is also true that Thailand experienced a massive economic boom starting in the late 1980s until the period of the Asian Financial Crisis in 1997. This rapid economic growth created a massive need for cheap labour in Thailand and a financial pull factor for many people from Myanmar. Following pressure from the business community, a series of temporary worker registration acts were passed to allow utilisation of the migrants as a source of low-cost labour (Caouette/Pack 2002).

Many of the forced migrants travel by the same routes as economic migrants, most would fit comfortably within the conventional definition of a refugee, and in many countries have been afforded UNHCR-acknowledged refugee status. Therefore, in the case of Myanmar's migrants, it can be said that the distinction between push and pull factors has become blurred to the point of being indeterminable in many cases (Karen Human Rights Group 2009).

2.3 Historical Development of the Royal Thai Government Policy Towards Displaced Persons

Thailand has a long history of providing shelter and asylum to the victims of political conflict in neighbouring countries, in some cases graciously offered and in others more reluctantly. The experience of hosting Indochinese refugees has proved to be a difficult and protracted situation to solve for Thailand. As a result, the policy towards displaced persons from Myanmar is based primarily on providing help on a temporary basis and discouraging long-term stay. There are huge numbers of displaced persons from Myanmar residing in the temporary shelters along the Thai–Myanmar border. Most of these have been granted permission to stay as displaced persons fleeing from fighting by the RTG, while a smaller portion have yet to have a status determination made.

As has been stated, Thailand is not a signatory country to the 1951 Convention on the Status of Refugees or other related international agreements and has no domestic legislation which directly defines the standards of treatment for refugees. Therefore, they are de facto illegal migrants in Thailand, residing in contradiction of the regulations of the Immigration Act B.E. 2522, and as a result can be subjected to capricious arrest, detention, prosecution and deportation.

However, for political and humanitarian reasons, the RTG has repeatedly made exceptions to its official policies and allowed continued temporary shelter for asylum seekers in Thailand. Vacillating between highly restrictive policies implemented based upon national security concerns and more pragmatic displays of tolerance driven by an understanding of the intractability of the different geopolitical crises faced by refugees, Thailand has in fact provided asylum to approximately 1.2 million refugees during the last four decades (Sciortino/Punpuing 2009).

As stated, the policy responses to refugee flows by the RTG have been very specific to the individual situations and actors involved. A notable example of this is exhibited by the contrast between the policy response to the refugee situation on the border with Myanmar and that of the Indochinese refugees. The refugees from Indochina were incontrovertibly ensnared within the complicated dynamics of cold war politics in the region as well as the service provision of a heavily politicised humanitarian aid programme, resulting in a highly internationalised situation in terms of decision-making, staffing and objectives. In comparison, the relief programmes provided to displaced persons on the Thai–Myanmar border have been a relatively little publicised, politicised or internationalised response, mostly managed and provided by local committees representing the displaced and NGO service providers, with only minor engagement of international organisations until the advent of resettlement operations (Lang 2002).

The differences in living conditions are also an outcome of the RTG's policy objective that the relief services and shelter provided on the Myanmar border are to be temporary and based on a sufficiency approach so as not to create a pull factor for additional displaced persons. MOI regulations for working in the camps require a minimum of international staff, that rations and other provisions are equivalent to the basic living standards in the area, that self-sufficiency be encouraged among the displaced and that a minimum of publicity be allowed for the camps. The RTG has required this quieter and smaller scale administrative structure for humanitarian relief by a consortium of NGOs partly with the intention of avoiding diplomatic conflict and misunderstandings with the government of Myanmar (Lang 2002).

In conclusion, it could be summarised that RTG policies delivered humanitarian need, with priority given to national security concerns, specific to the individual situation and actors involved. The progression of policies can be determined into three phrases.

2.3.1 Period 1: Origins of the Camps

Previous to the success of the Tatmadaw, Myanmar's armed forces, military campaigns in Eastern Myanmar during the 1980s, the border region of Myanmar was made up of a patchwork of territories controlled by ethnic insurgent groups fighting against the military government in Rangoon. The significant changes in the geopolitical landscape of the region since that time have caused a major shift in

Thailand's diplomatic relations with the government of Myanmar. While previously the RTG had attempted a delicate balancing act, dealing with both the insurgent groups on a practical level and the government in bureaucratic relations, more recently the RTG has reoriented its political relationship in favour of the government of Myanmar, as reflected by the reestablishment of official diplomatic relations between the two countries in 1988 (Lang 2002).

In 1984, changes from the previous patterns of forced migration began to occur on the Thai–Myanmar border. Whereas previously the border region of Thailand often played host to seasonal flows of displaced persons fleeing from fighting in Myanmar, they generally returned to their homes soon after the hostilities subsided. However, this model of seasonal migration was permanently disrupted during the dry season of 1983–1984 when the Tatmadaw launched a more aggressive and coordinated action against the ethnic insurgent groups with the goal of driving out combatants and civilians, disrupting the insurgent controlled black market economy and establishing a control point right on the Thai border itself. The RTG's policy response was to allow displaced persons from Myanmar who entered Thailand before 19th March 1976 to stay in Thailand (Cabinet Resolution 2005). Temporary asylum was generally in the form of informal hospitality on the part of the local community, with the displaced persons able to create a reasonably comfortable existence through utilising the surrounding natural resources and some assistance from humanitarian organisations.

Then, in February of 1984, approximately 9,000 displaced Karen crossed the border into Thailand at Tak Province and established what was to be the first of the longer term temporary shelters for displaced persons on the Western border of Thailand. The early policy response by the RTG was simply to grant temporary asylum in the hope that the displaced would soon return home after the conflict settled down as had occurred previously. The local community was also generally sympathetic due to their past involvement in trade with the Karen and the already existing social links between Thais and Karen living in the area.

To handle the immediate humanitarian needs, the MOI invited the CCSDPT, the committee coordinating services provided to the Indochinese refugees, to also provide emergency assistance to the displaced Karens. A small consortium of NGOs called the Burma Border Consortium (BBC; later the Thailand Burma Border Consortium, TBBC) was formed under the umbrella of the CCSDPT to provide the actual aid services in the camps. A Karen subcommittee of the CCSDPT was then established in April of 1984 to coordinate the BBC's work with the RTG. The BBC took a small footprint approach to providing services to the refugees, utilising the administrative structure of the Karen Refugee Committee in the shelters. Similar administrative structures were set up for subsequently established shelters, in 1989 in the form of The Karenni Refugee Committee, and in 1990 in the form of The Mon National Relief Committee. The administration in the shelters was an effort to mirror the traditional leadership structures that existed in the home villages of the displaced (Lang 2002).

The Karen Refugee Committee negotiated with the Governor of Tak Province and gained approval for the establishment of a basic shelters facility with the understanding that the Karen would return home as soon as safely possible. However, there was disagreement with this decision at the national level and at a meeting between the MOI, the military, and the Ministry of Foreign Affairs (MOFA), the decision was revoked and the Karen were ordered to return to Myanmar within 30 days. This decision was heavily influenced by concerns about the financial costs of providing humanitarian aid as well as the security-related concern that the Karen might establish permanent insurgency military bases in Thailand for cross-border operations. However, the decision was not strictly implemented on a practical level, and after negotiations were conducted, concessions were made to allow the Karen to remain in Thailand temporarily (Lang 2002).

In 1991, increase in displacement flows across the Thai–Myanmar border led to NGO service providers seeking permission to establish relief services in all four border provinces. The MOI agreed to this request to extend basic services including food, medicine and clothing to all of the border provinces, granting permission to the main NGOs working in the shelters to expand the scale of their services which included the BBC, replacing the original Consortium of Christian Agencies, COERR and MSF-France. The MOI subsequently gave authorisation in 1994 to add sanitation and educational services to the bundle of services allowed in the shelters (Cardno Agrisystems 2009). The MOI has slowly allowed the scope of the educational mandate to expand since that time to include some vocational training and agricultural projects for the shelters inhabitants. After 1997, the CCSDPT began to work exclusively with displaced persons from Myanmar, with 19 member organisations (TBBC 2004).

2.3.2 Period 2: The Fall of the Buffer Zone

Despite the intentionally basic level of services provided, the number of refugees seeking shelter in Thailand continued to rise due to intensification of Tatmadaw military operations along the border, and soon even the camps themselves were no longer places of safe refuge for the displaced communities. Between 1995 and 1998, shelling of the camps by the Tatmadaw and the renegade Democratic Buddhist Karen Army caused a new crisis in the camps for the displaced as well as their supporters (TBBC 2004).

The ground level situation in the camps changed dramatically when the border areas finally fell to the Burmese military during this period. With the end of the previous buffer area between Thailand and the Tatmadaw, and the clear and present danger created by the cross-border attacks, the Thai government began a series of shelter consolidations to help control the security situation. This meant the merging of the smaller and more village-like shelters into a greatly reduced number of larger resettlements facilities with an increased Thai security force surrounding their perimeters. The situation became worse in 1999 when two incidents happened: first, Burmese students raided the Embassy of Myanmar in

Bangkok, and then there was the hostage incident at a hospital in Ratchaburi Province. As a consequence, the RTG decided to review its current policy towards the displaced persons and foreign policy towards Myanmar (The Nation Newspaper 2000). At the border, the shelters were closed off from inside and out to restrict any movement from these areas (Viajar 2000). The change of the policy led to increasing of aid-dependency on services provided by the BBC and other NGOs working in the shelters (TBBC 2004).

These larger resettlements began to have a significant detrimental impact on the surrounding environment, though cooking fuels, bamboo and thatch for constructing shelters have been provided to displaced persons in order to prevent damage to the surrounding forests (ibid). Nutrition also became a more significant concern due to the restrictions on movement and livelihood opportunities (ibid). The RTG also increasingly insisted that it would only accept those displaced who met the Thai criteria for asylum, meaning only those *fleeing from fighting*. During this same period, the ethnic minorities within Burma were faced with increasingly dangerous and untenable conditions as the Tatmadaw continued its large-scale forced relocation plans which were designed to consolidate military control over the border regions and eliminate the remaining ethnic resistance forces. By 2004, 3,000 ethnic villages had been destroyed or relocated, affecting close to a million people (ibid).

Following this heightened concern with security in the shelters, in 1998 the Thai government granted UNHCR permission to play a role in the border camps for the first time, which brought with it full recognition from the international community of the refugee status of the camp inhabitants. Although the mandate established for UNHCR in the camps was strictly for protection rather than service provision or administration, the UN's presence brought with it international consultants which allowed the management and practices in the camps to be evaluated against international standards for the first time (ibid.).

By 1999, the UNHCR had begun official operations on the Thai–Myanmar border, with field offices located in Kanchanaburi, Mae Sot, and Mae Hong Son. Its first major activity was to undertake a registration process for the displaced persons in the shelters, working collaboratively with the MOI. UNHCR also worked with the relevant Thai authorities to clarify and formalise shelters admissions procedures which included establishing Provincial Admissions Boards (PAB) for status determination and construction of reception facilities within the camps themselves (Lang 2001).

2.3.3 Period 3: The Search for Solutions

The latter part of the last decade has seen a significant shift in policy by the RTG away from the previous *care and maintenance* model that defined the first two decades of policy responses, to the displaced person situation on the border, and towards a more *solutions-oriented* approach. Officially recognising the displaced communities as being a part of a protracted refugee situation, if not actual *refugees* themselves, has led to a liberalisation of many of the more stringent restrictions placed on the camp inhabitants. The most significant of these changes include: establishment of official procedures and assuming greater responsibility for receiving, determination of status and registration of shelter inhabitants; acceptance of resettlement as a viable durable solution to the situation; formal approval of increased opportunities for vocational training, education, and livelihood activities inside and outside of the shelters. However, progress has been very slow in practice on most of these fronts.

According to Adelman (2008), it should be noted that even approval of the resettlement programme, which would seem a very desirable solution from the perspective of the RTG, was not a foregone conclusion and was held up for a period due to a reluctance to issue exit visas without which the displaced persons would not have been allowed to leave Thailand. This was likely a part of concerns by the Thai government over creating a pull factor for additional *resettlement seekers* to come to the camps. More recently, however, the RTG has become more actively involved in the resettlement process, rarely denying permits and once again conducting registration and verification of the camp residents to allow for their consideration for resettlement.

In February of 2006, the Thai Prime Minister, together with diplomatic personnel from the international community, visited the shelter in Tak Province to assess the living conditions of the displaced persons living in the shelters. During this visit, the Prime Minister reaffirmed the RTG's commitment to implementing innovative and practical policy measures that would lead to progress towards attaining durable solutions for the situation. Emphasis was placed on the need to work in close collaboration with the international community and within the framework of international standards and practices (Duffy 2007).

The international community for the last several years has been increasingly focused on skills training and educational opportunities as well as income generation projects and employment, so called *self-reliance*, to supplement the resettlement solution. Though there has been an attempt to integrate refugee services with the health and educational institutions of the Thai system, as evidenced by the CCSDPT/UNHCR Comprehensive Plan (CCSDPT/UNHCR 2007), it has proved difficult to make real progress towards refugee self-reliance on the ground. This is at least partly related to the discontinuity in the RTG policy process caused by multiple regime changes since the 2006 (CCSDPT/UNHCR 2009).

According to Meyer, the international refugee regime has been considerably challenged in recent years by the increasing ubiquity of protracted refugee situations in the world, to the point where additional and more integrated strategy approaches became a necessity. These approaches were designed with the recognition of the frequently prolonged condition of asylum for refugees due to the obstacles to durable solutions, and therefore the need for adopting a developmental approach for aid and policy towards such refugee situations. The objective of this new approach is to encourage refugee self-reliance while simultaneously relieving a portion of the burden associated with hosting of refugee populations (Meyer 2006).

Several major UNHCR initiatives have attempted to formalise this approach to refugee situations in Thailand including Convention Plus and the Framework for Durable Solutions. Convention Plus provides an organising structure for the creation of a *comprehensive plan of action* (CPA) which utilises a combination of durable solutions to resolve refugee situations. The Framework for Durable Solutions also addresses the strategy for engagement with protracted refugee situations and attempts to remove some of the barriers to effective action that have arisen in the past. The Framework draws upon a combination of three new approaches to refugee interventions that have emerged in recent years: DAR (Development Assistance for Refugees), DLI (Development through Local Integration) which focuses on refugee self-reliance, and the 4R Approach (Repatriation, Reintegration, Rehabilitation and Reconstruction) which is to provide an overall framework that links the different phases of the UN's support to displaced populations (Loescher/Milner 2005a, b).

While the initial response to these proposals from the RTG was encouraging, progress since that time has been very slow primarily due to reluctance to allow greater freedom of movement in and out of the camps. As a result, everyday life for most of the refugees living in the camps has not changed significantly and donors have begun to express their frustration and fatigue with the situation by exerting financial pressures on NGOs working in the camps in hopes of encouraging progress. Perhaps more constructively, the donor working group also suggested that a way forward would be to hold an all-stakeholder workshop with representatives of the RTG in order to achieve consensus which took place in Chiang Mai on 4th November 2009 (TBBC 2010a, b).

Unfortunately, so far the increased level of deliberation has not resulted in policy changes that allow a plurality of durable solutions or an improved quality of life in the shelters. While the RTG remains sympathetic to these objectives, they have so far still been overridden by concerns for Thailand's national security, the impact on the local Thai community and the creation of a pull factor for additional asylum seekers. Consequently, until the encampment policies are altered in a significant way, there is little possibility that in the short-term dependency on humanitarian aid can be reduced (TBBC 2010a, b). Over three decades of hosting displaced persons from neighbouring countries, the RTG has become aware that outflow of displaced persons from Myanmar is unlikely to decrease. Kanyabarn has concluded that the unchanging RTG policy may be based on prioritisation of the interests of its own people and its relationship with the Government of Myanmar, and has kept the situation of displaced persons on the edge of acceptability (ibid).

2.4 RTG Policy Characteristic and Policy Stakeholders

RTG policy towards Burmese displaced persons has been shaped by relevant internal and external factors within the principle paradigm of traditional national security. The internal factors include concern for national security, economics, the impact on Thai citizens' benefits, and the fear of creating pull factors drawing more displaced persons. The state relationship with Myanmar Government, and RTG positioning on the international stage, are seen as the external factors. The different RTG sectors have contributed to formulate the development of the policy.

The responsibility for policy decision-making and implementation is spread across several institutions within the RTG. The main section of the RTG to oversee the day to day issue of displaced persons is the Foreign Affairs Division of the Ministry of Interior (MOI). Additionally, the ministries and government departments taking part in policy making are the Ministry of Foreign Affairs (MOFA), the Ministry of Defence (MOD) and the National Security Council (NSC).

The MOI is the primary civilian institution within the government responsible for the policy implementation process for displaced persons. The cabinet has established the Operation Center for Displaced Persons (OCDP) in giving the authority to MOI as the prime actor in dealing with the displaced persons fleeing from fighting from Myanmar. The centre is part of the Foreign Affairs Division, Office of The Permanent Secretary for Interior, MOI. The centre has the responsibility to carry out the RTG policy on security and administration responsibilities over all the routine camp activities relating to displaced persons and migrants. The OCDP persons is responsible for coordinating with international organisations, for managing the humanitarian aid providing system for displaced persons, and for providing information to assist in the formation of policy at the MOI.

The MOFA's involvement with displaced persons is coordinating and connecting with international organisations and other interested parties outside of the RTG, facilitating visits to the displaced persons. However, MOFA is seen to play only a minor operational and policy role in daily activities and issues involving the displaced persons (Lang 2002).

The issue of displaced persons is under the responsibility of the MOD's Department of Border Affairs (DBA) which oversees the security and situation of the border area, as well as coordinating with neighbouring countries on security issues along the border. The DBA is the secretary of the Joint Thai–Myanmar Boundary Committee, the body which two countries have set up to resolve the conflict and border issue.

The NSC is the central institution coordinating security policy and development in the border areas. The NSC acts in an advisory capacity to the prime minister and the cabinet on security issues and coordinates at policy level between different ministries and the military on security concerns. Two committees within the NSC are assigned to provide policy guidance on illegal labourers and displaced persons. The NSC is chaired by the Prime Minister in formal sessions. The other council members of the committee include the Deputy Prime Minister, Minister of Defence, Minister of Interior, Minister of Foreign Affairs, Minister of Finance, Minister of Transport, the Supreme Commander of the Armed Forces, and the Secretary General of the NSC. For special issues or particular situations to be considered, the NSC has set up subcommittees in response to which other relevant government agencies and academic are invited to join.

The different government sectors have their own and different mandates that contribute to the formulation or implementation the policy toward displaced persons differently but the principles of the policy will have to be complied by all sectors.

2.5 The Impact of the Policies

Having examined some of the key policy characteristics and institutions related to displaced persons in Thailand, it is quite difficult to describe the policy and practices definitively. Whereas the official asylum policies have often been characterised by their stringency, they are often implemented in a much more flexible and nuanced manner by local authorities as evidenced by the thousands of displaced persons who have entered Thailand and been granted temporary asylum. In sum, the words contained in the policies have frequently not been matched by the practices, as well as vice versa. Some of the significant practices contained within the policy implementation process including those related to registrations, basic services and freedom of movement.

2.5.1 Impact on Displaced Person Registration

Registration of the displaced persons in the camps has been conducted for various purposes by different organisations at different times. The first formal registration process for displaced persons in the border camps was conducted by the MOI and UNHCR in 1999. The initial intention was that identification cards would be issued for those over 12-year old, both for recognition of status and to allow for possible future permission pass to enter and leave the camp (CCSDPT-UNHCR 2009). At the same time, Provincial Admissions Boards (PABs) were established to handle status determination for new arrivals. However, the PABs were largely ineffective and by 2004 a large backlog of unprocessed new arrivals, as well those whose claims had been assessed and rejected, were living in the camps (Cardno Agrisystems 2009).

Since the 2004–2005 registration process, there have been major flows of new arrivals into the camps who have not had a status determination made as of yet. This is particularly significant because resettlement opportunities are restricted to the registered population of the camp. The PABs began screening again in late 2005 based on an expanded set of criteria established with the assistance of UNHCR. However, the halting pace of registrations in the camps has created problems for humanitarian aid organisations both in terms of operations and reporting on services provided to donor organisations.

In order to maintain accurate figures for service provision, TBBC began its own annual registration process for both registered and unregistered displaced persons staying in the camps at the end of 2007. In 2009, it was estimated that approximately 42,000 displaced persons were living in the camps that had not been registered by UNHCR. In March of that year, the MOI began a pre-screening exercise to help expedite the process, monitored by UNHCR staff. Those determined to have legitimate claims to asylum are handle to PAB for final determination. None of the results will be announced until the process has been completed in all of the camps in order to prevent rejected applicants from reapplying in other camp locations (Cardno Agrisystems 2009). It is hoped that the whole process will be completed in early 2010 (TBBC 2010a, b).

The other critical issue is the registration of children born in the shelters. Newborn babies are only registered with UNHCR, and there are no birth or official certificates provided for them. After the new laws on Personal Status Registration was launched in 2009, there followed the Cabinet Resolution on 18th January, 2005 and NSC strategy to solve the persons who have no registration status (NSC), all children regardless to their legal status are eligible to birth registration including the children in the shelters. To support this strategy, on 21st September 2010 the Cabinet lifted the reservation of Article 7 of Convention on Rights of the Child regarding to birth registration of all children. Thus, the displaced persons' children are now registered with Thai registration system and birth certificates have been provided which ensure their rights and identity, at least to proof as the new member of their origin family.

2.5.2 Impact on Freedom of Movement

According to the existing RTG policy, the residents of the shelters are not allowed to move freely in and out of the shelters without written permission from the Thai authorities. Written permission to leave the shelters can be obtained from the camp commander in the case of seeking healthcare in Thai local hospitals, to attend committee meetings, for students' access to education in other shelters, and for sports competition in local community (Mae La Shelter description document). The policy has restricted freedom of movement and many of the displaced people who do leave the shelters to work in their local Thai communities face possible extortion, arrest, detention and deportation.

2.5.3 Impact on Livelihood and Basic Services

With no freedom of movement, displaced persons are restricted from pursuing their choice of livelihood and effectively prevented from seeking employment outside the shelter at the risk of being caught and arrested by Thai authorities and the possibility of deportation. However, the limited quantity and variety of rations often drives those who are of working age to pursue employment outside of the camps on a daily basis despite the risks involved. Another basic motivating factor is that regular and productive employment is critically important to the self-esteem and social acceptance of the residents of the camp, just as it is for people everywhere (Duffy 2007). A livelihood study carried out in four of the camps by Cardno Agrisystems supported the fact that displaced persons have been provided sufficient nutrition but other needs were not met. Thus, instances of leaving the shelters to seek employment were found among male displaced persons, in order to send remittances back to their families (Brees 2008). This is a coping strategy that helps to minimise risk by leaving the most vulnerable family members in relative safety inside the camps while supplementing the food rations provided as well as covering other needed items with the additional income. This practice is often tolerated at the local level, which often benefits both the host community and the displaced persons, although to differing degrees. According to research conducted by Pongsawat (2007), the presence of the shelter near Mae Sot created a large pool of illegal workers in the border area. The displaced persons were illegally hired to work in every industrial sector of the border economy, especially in Mae Sot.

What needs to be emphasised is that the creation and formalisation of the displaced person category and the establishment of the temporary shelters did in fact institutionalise and expand the pool of illegal migrant workers ready to be employed and take the jobs in the area (ibid: 434).With permission and oversight from the RTG, NGOs provide settlement residents with food rations, primary care medical services, compulsory level education and housing assistance. However, some permanent infrastructure such as concrete floors and public power supplies are officially forbidden in the shelters (USCRI 2008).

A system of community-based healthcare has been established in the shelters, relying heavily upon involvement of the shelter population for service provision and management. For secondary and tertiary medical care, residents receive referral to local public hospitals outside the shelters (Sciortino/Punpuing 2009). However, though malnutrition rates for children have been lowered within the shelter community, they are still at higher levels than in the rest of Thailand (CCSDPT 2006). The crude mortality rate for the shelters as a whole is actually lower than those in Thailand or Myanmar (ibid). A study by Khin on reproductive health among adolescents in Karenni shelters shows that there are problems with Karenni youths suffering from reproductive tract infection and unwanted pregnancies (2002). There are cases of displaced persons suffering from accumulated stress caused by past abuse, trauma, and confinement, which has led to significant incidence of mental illness within the shelters (Sciortino, ibid). In the highly restrictive environment of the border shelters, increased levels of violence and human rights abuses have been documented. Significantly higher than normal levels of domestic violence, serious psychological disorders and sexual assaults have all been reported within the shelters.

Female Burmese refugees have few legal protections against such violence and the Thai legal system generally discourages displaced women from seeking legal recourse against perpetrators both among Thai authorities and their community. For example, in cases of statutory rape, the offender can choose to marry his victim rather than face punishment, financial compensation for rape of a married woman is given to the husband rather than the victim, and marital rape and domestic violence were only formally recognised as crimes under the Thai legal system in 2007 and are often only sporadically enforced by police (Immigration and Refugee Board of Canada 2007; Ward 2002).

Another obstacle to fair adjudication of gender-based violence (GBV) offences is that the internal mechanism within the shelters themselves for handling severe cases is to send them before the shelter committees which are always male dominated decision-making bodies. It should be noted that the traditional response to GBV within Burmese society is generally enacted between families rather than publicly in order to avoid the social stigma surrounding the issue. In Khin's study, young children are shown to be victims of sexual violence and in some rape cases the perpetrators are their close relatives (ibid). The shame for victims and their families associated with incidents of rape is so strong that Karenni women's groups have documented several occurrences of adolescent refugees choosing to commit suicide rather than reveal that they had been raped by Thai authorities (Ward, 2002).

Since 1998, the RTG has pursued the policy of providing education for displaced persons in the temporary shelters with support from NGOs. The education policy has been adjusted as appropriate and aligned with the National Education Plan used for Thai children, and the National Economic and Social Development Plan, and in accordance with the CRC to establish and enforce 9 years' basic education for every student (MOI-CCSDPT 2008). Besides the primary level education, RTG policy also supports part time education for any students who have been absent from school for some reason, as well as continuity specialty study programme for High School graduate students. The programmes provided in the graduate schools are Further Study, Special English, Agriculture School, Leadership and Management, Engineering, Economic Development, Teacher Preparation. However, these are not available in all shelters (ibid.).

The educational services in the shelter are primarily staffed and managed by the camp residents with assistance from the NGOs. Although the enrolment rates are quite high at 97.5 % of the school age children in the shelter, the actual attendance is much lower due to financial and language barriers to studying. The quality of education provided is also a significant problem because of poor facilities and equipment, inadequate curriculum and limited staff teaching capabilities. Native English speakers from outside the shelters are restricted from teaching in the schools, which is an additional drain on already limited teaching capacities. A final critical concern with the educational system in the shelters is that it remains completely unaccredited by Thailand, Myanmar or any other country. As a result, graduates of the system may not be eligible for higher education opportunities and their job prospects in the future may be very limited (Sciortino/Punpuing 2009).

A resolution of the Thai Cabinet in 2005 increased opportunity for migrant children to have equal right of access to education as local children regardless of their legal status, with budget allocated to support the policy. This policy should benefit children in the shelters but educational activity has since the beginning not been under the supervision of the Ministry of Education (MOE). All activities needed to be submitted for approval from the MOI, teaching are provided by displaced persons themselves. Educational opportunities which have been broadened by the Thai cabinet's resolution in 2005 do not permit displaced children to leave the shelters (Vungsiriphisal 2010). As well as academic education, vocational training has been permitted in the shelters since 2003 (Thai Education Foundation 2006). The objectives of the training are to provide and improve skill for displaced persons based on their interest, aiming to prepare them to be more self reliant.

2.6 Policy Responses to Changing Circumstances and Durable Solution

Historically, the three possible durable solutions for refugee situations have been repatriation, resettlement and local integration. Utilising these three strategies in a comprehensive and integrated approach to address protracted refugee situations is not a new paradigm. This approach was a critical part of the strategy that helped to resolve the refugee situations in Europe following World War II, and in Indochina and Central America during the 1980s (Loescher/Milner 2007). Past successes in resolving refugee situations can be said to be based upon three general principles: comprehensive, utilising the full range of durable solutions to the situation; cooperative, approaching with a spirit of burden sharing that recognises countries of first asylum cannot resolve refugee situations on their own and need the assistance of third party countries; and collaborative, involving the joint efforts of a variety of UN agencies and NGOs.

The UNHCR and humanitarian agencies focused on relief efforts are not capable of resolving refugee situations by themselves. A combination of peace, security and development agencies must commit to significant and sustained efforts to make truly durable solutions possible (Loescher/Milner 2007).

After years of hosting asylum seekers from neighbouring countries, Thailand has contributed to the three durable solutions directly or indirectly at different levels.

2.6.1 Local Integration

Limited local integration has been promoted by expanding of education from primary education to secondary level, the teaching of Thai language in the shelters which was permitted from 2006 and carried out by the MOE to enable communication skill between the displaced persons and the Thai authorities (MOE 2006). The ability to communicate in Thai is essential to bridge the communication gap between displaced persons, authorities and local community which may contribute to more integration with local community in the future, though the policy is not aimed to that purpose. As Jacobsen has remarked, because of the limited success of repatriation and resettlement strategies in global refugee situations, host countries have often pushed an integration approach without close investigation of the possible implications, with no public scrutiny from the national citizens, and, importantly, no strategic experience in dealing with national security issues that may emerge (Jacobsen 2001).

Local integration that leads towards a durable solution for refugees is regarded as a set of processes, legal, economic and social. The term *local integration* embodies the concept that refugees should not be required to abandon their own culture; in fact, refugees can *maintain their own identity, yet become part of the host society to the extent that host population and refugees can live together in an acceptable way*. Through legal process, refugees are granted a progressively wider range of rights and entitlements by the host state. Economic process should deliver a growing degree of self-reliance. Social process should lead to refugees living without fear of systematic discrimination, intimidation or exploitation by the authorities or people of the asylum country (Kuhlman 1994).

Local integration was recognised as the potential solution for refugee problems but the practice has been very limited, while resettlement and repatriation have been becoming the norm. This is due to perception within the refugees' host country of the negative impacts, such as economic and environmental impact of struggling to meet the needs of their own citizens, the more prosperous members of the international community not sufficiently committed to burden sharing, the fear of losing the ability to control the movement of people across international borders, and the belief that exiled populations represent a threat to local, national and regional security, especially in the situations where bona fide refugees are mixed with armed elements.

In the debate regarding whether hosting of refugee populations is a burden or benefit (Meyer 2006), a number of studies have shown that *the impact on differing sectors of the host population and spheres of government, as well as differing elements of this impact—for example, on security, the environment or infrastructure—precludes any generalisation regarding the 'burden' or 'benefit' of refugee-hosting on local communities and host states. In fact, in some spheres, refugee influx can create opportunities and broader social, political and economic development in the area. Contrary to popular readings of refugee situations, the potential for refugees to present a burden is often due to host government restrictions on livelihood opportunities*" (ibid).

Jacobson concludes that local integration will only work if it is acceptable to host governments, to the local community and to refugees. Local integration can be encouraged through assistance programmes that benefit both refugees and local communities. Jacobson also proposes an approach which embraces refugees and views them as a potential asset, assisting them to become integrated in the community. Local integration can be pursued, also, if host governments are supported and on the agendas of development organisations such as the World Bank and UNDP persons as well as bilateral donors.

In the case of Thailand, the acceptance by local people of displaced persons is a doubt, as reflected in a research paper on the attitude of Thais to the refugees from Myanmar. It was found that the majority of the respondents had a negative perception of the refugees: over 88 % prefer the refugee to repatriate when the situation in their homeland improves. They were also fearful of the social chaos and danger to the society if permission is given to refugees to work outside the camps, considering refugees as carriers of epidemics, a burden to the nation, a threat to national security, and competitors for job opportunities with Thai worker. Nevertheless, there is also positive perception of the refugees on some points: that refugees should value themselves by working to take care their families, contribute to the country's economic growth, capable refugee youth should have access to Thai education institutes, should have access to insurance system, and others (Assumption University 2007).

However, there are situations in which the promotion of local integration has particular potential to succeed if the refugees share a language, a culture or ethnic background with the host community, or bring particular skills, or can attract resources and investment to their country of asylum (Crips 2004). Refugees who have particular skills and knowledge that can contribute to local communities of asylum countries are more accepted (UNHCR 2002).

Though the RTG has never publicised its asylum policy, it is clear that the principles of the policy are based on temporary acceptance basis, repatriate on the first occasion, limit the number of new arrivals and keep remaining displaced persons to the minimum.

In another aspect of protection, the RTG has supported the displaced persons to access the Thai judicial system since 2007 in order to control the violation of the laws inside the shelters. The permission has given to set up Legal Assistance Centres (LAC) parallel with the shelters' traditional govern legal systems to ensure the standard protection of the displaced persons from increasing domestic violence, sexual violence and other criminal cases occurring in the shelters which the old system seemed not to be dealing with appropriately.

In 2009, CCSDPT and UNHCR collaborated in the creation of a new 5-year strategic plan for coordination of all service sectors aimed at increasing refugee self-reliance and, where possible, integrating refugee services within the Thai system. Despite this plan, however, the RTG has given little indication that its policy direction will change any time soon (TBBC 2009a, b), but it will provide a good basis for dialogue with the RTG on finding sustainable solutions for the refugees. In 2009, the European Commission (EC) started scaling down the EU contribution to the temporary shelters in Thailand, a total of €8.75 million, slightly lower than the 2008 figure of €9.5 million. The EC's strategy has been coordinated with other EU instruments and donors, and is searching for the most effective way to accompany early implementation of the 5-year strategic plan of the CCSDPT and UNHCR (EC 2010).

2.6.2 Voluntary Repatriation

In relation to the other options for durable solutions, voluntary repatriation has come to be seen by many academics, international organisations and governments as the favourite choice both in terms of practicality and preference. The hierarchy of durable solutions has seen the demotion of local integration as a feasible policy option and has led to an increased focus on the use of repatriation to resolve refugee situations (Meyer 2008). While the US and other donor countries have attempted to utilise resettlement to encourage increased consideration of local integration as a share of the solution to refugee situations, there is still significant reluctance on the part of many host countries to change encampment policies (US Department of State 2009).

The ideal international standard for repatriation is *voluntary repatriation in safety and dignity* to an environment in which *the causes of flight have been definitively and permanently removed* (UNHCR 1993). A broad theoretical discourse that has been applied to refugee repatriation over the last decade has been the concept of human security. Despite the significant political and practical obstacles, the human security approach attempts to engage with the situation in a holistic manner, addressing the problems and concerns faced by hosting nations, the needs and quality of life concerns of refugees and their communities, and the requirements for repatriation, reconstruction, and reconciliation in countries of origin. Human security is conceived as resting upon three conditions that must be met for a safe and lasting repatriation to be completed (Lang 2002). A further issue that will need to be addressed if a future repatriation is to take place is that the Myanmar authorities have already indicated that they will require Thailand to submit names, home addresses in Myanmar, photographs, and identity cards in order to verify citizenship before return. Significant problems with registration records and proof of citizenship are sure to arise among the mostly ethnic minority displaced population. In Thailand, a large number of the displaced have never completed the registration process to establish their citizenship and are becoming stateless as a result of their migration to Thailand where their children are also born without birth registration or other documentation of citizenship (Caouette/Pack 2002).

To respond the birth registration concern, the RTG through a Cabinet resolution on 21st September 2010 will commit provide birth certificates to all children regardless their legal status. This practice will ensure displaced persons' children have proof their citizenship when returning to Myanmar or elsewhere in the future.

The RTG's permission for humanitarian agencies to provide vocational training in the shelters is a measure to ensure displaced persons obtain necessary skills for their future income (Thai Education Foundation 2006). The skills obtained in training will either support their repatriation, resettlement or possible employment in Thailand.

2.6.3 Resettlement

Currently, resettlement is the only one of the three durable solutions available in the border shelters, and RTG policy has also had significant impacts on how the resettlement programme has been conducted or contributed to the success in depopulating the shelters. Despite over 64,000 displaced persons being resettled (IOM 2010), actual shelter populations, if not the registered populations, have not decreased since resettlement began in 2005. This indicates that displaced persons continue to seek asylum in Thailand from Myanmar (Sciortino/Punpuing 2009). The ideal result for the resettlement programme would be for the population of the shelters to gradually draw down until they are no longer needed. However, the combination of high birth-rates and new arrivals has made this appear to be a distant outcome for the programme at present.

While Jacobsen presents the resettlement option as the policy pursued most often by third countries, the desire of displaced persons and support from the first asylum country also play key roles in driving the programme. Asylum seekers might have the desire to settle abroad but their desire is limited by the fear of self adaptation into a country with a distinct and potentially very different culture, and by an unwillingness to be separated from family (Jacobsen 2001).

Additionally, without formal status, displaced persons like ones from Shan State cannot participate in the resettlement programme (ibid.). The current resettlement programme only includes registered population arriving in the shelters up to 2005 as eligible applicants. The vacuum of registration process after that has left many non-registered asylum seekers not eligible for the resettlement programme. In addition to the pre-screening programme, aiming to fill the registration gap has prolonged the result for over a year now. The potential of residents leaving to resettle has had an impact on the remainder and there are no clear improvements to the living conditions for those refugees who have decided not to apply for resettlement (Garcia/Lynch 2009).

References

Adelman, H. (Ed.), 2008: *Protracted Displacement in Asia* (Aldershot: Ashgate).

Assumption University, 2007: *Refugee in Thailand in Public awareness and perception* (Bangkok: Assumption University Social Innovation in Management and Business Analysis Research Centre).

Brees, I. 2008: "Towards sustainable livelihoods: Vocational training and access to work on the Thai–Burmese border", in: *ZOA Issue Papers,*1: 1.

Caouette, T.; Pack, M., 2002: *Pushing Past the Definitions: Migration from Burma to Thailand* (Washington DC: Refugees International).

Cardno Agrisystems, 2009: *Livelihoods Vulnerability Analysis in Burmese Refugee Camps in Thailand* (Bangkok: Cardno Agrisystems).

CCSDPT, 2006: *2006 Annual Health Information Short Report* (Bangkok: TBBC).

CCSDPT, 2007: *CCSDPT Planning for the Future: The Impact of Resettlement on the Remaining Camp Population* (Bangkok: CCSDPT).

CCSDPT/UNHCR, 2007: *A Comprehensive Plan Addressing the Needs of Displaced Persons on the Thailand/Myanmar (Burma) Border in 2007/2008* (Bangkok: CCSDPT/UNHCR).

CCSDPT/UNHCR, 2009: *Five-Year Strategic Plan* (Bangkok: CCSDPT/UNHCR).

Chumak, S.; Nualsuwan, O., 1982: *The problem of Indo China Refugees: The Response of Other Countries and the International Organisation* (Bangkok: Chulalongkorn University).

Colm, S., 2004: "Out of Sight, Out of Mind: Thai Policy toward Burmese Refugees", in: *Human Rights Watch,*16, 2: 1–46.

Crips, J., 2004: "The Local Integration and Local Settlement of Refugees: A Conceptual and Historical Analysis", in: *New Issues in Refugee Research, Working Paper No. 102* (Geneva: UNHCR).

Duffy, R., 2007: *Strengthening Protection Capacity Project: Livelihoods Component* (Bangkok: UNHCR/ILO).

Eick, M., n.d.: *Thailand—World Refugee Day 20 June 2010: Refugees in Thailand: Another 25 years in limbo?* at: http://ec.europa.eu/echo/aid/stories/asia30_en.htm.

European Commission, 2010: *Aid in action—Thailand*; at: http://ec.europa.eu/echo/aid/asia/thailand_en.htm.

Immigration and Refugee Board of Canada, 2007: *Thailand: Domestic Violence, State Protection and Resources Available to Victims of Domestic Abuse*; at: http://www.unhcr.org/refworld/docid/47d6547b23.html.

IOM, 2008: *Situation Report on International Migration in East and South-East Asia* (Bangkok: IOM).

IOM, 2010: *IOM Resettles over 74,000 Refugees from Thailand Since 2004*; at: http://www.iom.int/jahia/Jahia/media/press-briefing-notes/pbnAS/cache/offonce?entryId=26824.

Jacobsen, K., 2001: "The Forgotten Solution: Local Integration for Refugees in Developing Countries", in: *New Issues in Refugee Research, Working Paper No. 45* (Geneva: UNHCR).

Kanyabarn, P., 1998: *The Problem of Displaced Persons in Thailand: Study the Past, Present for the Future: Research Report: Academic Year 1997–1998* (Bangkok: National College of Thailand).

Karen Human Rights Group, 2009: *Abuse, Poverty, and Migration: Investigating Migrants' Motivations to Leave Home in Burma* (Bangkok: Karen Human Rights Group).

Lang, H., 2001: "The Repatriation Predicament of Burmese Refugees in Thailand: A Preliminary Analysis", in: *New Issues in Refugee Research: Working Paper No 46* (Geneva: UNHCR).

Lang, H., 2002: (Ithaca: Cornell Southeast Asia Programme). *Fear and Sanctuary: Burmese Refugees in Thailand*

Loescher, G.; Milner, J., 2005a: *Protracted Refugee Situations: Domestic and International Security Implications* (London: International Institute for Strategic Studies).

Loescher, G.; Milner, J., 2005b: *Security and Forced Migration: Developing DFID's Policy Approach to Refugees and Internally Displaced Persons* (Oxford: Refugee Studies Centre).

Loescher, G.; Milner, J., 2007a: "Protracted Refugee Situations: Causes, Consequences, and Trends", Paper Presented at the RSC 25th Anniversary Conference.

Loescher, G.; Milner, J., 2007b: "Protracted Refugee Situations: Towards a New Research Agenda", Paper Presented at the RSC 25th Anniversary Conference.

Meyer, S., 2006: "The 'Refugee Aid and Development' Approach in Uganda: Empowerment and Self-reliance of Refugees in Practice", in: *New Issues in Refugee Research, Working Paper No 313* (Geneva: UNHCR).

Meyer, S., 2008: *FMO Research Guide on Local Integration*; at: http://www.forcedmigration.org/guides/fmo045/.

Ministry of Education, 2006: *Report on Thai Language Teaching in the Shelters* (Bangkok: Ministry of Education).

MOI/CCSDPT, 2008: *The Government and Humanitarian Organisations seminar on Working Practices under the Government's Policy on the Displaced Persons from Burma* (Bangkok: Ministry of Interior).

Pongsawat, P. 2007: *Border Partial Citizenship, Border Towns, and Thai–Myanmar Cross-Border Development: Case Studies at the Thai Border Towns* (Berkeley: UC Berkeley).
Sciortino, R.; Punpuing, S., 2009: *International Migration in Thailand 2009* (Bangkok: IOM).
TBBC, 2004: *Between Worlds: Twenty Years on the Border*; at: http://www.tbbc.org/resources/2004-between-worlds.zip.
TBBC, 2009a: *Programme Report, January–June 2009* (Bangkok: TBBC).
TBBC, 2009b: *Programme Report, July–December 2009* (Bangkok: TBBC).
TBBC, 2010a: *Programme Report, January–June 2010* (Bangkok: TBBC).
TBBC, 2010b: *Programme Report, July–December 2010* (Bangkok: TBBC).
Thailand Education Foundation, 2006: *Mid Term Review of the Vocational Training for the Burmese Displaced Persons, 2006* (Bangkok: Thai Education Foundation).
The Nation, 2000: *Officials Outraged by Lapse in Security* (Bangkok: The Nation).
Trichot, P., 2003: *A Journey of Ethnic Minority* (Bangkok: Institute of Asian Studies, Chulalongkorn University).
UNHCR, 1993: *The State of the World's Refugees: The Challenge of Protection* (Geneva: UNHCR).
US Department of State, Bureau of Population, Refugees and Migration, 2009: *FY 2010 General NGO Guidelines for Overseas Assistance*; at: http://www.state.gov/g/prm/130740.htm#policy.
Vungsiriphisal, P., 2010: "The Challenge of Education Policy for Migrant Children in Thailand from Security Standpoints", Paper Presented at the Workshop on "Human Security in Migrant Population for the Reconciliation of Society; A Case Study of Unskilled Migrant Workers and Refugees, Kyoto University, Kyoto, Japan, 18–19 January.

Chapter 3
RTG Policy Towards Displaced Persons from Myanmar: Development and Current Status

Premjai Vungsiriphisal, Graham Bennett, Chanarat Poomkacha, Waranya Jitpong and Kamonwan Reungsamran

Abstract The history of the displaced persons issue is traced, from its origins in localised flight from fighting in Myanmar, to large-scale influxes of refugees, or displaced persons as the RTG has termed them. Thailand's history of providing refuge to refugee populations, notably those from Indochina, is outlined, and partly explains the RTG's reluctance to once again bear the burden of another large-scale refugee issue. The RTG's status as a non-signatory to the 1951 Refugee Convention, and the policy issues that have arisen from this, is explored. The evolution of the RTG's practice is also mapped, where areas such as education and health care have developed in spite of formal policy restricting self-reliance and any move towards local integration.

Keywords Thai refugee policy · UN conventions · Displaced persons · Refugee camps · Indochina refugees · Confinement · Thai government departments · Maneeloy · Burmese refugees

P. Vungsiriphisal (✉) · G. Bennett · C. Poomkacha · W. Jitpong · K. Reungsamran
Asian Research Center for Migration, Institute of Asian Studies, Chulalongkorn University,
3rd floor, Prachadhipok Rambhai-Barni Building, Bangkok 10330, Thailand
e-mail: premjai.v@chula.ac.th

G. Bennett
e-mail: grahambennett777@hotmail.co.uk

C. Poomkacha
e-mail: cpoomkacha@abeam.com

W. Jitpong
e-mail: wec135@hotmail.com

K. Reungsamran
e-mail: kamonwan24@yahoo.com

P. Vungsiriphisal et al. (eds.), *Humanitarian Assistance for Displaced Persons from Myanmar*, SpringerBriefs in Environment, Security, Development and Peace 17,
DOI: 10.1007/978-3-319-02795-1_3,

3.1 Introduction

Historically, Thailand has hosted millions of displaced persons seeking asylum. The policy towards different groups has varied according to their particular situation but, certainly, Thailand has accommodated many displaced persons over time, including those who came from Myanmar in earlier periods. Until now, Thailand has no particular laws or solutions for asylum seekers but other forms of legislative provision have been adapted to address the situation and these solutions are subject to change according to circumstances.

In addition to the displaced persons from Myanmar, Thailand has already faced the situation of hosting great numbers of stateless persons including hill-tribe groups, non-Thai population and various displaced persons groups from Indochina. The situation was first addressed by different government sectors authorised or responsible for each particular group. Later, the RTG issued cabinet resolutions as a mechanism to establish the legal status of each group.

The various groups of displaced persons included Shang Kai Chek ex-militants and families, Vietnam Dien Bien Phu and Nepalese. To focus only on displaced persons from Myanmar, an MOI announcement was used to categorise the groups who entered at different periods. The RTG adopted the timeframe that Thailand used to solve the status of many hill tribes in the country to define status for Myanmar displaced persons.

In the case of displaced persons from Myanmar, the RTG has maintained the line that those coming from Myanmar are not *refugee*s but are *displaced persons fleeing fighting,* and its non-membership of the 1951 Convention has enabled the RTG to avoid some of the responsibilities it would have to those crossing the border from Myanmar if they were to have full status as refugees. However, the RTG's policy does embrace many of the principles of the 1951 Convention; and its practice does, in many cases, extend beyond its own policy as it has sought to respond and manage an often difficult situation.

In examining why the RTG's policy has evolved as it has, this study looks at a number of far-reaching and intertwined factors to move closer to a long-term solution. Its aim is to identify real, practical steps that would contribute to that solution and would be both acceptable and beneficial towards all the various stakeholders. These stakeholders include the RTG, the displaced persons themselves, international agencies and NGOs, and other countries that have offered resettlement, such as the USA and the UK. But they must also include local Thai communities directly affected by the shelters, wider Thai public opinion, and, crucially, the government of Myanmar and the ethnic communities in Myanmar that have been and continue to be the source of the displaced persons. Critical to both understanding the problem and finding practical solutions is that the RTG is not a uniform body; it has various parts and interests, with their own perspectives and priorities.

3.2 Formulation of RTG Policy and Responsible Bodies

With the absence of formal law, RTG policy on displaced persons is governed by a variety of legislative provisions, including cabinet resolutions, announcement of authorised sectors and other measures. The irregular migration experienced by Thailand, including displacement from Myanmar, has been treated as a *security issue* because of the illegality of entry, as per National Security Policy. Various government actors addressed the issue of displaced persons from their own mandate and regulations. The National Security Council (NSC), the Ministry of the Interior (MOI), the Ministry of Foreign Affairs (MOFA) and the military have responsibilities on the security issue, for instance. The displaced persons, especially those with links to armed groups in Myanmar, might pose a threat to national security. Government actors need to take account of Thailand's foreign and economic relations with Myanmar and how these have shifted over the past 20 years, and the current geopolitical situation involving regional organisation like ASEAN and the wider international community.

The NSC as the consultative body to the government has been assigned by its mandate to be the leading organisation on the policy towards irregular displacement from neighbouring countries and other relevant matters, as well as security issues. The NSC has carried this role from the Indochina period. NSC is responsible for providing a policy framework, guidelines and suggestions to the Cabinet and other government sectors. The NSC has several permanent committees including the Screening Committee, headed by the NSC Secretary General. In March 2004, a subcommittee was set up by the NSC Screening Committee to oversee the issue of displaced persons from Myanmar (Order No.13/2546 dated 4/8/2003). The subcommittee comprised of members from MOFA, MOI, Ministry of Defence (MOD), Ministry of Justice (MOJ), Royal Police Office, Ministry of Public Health (MOPH) and the Immigration Office. The subcommittee meetings have served as the platform for relevant RTG actors to contribute to policy formulation. The policy recommendations from the subcommittee meeting are submitted to the NSC Board or the Cabinet for approval and apply to implementation by relevant sectors (Interview NSC officer, 24/9/10). The assignment of responsibility to the NSC gave the policy and administration of displaced persons a clearer direction.

The MOI carried on its role from the Indochinese refugees and assumed responsibility to administer displaced persons from Myanmar (Cabinet Resolution June 3, 1975). In the case of displaced persons from Myanmar, the MOI, as the authorised body, administered displaced persons from Myanmar who entered Thailand at different period with different approaches. The Foreign Division of the Permanent Secretary of MOI, through its OCDP, has continued to administer the day to day activities of the shelters. In 2002 the MOI restructured, and the administration of displaced persons was divided between two departments: the Foreign Affairs Division Office of the Permanent Secretary for Interior, and Department of Provincial Administration (DPA). The OCDP responsibility includes the coordination of external resources to the shelters. The DPA is responsible mainly for the administration of the shelters. The OCDP has set up its committee to responsible for policy implementation and administration of displaced persons. The OCDP committee members are from various government sectors including the NSC, Ministry of Social Development and Human Security, Immigration Office, MOPH, Ministry of Education, Ministry of Labour, Red Cross, Border Police and others.

MOFA and MOD deal with Myanmar from different perspectives. MOFA's Department of International Organisation and Department of East Asian Affairs are members of the NSC subcommittee whenever relevant issues are on the agenda. The subcommittee meeting is the channel to propose policy as well as information sharing among relevant government sectors with (Interview MOFA Officers 26/11/10, 9/12/10). MOFA also engages in regional cooperation and international bodies such as ASEAN. The problem of Rohingya displaced persons has been brought to the ASEAN Foreign Ministers meeting, unlike the issue of displaced persons in Thailand which is addressed at bilateral level and has never been brought up to a regional platform.

The MOD, through Department of Border Affairs, is responsible for the cooperation between Thailand and Myanmar on border affairs. The MOD role is about implementing rather than formulating RTG policy on displaced persons but information from the MOD has played an important role in contribution to policy making, especially regarding the conflict situation in Myanmar (Interview Department of Border Affairs Officer, 20/12/10).

The Internal Security Operations Command (ISOC), another unit under the Office of the Prime Minister, is working at both policy and implementation levels. At a practical level, its role is to promote voluntary repatriation for the displaced persons population and searching for information (Interview shelter committee, 7/7/10).

Policy can be proposed at NSC subcommittee meetings, to cabinet through Ministers, and through subcommittees of the parliament. As an example, the coordination with UNHCR for repatriation of displaced persons was proposed to cabinet meeting (Cabinet resolution, March 23, 2004). The NSC Board and subcommittee overseeing displaced persons will be consulted for particular issues; for example, the proposal for displaced persons to work outside the shelters (Interview NSC officers, 23/9/10). The consultation with the NSC by relevant sectors has been made on particular issues that need more consideration, for example, education for children in local schools and training programmes (Interview MOI officer 19/10/10). NSC subcommittee is authorised to set up working committees or consulting boards to study or consider specific issues. Each proposal may not always be approved by the committee or additional information may be required to support the decision. In some cases, the proposal approved by the NSC board or subcommittee will be submitted to the cabinet for acknowledgment or final decision.

It can be concluded that various government sectors have contributed to policy formulation, from the different mandate of each sector. The policy has been formulated through the structure and mechanism set by RTG through NSC board, subcommittee, working committee or OCDA Committee. These platforms can serve as the policy formulation and amendment, information sharing and consultation. Some policies can be finalised or rejected at the meetings or will be passed to government or cabinet for final decision.

3.3 Development of RTG Policy Towards Displaced Persons from Myanmar

3.3.1 Flexibility at the Beginning

Displacement from Myanmar has taken place from time to time, but the number of displaced persons who arrived at Thailand in earlier periods was small and resided with Thai community. At the beginning, the displacement from Myanmar was considered temporary and seasonal. The issue was treated locally because at that time the Indochinese refugee issue was a huge problem. Later, when the situation got worse, the RTG took the issue of displacement from Myanmar more seriously. From 1984, MOI as the authorised body agreed to set up small settlements along the border for remaining displaced persons and called upon humanitarian organisations helping Indochinese displaced persons at that time to provide assistance.

After the nationwide protest in Myanmar in 1988 and mass suppression by the government, the Burmese students, activists and opposition group leaders fled to Thailand. Some managed to go to UNHCR in Bangkok and were granted Person of Concern (POC) status; some were reported to Thai authorities. The RTG set up Maneeloy shelter in Rajburi province to host this group in 1992 (Cabinet resolution, August 31, 2010). The student activists were permitted to stay with the exemption of Immigration Act, 1979. They got permission to move freely in the province and other areas for a certain period and were eligible to study in Bangkok. This group continued their political activities until the two incidents in 1999, in which members of the group were involved: the hostage siege of the Burmese embassy, and the invasion of Rajburi hospital. The POCs were transferred to Maneeloy in 2000 and their movements were controlled after that.

In addition, the Democratic Karen Buddhist Army (DKBA) and Burmese military made several attacks on the displaced persons settlements along the border in the 1990s. Thus, in 1995 the small settlements were consolidated into fewer, larger safe shelters (NSC meeting, 16/3/1995–22/5/1995, cited in Kanyaban 2004). It should be noted that Thailand was always accused by Myanmar government in hosting ethnic groups and supporting ethnic armed groups. The enforcement of the confinement policy may have been tightened up because the relationship between Thailand and Myanmar has changed from confronting to trading and cooperating.

3.3.2 Movement Tightened Up

After the shelters were consolidated, the displaced peoples' movements were restricted, they were registered, and the shelters were regularly raided to prevent any hoarding of arms (Kanyaban, ibid.). Currently, three principles underpin RTG policy: upholding the encampment, minimising or relieving the burden on Thailand, and solving the root cause of the problem (MOI). The problems of displaced persons from Myanmar became a challenge and threat to security and the burden become greater. In 1998, the RTG invited UNHCR, which was operating in Thailand for Indochinese refugee at that time, to provide protection for the displaced persons from Myanmar. The role of UNHCR was to support the registration system, assist voluntary repatriation when the situation allowed, support the RTG decision to relocate or consolidate the shelters, and negotiate with Myanmar government to increase its role in Myanmar to facilitate the repatriation and support the reintegration.

3.3.3 Internationalising the Issue

The admission to the shelters was first decided by local authorities. The registration was done with MOI. In order to support the formal registration system, the RTG set up the Provincial Admission Board (PAB), a formal body for status determination in 1998. When the PAB was set up, the local investigation team would submit the application to PAB to consider and determine *displaced person* status. The PAB has eight members from provincial government sectors, with a UNHCR representative. The UNHCR role is to provide support data and advocate for displaced persons applications.

The approved cases are granted displaced persons status, with the registration based on family unit. Until 2007, an individual identity card was issued to each displaced person. The ID card is issued by MOI with support from UNHCR. The presence of UNHCR and formal screening procedure has changed the status determination from localised to internationalised level. The rejected applicants can appeal to the Appeal Board within 7 days with the assistance of UNHCR to submit additional documents. The Appeal Board has 12 members, headed by an Inspector of the MOI, and it considers PAB reports and UNHCR filed documents. The board's decision is final. According to circumstances, most of rejected applicants are not likely to appeal unless they have additional data to support their appeal.

In order to provide more precise information on applicants and improve the screening procedure, the pre-screening programme has been initiated to standardise the interview and screening process in 2009. The authorised interviewers are fully trained and provided with guidelines, UNHCR was one of the trainers; and interviews were done at the same time in four pilot shelters to prevent duplicated applicants from moving from one shelter to another. The results of the pre-screening are confidential and pass to the PAB.

3.3.4 Resettlement Permitted

Status determination became an important issue when the RTG agreed to a mass resettlement programme for displaced persons in 2005. Earlier, permission was given to POC or Burmese students on case by case basis. The lack of a PAB to prove the displaced persons' status not only obscured the displaced person's identity but also eligibility for protection and resettlement opportunity. The non-registered may also cause tension in the shelters. As the funding is declining, NGOs restricted food items and rations only to registered displaced persons, though negotiating for the vulnerable cases are permitted (Interview NGO, 6/8/10).

Prior to the consolidation of the shelters, the encampment policy was not strictly enforced, and the displaced persons' movements were allowed to seek for surplus food from surrounding forest and work in agriculture farms nearby. The consolidation and encampment policy have made it more difficult for displaced to work outside. Some displaced persons were arrested and deported, to the areas not controlled by Burmese authorities, but most managed to go back to the shelters (Interview Border Police, 6/9/10).

3.3.5 Displaced Person, Not a Recognised Refugee

As noted, the RTG has adopted its own term *displaced persons* for those *fleeing fighting*. In principle, then, the RTG puts a higher threshold of threat for those it considers are in need of the protection it affords. The RTG does not use the term *refugees* at all; and the shelters it has set up to house the displaced persons are *temporary settlements* rather than refugee camps.

Though not granting refugee recognition to asylum seekers from Myanmar, Thailand has adopted certain protection measures for displaced persons whose status has been determined, one of which is non-refoulement. The Cardno Agri-systems report (2009) showed the displaced persons who failed the screening process are still living in the shelters.

Despite hosting millions of asylum seekers over decades, Thailand has never made public any formal asylum policy. In the period of the Indochinese refugees there were discussions of possible solutions, including the issue of an Asylum Act, proposed by some parliament members, but the act was not taken forward. The RTG has issued other legislative provisions to deal with certain circumstances of displacement from Myanmar.

In conclusion, the RTG policy towards displaced persons comprises temporary asylum, confinement and assigned status of displaced persons rather than refugees. It is a purposive policy, has clear principles, but has been formulated by ad hoc mechanism, flexible at first, and tightened up at some key turning points. The rationale for this situation is that Thailand was faced with finding a solution for Indochinese displaced persons at that time and considered the displacement from

Myanmar as temporary. The RTG wanted to maintain a good image in dealing with refugees. The more rigid policy was enforced after the political activities of Burmese activists against their government that took place in Bangkok became too frequent and too serious with the Embassy and hospital hostages. Also, the RTG has wanted to keep constructive engagement with Myanmar government, and to strengthen it.

3.3.6 Chronology of the RTG Policy Towards Displaced Persons from Myanmar

- 1984: RTG permitted the first shelter for displaced persons from Myanmar to be established
- 1992: RTG set up Maneeloy shelter to host Burmese students, and activists
- 1995–1998: consolidated small shelters and moved shelter locations after several cross border attacks from Burma military and DKBA
- 1998: RTG invited UNHCR to provide protection for displaced persons from Myanmar
- 1998–1999: PAB was set up, official screening and status determination started. PAB determined only those *fleeing fighting* at the beginning. Later the definition was expanded to *fleeing persecution*
- 2000: MOI and UNHCR agreed to transfer POCs from urban areas to Maneeloy shelter
- 2002: Vocational training (VT) was provided as a pilot project in Suan Pueng shelter
- 2002: RTG planned to repatriate displaced persons in border areas and resettle Burmese students
- 2003: Closed Maneeloy shelter, transferred POCs to Tham Hin shelter
- 2003: Appeal Board was set up for displaced persons to appeal for their status determination
- 2005: MOI signed MOU with UNHCR to set up the registration system
- 2005: MOI and UNHCR transferred the remaining POCs to border shelters. RTG permitted the mass resettlement programme
- 2006: MOI gave permission to start VT in some shelters
- 2006: More government agencies started involvement in displaced persons issue. MOE started its teaching Thai project in the shelters
- 2007: MOI issued displaced persons individual identity cards
- 2009: Pre-screening programme starts in four shelters at Nupo, Tham Hin, Ban Mai Nai, Soi Site 1 and Ban Don Yang

3.4 Policy and Practice, Realities on the Ground

The policy of the RTG towards displaced persons Myanmar, though it has some ambiguities, is fairly clear in the settlements, where displaced persons have faced various restrictions on their freedom of movement, access to law, education and health care, and earning a living. In particular, if they leave the settlement they will be considered an illegal immigrant, and be subject to deportation back to Myanmar. The protection and rights afforded to the displaced persons are therefore less than would be guaranteed if Thailand had signed the 1951 Refugee Convention.

In practice, however, the actions of the RTG towards the displaced persons have always been more positive than the stated policy on particular issues, and have varied according to local administrations and circumstances, for example variations in the approach of different settlement administrators. Practice over time has also evolved, partly to cope with new problems, partly in response to international opinion, and partly as a result of different national governments in Thailand. The RTG has learned lessons from dealing practically for so long with hosting Indochinese refugee.

3.4.1 Confinement

Practice on confinement has varied over time, and has become tighter as the displaced persons issue became more politicised. The RTG has made clear from the start that the acceptance of displaced persons is temporary and asylum seekers need to be confined to the temporary shelters (MOI). This regulation was not strictly enforced in the first 10 years and many of the displaced persons enjoyed freedom of movement to some extent. After a higher risk was placed on the displaced persons' security, confinement became real and put into practice.

In practice, current reports state that many of the displaced persons have managed to leave the shelters for work (IRC 2008). Thai security to guard or control the movement of displaced persons is small when compared to the displaced persons population; in Mae La shelter, there are only 62 territory voluntary guards, only half of the required number, and they work in shifts, while the displaced persons population is 46,673. The number is insufficient to patrol the shelter strictly, and reflects the flexibility of the shelter control in practice (Interview RTG officer, 20/12/10). The movement in and out of the shelters is unofficial but the confinement policy is not effective, and can lead to abuse and corruption. Normally, the movement between shelters for the purpose of shelter administration, education and training are permitted.

Consequently, the legal status of displaced persons remains *illegal* because Thailand has no other applicable law than its Immigration Act to address immigrant entry including displaced persons from Myanmar seeking asylum. In practice, this means displaced persons are confined to *settlements* as a condition of the protection offered. Those who leave the shelters are subject to arrest and deportation. Arguably, the repatriation of Karen displaced persons that took place, *informal deportation* as it has been termed, did not place displaced persons into danger as they were not handed to Myanmar authorities but rather through informal channels along the border (Interview MOD officer, 20/12/10). But in most cases the RTG has broadly kept to the principle of non-refoulement.

3.4.2 Status Determination and Registration

The official screening procedure started in 1998, with UNHCR's participation, but has ceased functioning from time to time. The screening is based on interview information which varies according to each shelter and interview team. The pre-screening programme has been introduced with the aims to increase the capacity of interviewer and standardise the procedure.

Admission to the shelters was restricted initially to people fleeing from the fighting between ethnic insurgents and Burmese military but later the criteria broadened to the two definitions of displaced persons defined earlier, fleeing from *fighting* and *political persecution* (MOI). PAB was regularly meeting on monthly basis during 1999–2001 but less frequently after 2002 and resumed full function again in 2004, only to re-register and transfer the cases to new database system, only small number of new cases. The PAB status determination was considered on group basis during the first period but after 2005, the meetings were rare, one or two per year but the consideration was made on case basis; the last meeting was held on 16 August 2010 (PAB meeting report, 16/8/10).

Though the newcomers still arrive at the shelters, they are a mixture of vulnerable groups, seekers for resettlement, and job seekers; without the status determined, there are no other mechanisms to screen out those not eligible to displaced persons status (Interview NGO staff, 8/9/10). The reasons why the PAB often fails to function are various; in a view of MOI officer, the status determination has become meaningless with the failure to deport the *screened out* cases, and UNHCR is not able to guarantee safe return (Interview MOI field officer, 4/11/10). The ineffective screening process is reported in an earlier study of Cardno Agrisystems (2009). The difficulty, on the other hand, can come from an MOI attitude of not wanting to force any deportation, so that a stronger operation may be necessary (Interview MOD officer 11/12/10). The pre-screening programme that aims to fill the PAB gap is in doubt. Training was provided before the programme started but after a year the result of the pilot programme has not yet been finalised.

Registration of displaced persons in the shelters has been conducted for various purposes by different organisations at different times. The first formal registration process for displaced persons in the border shelters was conducted by the MOI and UNHCR in 1999. Only in 2007 was each displaced person issued with an individual ID card rather than a family registration form. The ID cards, which come with a photo and a magnetic strip issued by DPA, are issued to all refugees over the age of 12. The card contains the name and age of the displaced person, as well as the settlement where he or she is registered, together with the left and right thumbprints encoded on the magnetic strip. Holding the card, the displaced person will be able to return to the settlement safely if he or she is arrested outside.

Though the initial intention was that ID cards would be issued for those over 12-year old, the latest registration process, from 2009, applied to newborn children in the shelters. It was the first time that the official birth registration for displaced persons fitted with the Thai registration system. The providing of birth certificates in the settlements is perhaps the most significant practical change. As has been noted, the CRC, to which Thailand is a signatory, requires this as a right for all children; and arguably the Thai constitution also guarantees this basic right. Before, the newborn was registered on the family registration form. The RTG's reluctance to include the newborn within the official Thai system is often seen as due to the risk of being forced later to grant them Thai citizenship. However, the absence of clear documentation of identify those in the camps also ran the risk, for instance, of making any subsequent resettlement more difficult. It would potentially even complicate voluntary repatriation, giving Myanmar an easy excuse for not accepting any displaced persons who lacked formal identification. In 2009, the RTG began formally to issue birth certificates to those children born in the camps. The reservation of CRC, article 7, was lifted in a cabinet meeting in September, 2010. The issue of a formal system for registering births has been one of the most controversial in relation to the Burmese displaced persons.

3.4.3 Education

Education has been another area where practice has evolved. All children and young people in the settlements have been guaranteed primary and secondary education, though attendance has sometimes been patchy. The education system, though, was geared towards voluntary repatriation as the only solution, and it was therefore not linked to the Thai education system and curriculum, but rather to that in Myanmar. The fact that, increasingly, many of the young people in the settlements had never lived in Myanmar was an unfortunate truth. Again, for the RTG, harmonising education in the settlements with the Thai system, including teaching Thai language, could be seen as another step to granting mass right to remain in Thailand, perhaps partly as a result of international pressure for a solution from donor countries.

Access to tertiary level education is very restricted for the Burmese displaced persons because of the policy of confinement to the settlements. However, the 2006 visit to the settlements by the ex-Thai Prime Minister led to an idea that Thai universities and colleges might sponsor selected Burmese displaced persons and bring them to Bangkok. However, this has not been put into practice. Tertiary level education is still restricted, but many courses under the term *Post 10* or training course have taken place in some shelters.

In 2005, the NSC and MOE together with Provincial Governors of the border provinces and other relevant organisations planned to work jointly on the *Education for displaced persons* programme (Source: MOE). The agreed strategy was firstly to prioritise education for communication, both in reading and writing, rather than focus to academic matters. Secondly, it was agreed to encourage the understanding of tradition between two countries, Thailand and Myanmar. Later, the MOE was able to set up Thai Language Study Centres in the settlements, teaching Thai language to displaced persons adult and children.

The Thai language courses are arranged into three grades; basic, intermediate and advanced; and there is 96 h learning for each grade. Besides those, there are supplementary activities on Thai culture and language organised. Classes are conducted by territorial security corps, volunteers and teachers from office of the Non-Formal and Informal Education. Thai language study is a supplementary subject in secondary level at schools (MOI-CCSDPT Annual Workshop 2008). The Special Study programme accepts grade 10 graduated students, and is categorised into seven special programmes, but due to the lack of human resources, the programme is open in some camps only.

Graduation in the settlements is not recognised by the Thai education bureau yet. The attempt to adapt the shelter curriculum to Thai curriculum is ongoing. An interview with the MOE suggested a possible approach is to arrange a placement test (Interview with Office of The Basic Education Commission, MOE 2010).

3.4.4 Employment

Employment, a key part of self-reliance, has been the biggest stumbling block for the displaced persons. The right to earn a livelihood has effectively been denied, resulting in all sorts of problems, not least one of dependency on supplies from the various NGOs that operate in the settlements. Again, arguably, the resistance to the displaced persons being able to legally work can be viewed as consistent with the RTG's attempts to limit the move towards local integration. Under the current Thai national legislation, any displaced persons that leave the settlements to seek work or for any other reason become illegal immigrants and can be deported. In practice, many of the displaced persons do have jobs, and are able to leave the settlements to work for local employers, usually in agriculture and manufacturing. This practice is widespread, if not officially sanctioned. Practice also varies locally, reflecting the relative autonomy that the RTG gives to different local officials. Attempts to create work opportunities in the settlements, other than for tasks related directly to settlement functions, such as administrators, nurses and teachers, have been relatively unsuccessful, partly because of the logistical challenges of, for example, bringing raw materials into the settlements in order to run manufacturing operations using the displaced persons as labour. The tolerance of displaced persons going outside to work can be partly seen as a way of reducing unhealthy and potentially disruptive tensions in the settlements, with so many confined displaced persons. Displaced persons can work legally; but only inside the settlements, such as working with NGOs, trading and agriculture. Inevitably, numbers are limited; not all displaced persons can find work in the settlements. So far, there is not so much real change viewed from the UN and NGO perspective; the CCSDPT/UNHCR 5-year strategy plan emphasises more employment, but there has been little real progress.

3.4.5 Vocational Education and Training

The issue of vocational education has also been one where policy has changed. Again, this area has been one where the RTG has seemingly been reluctant to sanction an activity that might seem to support the idea of local integration. Nevertheless, the teaching of practical skills such as weaving and carpentry has been introduced. Skills acquired could equally be applied back in Myanmar, of course, should voluntary repatriation become an option. There are income generating programmes in many shelters, with displaced persons given training on sewing, electronics, and agriculture. Handicraft shops are open in shelters to sell products produced by displaced persons. The MOI has permitted renting of land for training agricultural skills and generating income. These all are part of the self-reliance initiative, being an investment in resettlement as well as eventual repatriation, as viewed by the RTG.

The lack of progress in conflict resolution in Myanmar has led to a change in the position of the previous Thai government regarding burden sharing through resettlement programmes and capacity building of the refugees while in Thailand. VT is a way of working towards sustainable livelihoods by fostering economic self-reliance. This major shift in thinking requires a different focus for the VT courses. VT needs to be balanced between training for independence within the refugee situation and training for repatriation and resettlement. As of now, VT is provided by both NGOs and Community-Based Organisations (CBOs), and programmes vary from income generation to improving the food basket to merely teaching new skills, such as auto mechanics, baking and cooking, carpentry and computers and IT. Some training courses such as agriculture, animal husbandry and fish breeding require access to land leased from the Thai Forestry Department near the settlements, and also support from local citizens in the villages around the settlements. Arguably, some of this training may need to be revised to better meet displaced persons' needs and create opportunity for income. Microfinance has been initiated in some settlements in the form of Village Saving and Loan Associations (VSLA) for those who are more interested in setting up their own small businesses than looking for waged employment.

3.4.6 Internationalisation and the Role of UNHCR

The invitation to UNHCR to oversee the temporary settlements in 1998 was in itself a change in policy, and the UN body now plays an active role in monitoring the settlements, and in seeking durable solutions. Its initial role in *screening in* Burmese displaced persons who reached its offices in Bangkok, the POCs, became less important in 1996 when the Maneeloy Camp was closed and all remaining POCs were transferred to the border settlements. The status of POCs was a problem because it provided protection that should not be binding in Thai law, and it tended to be assigned to political activists who could be embarrassing to the RTG, especially as POCs did not have to be confined to settlements. In practice, the case of POCs has been flexibly treated. Currently, the POC status is used not only for asylum from Burma, but asylum from other parts of the world such as North Korea, the Middle East and Africa. Local criticism maintained that the POC status was easier to obtain in Thailand than in most other places (Interview RTG officer 10/11/10). Since the RTG accepted resettlement as one of the solutions to the displaced persons issue, international agencies have played a major role, and over 64,000 displaced persons have settled in many countries. However, case load has not reduced, and resettlement has been considered as a pull factor, making it unsatisfactory to the RTG. As a result, though the policy was not changed, the resettlement process has slowed down, with numbers expected to be around 10,000 in 2010 (interview with TBBC 2010a, b).

3.5 Factors Influencing RTG Policy

The RTG's formal policy stance on the displaced persons from Myanmar has been shaped by a number of historical factors, notably its experience with the Indochinese refugees in the 1970s. At the same time, the difference in treatment of the Indochinese and ethnic displaced persons from Myanmar by the RTG may have contributed in some measure to the protracted nature of the current displaced persons issue. The apparent reluctance, as some commentators have seen it, in *internationalising* the current situation, such as involving UNHCR and rejecting resettlement, may have made the situation more complex and solutions harder to find.

There are particular circumstances, from the national perspective, that the RTG feels justifies its decision in the face of such international criticism. Of these, the most crucial is the concern that the exercise of full refugee rights will cause more political chaos; the protest of the anti-Burmese government movement and the seizure of the Burmese embassy in Bangkok support this concern.

3.5.1 Internal Factors

Since the Indochinese refugee experience, Thailand had a clear *preventing policy* for asylum seekers, though permission for humanitarian assistance has not been denied. The long period of struggling with local protest, the difficulties dealing with different humanitarian agencies, conflict between refugee groups, the assumed autonomy of UN agencies which led to violence among refugees against local Thai authorities, the pressure from the international community to open up more local integration, are all pressures that Thailand has had to face for a long time. This historical experience has shaped the policy toward displaced persons from Myanmar who entered at later period.

The local resistance during the Indochinese period came from the poor standard of living among local communities that were themselves struggling to survive. The assistance offered to the refugees was seen as a free gift. There was also a fear of political ideology at that period. Villagers also had to move to make way for shelters to be established. All these factors increased Thai community unwillingness to accept the Indochinese refugees.

Thailand's experience of dealing with the huge numbers of Indochinese refugees from the 1970s has had some impact on how the RTG deals with the protracted Burmese displaced persons situation. For example, the aggressive attitude of Vietnamese refugees against Thai authority was considered to result from UN protection and autonomy. The RTG has shown a reluctance to involve UN and international organisations too soon because the RTG resists external pressure that will override its own interests.

The fear of politics may not be a problem with displaced persons from Myanmar nowadays, but modernisation has made the way of living more costly. Though the economy in Thailand has improved, income inequality still remains a problem between rural people and urban. The increasing population has made land and natural resources a crucial problem for every Thai government. The use of land among locals becomes competitive, not only for daily consumption but also for living and business. When the displaced persons are included in the competition, either as labourers or users of natural resources, negative feelings towards displaced persons among local community are increased (Interview local administration officer 12/7/10).

Thai public and local opinions have remained a critical factor for the RTG, and surveys have consistently showed that strategies of local integration are a challenge (Assumption University 2007; Pettra 2008). This is especially true of the Thai communities in the border areas, who have experienced competition for agricultural land and pollution as a result of the settlements, and who believe in many cases that the displaced persons have better access to local resources. The resistance and reaction to displaced persons settlement can happen long after the local settlement has taken place, as in the case of Vietnam refugees settled in Thailand. They also considered the existence of displaced persons settlements had caused the spread of disease and crime (Khanchai 2003; Pettra, ibid).

The attempt to increase displaced persons access to social services, as stated in UNHCR/CCSDPT 5-year strategy, is another challenge to Thailand. Rural health services are planned for a certain amount of people, not only the materials and equipment but numbers of health personnel to serve local communities. Basic health problems are better addressed in the shelters but the prevention and report system may need to be coordinated more with Thai health systems for better collaboration (Interview MOPH officer 25/11/10). Therefore, the RTG is reluctant to include displaced persons to local public services.

Access to higher education is beyond the basic education that RTG has provided to local children, in addition to the different education system and language of instructions. The adjustment of existing education curriculum to Thai education system will be helpful for accreditation only if the language barrier is overcome, and access to local or Thai schools will be a challenge for cultural identity and assimilation to Karen, Karenni or other ethnic displaced persons. The RTG budget for education does not cover tertiary education, thus financial matters will be another constraint for displaced persons access to higher education.

The difficulty in management of migrant workers from Myanmar is undeniably a factor connected to policy on displaced persons. As earlier mentioned, Thailand has struggled with problematic administration over the migrant issue for a long time. The control approach used to administer migrant workers has proved unsuccessful and another approach is needed. The addition of the displaced persons, with its political dimension, makes the migrant situation more complicated. Combining migrant and displaced persons issues, in some RTG officers view, will provide double protection to displaced persons and make them difficult to administer, because migrants have limited term of services and can be deported but displaced persons have international protection that makes deportation more difficult (Interview NSC Officer, 13/11/10). The same view is cited about the economic uncertainty, whether displaced persons are willing not to receive support in the shelter or to survive by themselves if the economic downturns (Interview MOFA Officer). This question remains for all stakeholders to consider, not only displaced persons.

The RTG has most often cited national security as a critical issue in defining its policy towards the displaced persons. However, there have been instances, notably the Myanmar Embassy incident, which have both embarrassed and unnerved the Thai authorities. The regular search to prevent some opposition groups who were active in the armed movement in Myanmar from using the shelters to support their activities reflects the RTG concern, and this has legitimately helped shape its policy.

3.5.2 External Factors

The RTG's resistance to signing the 1951 Refugee Convention has provided a means to refuse protection to some displaced persons. The reason for not signing has been the source of speculation: by being a non-signatory, for example, the

RTG avoids being subject to the rulings of the International Court of Justice on refugee issues, and the RTG has had some experience of rulings from that court going against it. Another possibility, raised in interviews with RTG representatives, is that Thailand cannot cope with the freedom of movement of *refugees*, especially in being politically active against Myanmar. There is also a feeling that signing the Convention, and therefore treating displaced persons from Myanmar formally as refugees, might be seen as an unfriendly act by Myanmar, something to be avoided as Thailand continues to manage its complex relationship with its neighbour. Or maybe the RTG merely wishes to maintain its large margin of discretion to deal with the flows of displaced persons.

Thailand has signed other international declaration and conventions, some of which do have relevance for the displaced persons, including the Universal Declaration of Human Rights (UDHR), the Convention on the Rights of the Child (CRC), International Covenant on Civil and Political Rights (ICCPR) and the Convention on the Elimination of All Forms of Discrimination Against Women (CEDAW). Part of CRC is cited by the RTG as its commitment to protect displaced children. However, the RTG posted reservations to the relevant Articles 7 and 22; the former confers rights of birth registration and nationality for all children and the latter deals directly with refugee children. The Cabinet has now lifted the reservation of Article 7 to register birth of all children on Thai soil, including refugee children which does not biding to grant them nationality. The issue of a formal system for registering births has been one of the most controversial in relation to the Burmese displaced persons.

In the absence of the framework that the UN Refugee Convention would provide, the displaced persons have in essence been subject to Thai national laws, notably the Immigration Act 1979 which clarifies the classification of *illegal immigrant*. Section 17 of the Act does allow for decisions by the RTG Cabinet to overrule the Act in special cases, and this was used in some cases in the 1970s and 1980s for some Indochinese refugees, but it has been little used more recently and does not apply to the displaced persons residing in the shelters. The Constitution of Thailand, in principle covering all who reside in the country, Thai and non-Thai, ought to offer some protection to the Burmese displaced persons, since it mentions human rights and human dignity; in practice, though, it applies to citizens, and displaced persons are classified as illegal. It has not been tested in the Courts.

The relationship with Myanmar is certainly an influence factor to the RTG policy, and RTG foreign policy towards Myanmar has been altered from time to time. During 1980–1988 the policy emphasised partnership to protect the country from the Socialist Vietnam influence in the region. From 1988 onwards, Thailand gave priority to economic growth, and Thailand adjusted its national development policy from producing for internal consumption to producing for export. Thailand foreign policy during 1988–1991, was to build a *trading market instead of war zone* with neighbouring countries. In 1996, Thailand signed an agreement with Myanmar to build the first friendship bridge in Mae Sod district, Tak, and signed Memorandum of Understanding (MOU) with Myanmar in 2004 to collaborate in solving the migrant worker issue. Thailand's intention to strengthen relationship with Myanmar was stated in its Security Policy towards Myanmar 2003–2005, as well as to prevent any operation against Myanmar government to take place in Thailand.

Thailand had to search for more resources and markets, which led to more constructive engagement with Myanmar. Myanmar's fertile land, minerals, oil and gas were attractive to Thai business investors. Most of the huge projects between Thai and Myanmar focused on the land of ethnic minority groups. Economic factors have been criticised as becoming overly important in Thailand's relationship with Myanmar, leading Thai policy makers to go along with the Myanmar government rather than confront it, for example on human rights issues.

Thailand was in a uniquely difficult position with regard to the conflicts in Indochina, with the geopolitical context, *stopping the march of communism*, and the resulting refugee influx from Vietnam, Cambodia and elsewhere. The RTG did afford protection to those seeking it on a large scale and in a way that mainly accorded with international humanitarian law and the spirit and letter of the 1951 UN Refugee Convention. The Comprehensive Plan of Action (CPA) that ultimately was put in place to deal with the situation involved huge international cooperation, including a significant resettlement programme, and arguably only came about with the media focus on boatloads of Vietnamese refugees being turned away from ports or interred, as well as a desire by all countries to end the problem and move on. Partly for its own reasons, relating perhaps to its relationship with Myanmar, the RTG has deliberately sought not to draw attention to the displaced persons from that country, to the extent of not inviting UNHCR to the border settlements until 1998. From interviews with RTG representatives, it seems clear also that the RTG did not expect the situation would last so long and become protracted (interview, MOFA officer, 10/11/10).

The engagement in regional cooperation and international bodies such as ASEAN can contribute to RTG policies both positively and negatively. With the success of Thailand in supporting Myanmar to be a member of ASEAN, the recent meeting of the Foreign Ministers of ASEAN has stressed the importance of having a dialogue of all parties concerned in Myanmar's further development. The strengthening of the economy could promote reconciliation and democracy in Myanmar; which in turn may create, eventually, conditions for voluntary repatriation of the displaced persons.

The role of ASEAN in positively engaging with Myanmar is significantly increasing. During the ASEAN Summit which was held in Thailand in 2009, all the countries agreed that in order to gain a durable solution for the Rohingya problem in Bangladesh, discussion and agreement at the regional level was critical to ultimate success. A regional mechanism has been set up to monitor respect for human rights. One outcome was that the Prime Minister of Myanmar accepted the approach of setting up a contact group and bringing the issue on to the region panel. The practice that follows this promise needs to be seen. Another attempt can be seen from the recent meeting among the ASEAN's Minister of Foreign Affairs in Indonesia in January 2011(MOFA). ASEAN will seek international cooperation to remove sanctions that have been applied on Myanmar by some countries, and push forward compromises between the Myanmar Military Government and Aung San SuuKyi, the pro-democracy leader. The latest visit to Aung San SuuKyi and high ranking officers in the Myanmar government by the Thai Foreign Minister in mid January 2011 is a sign that Thailand also prefers Myanmar to solve its internal conflict peacefully. There is a possibility that, in the near future, Myanmar will take its turn to become the president of ASEAN, so there is a need for Myanmar to gain credit from the international community. All this may lead, ultimately, to safer conditions for repatriation for the displaced persons.

The ratification by the RTG of international conventions is another influence on RTG Policy. Since 1998, in accordance with the CRC, National Education Plan and the National Economic and Social Development Plan, the RTG established and enforced 12 years' basic education for every student including displaced persons, and permission has given to education expansion in the shelters.

UNHCR's involvement has had an impact on the displaced persons situation since 1998, and has had some influence on the policy of RTG. The formal registration and establish of PAB was the RTG response to a UNHCR proposal to provide protection to displaced persons. Involvement of UNHCR to solve the displaced persons' problem from Myanmar has also given some support for repatriation as a durable solution (UNHCR-RTG 2nd meeting, 1998), though UNHCR will only support RTG policy for voluntary repatriation, for example, if certain basic conditions are met (Interview with UNHCR, 17/6/2010).The contribution of UNHCR as well as other UN agencies and NGOs has resulted in the shifting of some RTG policy. But the relationship between Thailand and UN agencies is not always positive, and there were times that the RTG expressed its unwillingness to receive any support which was accompanied by conditions, considering it was not an equal partnership (Cabinet Resolution, 23/12/2003).

It is not yet clear what impact the election of November 2010 and its aftermath may have, both on political processes in Myanmar and, ultimately, on the 150,000 or so Burmese displaced persons living in the temporary settlements across the Thai border. In particular, the release from house arrest of Aung San SuuKyi, the symbolic leader of Myanmar's opposition and the daughter of its greatest national hero and anti-imperialist liberation fighter, may have the potential of being a game changer for the political impasse. Many analysts are speculating that the regime cannot easily reverse its decision; reimposing restrictions on SuuKyi might lead to a new level of civil unrest. At the same time, it has been remarked that Aung San SuuKyi has been taking a noticeably more conciliatory tone towards the regime since her release, and that there is more potential for positive action and democratisation than there has been in the last 20 years. Whether this means, for example, that the opportunity for voluntary repatriation for those Burmese displaced persons in Thailand is closer, remains to be seen. However, initial signs that the Myanmar army, post November 2010 election, is stepping up action against armed groups from the Karen, Wa and Kachin ethnic groupings is not encouraging. Against this, the ASEAN regional group, of which Myanmar is a member, is showing a willingness to engage as it has not done before.

References

Assumption University, 2007: *Refugee in Thailand in Public awareness and perception* (Bangkok: Assumption University Social Innovation in Management and Business Analysis Research Centre).

Cardno Agrisystems, 2009: *Livelihoods Vulnerability Analysis in Burmese Refugee Camps in Thailand* (Bangkok: Cardno Agrisystems).

Kanyabarn, P., 1998: *The problem of displaced persons in Thailand: study the past, present for the future. Research report. Academic year 1997–1998* (Bangkok: National College of Thailand).

Khanchai, S. et al., 2003: *Needs evaluation of communities in shelters surrounding areas in Thasongyang and Pobphra districts, Tak provinces* (Bangkok: Asian Research Center for Migration).

MOI, 1954: Document 1678/2497, issued on 8 April (Bangkok: Ministry of Interior).

MOI/CCSDPT, 2008: *The Government and Humanitarian Organisations seminar on Working Practices under the Government's Policy on the Displaced Persons from Burma* (Bangkok: Ministry of Interior).

TBBC, 2010a: *Programme Report, January-June 2010* (Bangkok: TBBC).

TBBC, 2010b: *Programme Report, July-December 2010* (Bangkok: TBBC).

Chapter 4
RTG Policy and the Needs of the Displaced Persons

Premjai Vungsiriphisal, Graham Bennett, Chanarat Poomkacha, Waranya Jitpong and Kamonwan Reungsamran

Abstract The effects of the confinement policy of the RTG are described, with displaced persons formally restricted to the settlements and forced to rely entirely on humanitarian aid. The opinions of the camp residents are sought on a range of needs, including protection, health care, education, well-being and livelihoods. In most cases, people have been treated well; it is the issue of confinement that is the problem. The displaced persons are also asked about which of the durable solutions would be most acceptable; this varies by age and experience, but many would wish to return to Myanmar if safety could be ensured.

Keywords Confinement · Aid dependency · NGOs · UNHCR · Refugee health care · Vocational education · Welfare · Access to justice · Gender

P. Vungsiriphisal (✉) · G. Bennett · C. Poomkacha · W. Jitpong · K. Reungsamran
Asian Research Center for Migration, Institute of Asian Studies, Chulalongkorn University, 3rd floor, Prachadhipok Rambhai-Barni Building, Bangkok 10330, Thailand
e-mail: premjai.v@chula.ac.th

G. Bennett
e-mail: grahambennett777@hotmail.co.uk

C. Poomkacha
e-mail: cpoomkacha@abeam.com

W. Jitpong
e-mail: wec135@hotmail.com

K. Reungsamran
e-mail: kamonwan24@yahoo.com

P. Vungsiriphisal et al. (eds.), *Humanitarian Assistance for Displaced Persons from Myanmar*, SpringerBriefs in Environment, Security, Development and Peace 17,
DOI: 10.1007/978-3-319-02795-1_4,

4.1 Introduction

The earlier chapter explained the formulation of the RTG policy towards displaced persons, the rationale and factors that have influenced the policy development. This chapter will explore how the existing policy has responded to the needs of the displaced persons, how it has contributed or affected the living conditions and well-being of the displaced persons, and what is the gap that needs to be considered for improvement.

4.2 Needs of Displaced Persons

4.2.1 Protection

Considering the situation that drives displaced persons out of Myanmar, the first need of those fleeing from perceived danger is a safe sanctuary in Thailand as their refuge country. The RTG has consolidated the various earlier small shelters close to the Thai–Myanmar border after several attacks from the DKBA. Though criticised for placing more restrictions on displaced persons, the consolidated settlements have proved easier to defend as well as to providing more safety. The survey indicates that the main reason for most of the respondents, 61.5 %, to remain in the shelter is safety, followed by family unity, children's education, food rations and having no choice. The findings show that most of the respondents feel physically safe, and only a small number feel unsafe, with no difference between the registered and non-registered displaced persons (Figs. 4.1, 4.2, 4.3).

In order to ensure the shelters safety, regulations to control security have been put into practice: such as placing security guards. The regulations to control the shelters are acceptable to most of the displaced persons.

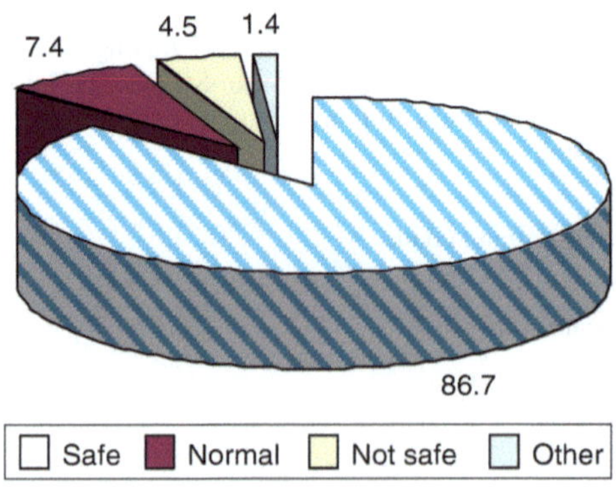

Fig. 4.1 Displaced persons' feeling safe residing in the shelter. *Source* The authors

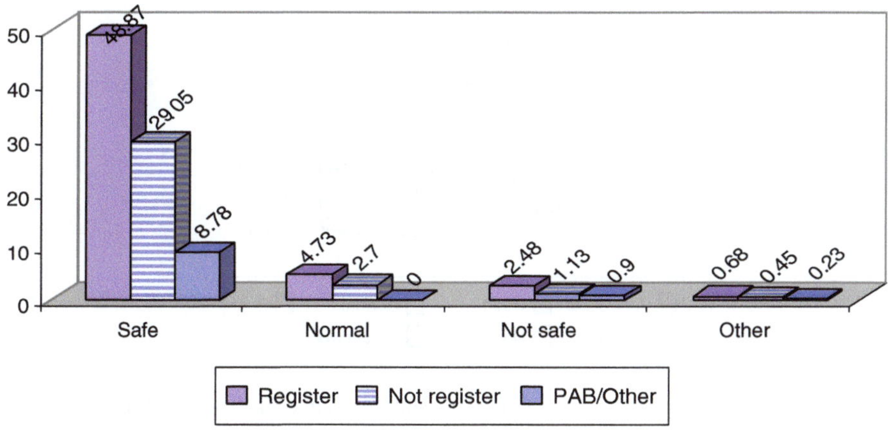

Fig. 4.2 Feeling safe among respondents' different status. *Source* The authors

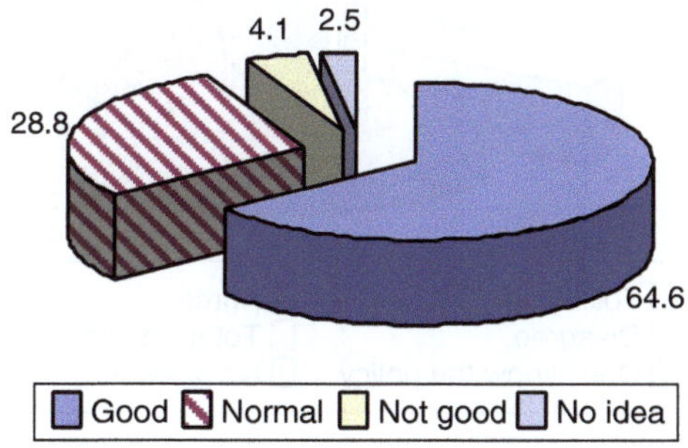

Fig. 4.3 Displaced persons' opinion toward security control policy. *Source* The authors

Another factor that can contribute to secure feeling of displaced persons is the relationship with Thai authorities who are responsible for shelter control. The survey finds that two-thirds of the respondents consider they have a good relationship with Thai authorities, and a much smaller group of 4 % feel their relationship is rather poor (Fig. 4.4).

It should be noted that the good relationship between displaced persons and authorities does not necessarily indicate personal contact but it may be only normal or good cooperation between them. The shelter administration system does not require displaced persons to contact the authorities directly.

Compared to the earlier period, more restricted regulation has been applied to displaced persons' movement. Although the confinement policy has been criticised negatively by different stakeholders, the restriction may be perceived as the means to achieve shelter security. The findings show that almost two-thirds of displaced persons who participate in this study agree to the policy and only a small number disagree (Fig. 4.5).

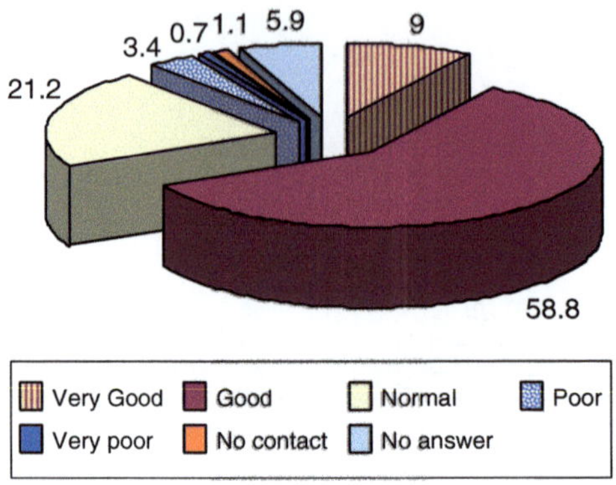

Fig. 4.4 Relationship between displaced persons and Thai authorities. *Source* The authors

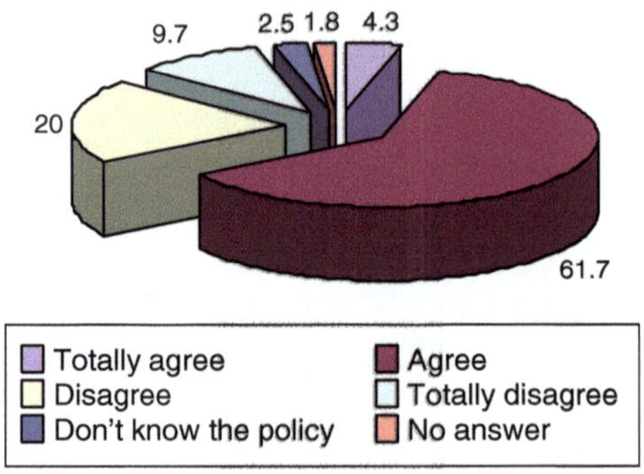

Fig. 4.5 Displaced persons opinion towards policy of restricted movement. *Source* The authors

Though the majority of respondents seem to accept the confinement policy, some of them still want it to change. Asking them to prioritise the policy element they want to change, some 20.3 % of the respondents want the confinement policy to change, more respondents as 25.9 % want change in education policy and 17.6 % policy of employment (Fig. 4.6).

The above answers, it could be argued, indicate acceptance by the displaced persons of the policy that restricts their movement. It is likely that they accept the policy because, in reality, they are not completely confined to the shelters; there is some flexibility on the ground or, in the worst case, they accept it as having no other alternative.

Information from focus group interviews can support or explain the reasons for policies that respondents want to see some changes. The long waiting time for resettlement application and the fact that non-registered displaced persons are not eligible to apply are reasons they want to see change in resettlement policy as well as to be informed of the reason for rejected cases. Some look for more

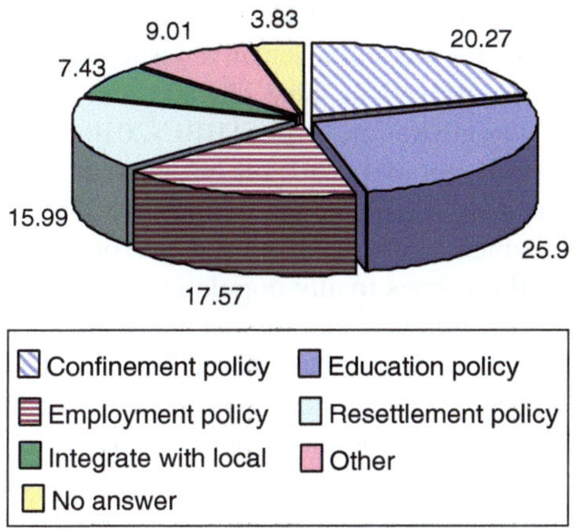

Fig. 4.6 The policy that respondents want to change at first priority. *Source* The authors

opportunities to study outside the shelter and study at a higher level in a Thai institute, while some want permission to be employed outside the shelter and not be arrested.

4.2.2 Administration in the Settlements

From the beginning, the MOI has tried to give the displaced persons a high degree of self-management in the settlements, especially as the settlements have become formally established. Attempts have been made to involve the displaced persons directly in the committee structures that govern the settlements, while maintaining overall RTG control. Also, probably as a consequence of the natural flow of displaced persons, the settlements tend to be dominated by one ethnic group, whether it is Karen, Karenni, or other. In fact, the Karen is the most numerous group of displaced persons. In most cases, the committees have been shaped to reflect the traditional structures of the ethnic groups themselves. One particular issue that needs more attention is the diversity of population. The other ethnic populations other than Karen and Karenni are increasing: Burman, 2.1 % in 2006, increased to 4.1 % in 2010, Mon 0.3 to 1.0 %, Chin and Kachin from very small numbers to 0.4 and 0.3 %, while Karen and Karenni has decreased (TBBC 2010a, b). Christian Karen was the majority population but currently, the proportion of other religious groups such as Buddhism and Islam has increased (TBBC 2010a, b). These changes need more awareness and careful consideration to cover this diversity.

In terms of gender balance in internal administration, women did not hold much decision-making authority in the past. In many shelters, the proportion of female members in shelter committees was small, for example 3 female among 15 members (MOI document 2009), and only 23 % of female participants had taken part in camp management trainings (TBBC 2009a, b). This practice may lead to the downplaying of the seriousness of a sensitive issue like gender-based violence. The situation has been improved in most shelters and women now have more shares in the shelters' administration level (TBBC 2010a, b).

While the RTG, in collaboration with the military, is able to ensure external security, the internal security is a challenge that needs to be considered, especially in the area of crime which leads to displaced persons feeling insecurity. The shelters experience similar crimes to any population, but there are indications that crimes such as domestic violence and sexual harassment may be more acute because of the displaced persons' psychosocial difficulties. Gender-based violence is seen as a particular problem in the closed communities of the confined shelters. Ninety-three cases of abuse and violence incidents occurred during 2002–2004, including 18 cases of domestic violence and 11 child rape cases (Vungsiriphisal 2010). In 2006, the incidents increased to 199 cases and domestic violence came up to 122 (UNHCR 2006). The concern over this matter is reflected in interviews:

> Domestic violence came from drinking alcohol, quarrel and violence in the families (Focus Group Interview, Nai Soi 11/8/10).
>
> Scolding, sometimes fighting between husband and wife become more frequent, mostly from drinking (Focus Group Interview, Mae La, 4/9/2010).

The other area of protection that is linked to actual and perception of security and safety for the displaced persons is access to justice. Earlier, law and order systems in the settlements operated largely on traditional justice lines but the increasing incidents and sensitive cases require more formal legal mechanisms to deal with them. In late 2002, the UNHCR Gender-Based Violence Programme was launched in the shelters to address the problem of violence against women. The programme organised several awareness raising activities which are positively accepted by many displaced persons, 64.6 % of the respondents in the survey. In 2006, the RTG gave permission to establish the Legal Assistance Centre (LAC), which is run by an NGO, International Rescue Committee (IRC). The centre is intended to provide a systematic justice system to respond to the need of displaced persons to access to the Thai legal system and ensure rights for fair and equal treatment across diverse ethnic groups. Having access to the formal system has been perceived by displaced persons positively (Fig. 4.7).

But the access of increasing numbers of clients may also emphasise the need for more prevention and tackling the root causes of the problems; either from the protracted nature of the confinement, the unawareness of the gender sensitivity or other underlying. The MOI has facilitated the establishment of legal assistance and access to Thai justice system and the collaboration of UNHCR, IRC and MOJ in order to assure displaced persons better protection when the perpetrators are local people or authorities whom the traditional justice system will have little chance of charging the perpetrators (Interview MOI officer, 8/11/10).

Though the displaced persons community has a strong administrative structure, this may be changing and growing weaker as the young generation, by exposure to external influences, tend to lose their respect for their seniors and have less

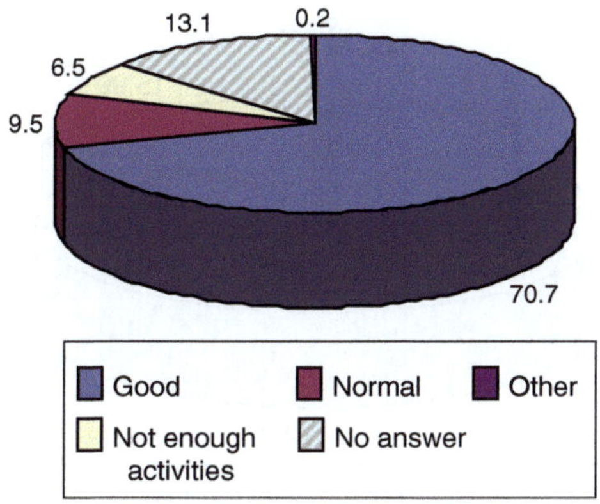

Fig. 4.7 Displaced persons opinion toward formal legal assistance. *Source* The authors

discipline. The prevalence of youth gangs inside the shelters has increased (TBBC 2010a, b). The young displaced persons' behaviour has raised concerns for displaced persons, adults and their leaders, but the external factor has been perceived as the key influence:

> Young ones mixing with outsiders, there were disputes sometimes and caused trouble (Focus group interview, Mae La, 3/9/10).

The mixing of displaced persons youth with outsiders can reflect the flexibility of administration system to allow visits of local people to the shelters but also can be perceived as the loose security control of the shelters.

4.2.3 Well-Being

4.2.3.1 Basic Needs

The well-being of displaced persons is a critical issue in terms of their feelings of security and safety, and focuses on basic needs provided to them. In this aspect, the RTG has permitted humanitarian organisations to provide food, clothes and material for shelters to displaced persons. The main provider for basic needs is Thailand Burma Border Consortium (TBBC) with funding majority from various government donors: Australia, Canada, Czech Republic, the European Union, Denmark, Great Britain, Ireland, Netherlands, New Zealand, Norway, Poland, Spain, Sweden, Switzerland, Taiwan and United State of America (TBBC 2009a, b).

Though the assistance is at a basic level, most displaced persons consider the policy regarding their well-being is good, and only a very small number disagree and regard it as bad policy (Fig. 4.8).

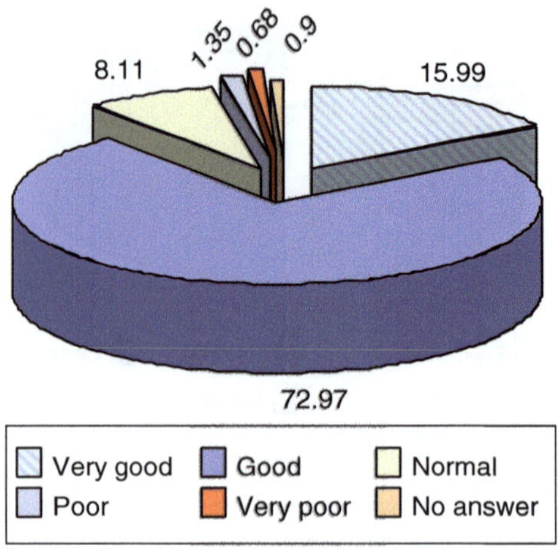

Fig. 4.8 Displaced persons opinion toward well-being policy. *Source* The authors

4.2.3.2 Health Services

There are several humanitarian agencies which are responsible for health care in the shelters: Aide Médicale Internationale (AMI), ARC International, Catholic Office for Emergency, Relief and Refugees (COERR), Handicap International (HI), IRC, Malteser International, Solidarités, Ruammit Foundation for Youth and Children: Drug & Alcohol Recovery & Education, Solidarités (Source: CCSDPT). Statistics have shown that the general health of the displaced persons is in equivalent to international standards. The crude mortality rate in all shelters 2003–2006 is 3.6–4.9 per 1,000 populations, lower than the UNHCR standard of 5 per 1,000. Infant mortality rate has decreased from 28.7 to 20.2 per 1,000, but still higher than Thailand rate which is 18 per 1,000 and much lower than Myanmar which is 75 per 1,000 (CCSDPT 2006). The coverage of vaccination of all types is over 95.5 %, close to UNHCR standard (100 %) and Thailand rate (96 %) but better than Myanmar.

For certain categories of physical health, therefore, the displaced persons are actually close to or perhaps better than the surrounding Thai communities. The reasons for the relatively good state of general health are related to reliable food supplies being provided and the fact that primary health care clinics are permitted in the settlements themselves. This assumption is supported by the survey findings that two-thirds of the respondents consider health care policy is good and only very small do not think it is good (Fig. 4.9).

The key challenge for displaced persons' health condition is the high birth rate in the shelters which is 30–34 per 1,000, double that for Thailand, which contributes to the increasing population. The outbreak of infectious diseases such as cholera, diarrhoea, upper respiratory infection and others may be caused from the problem of waste disposal and other environmental factors, especially given the

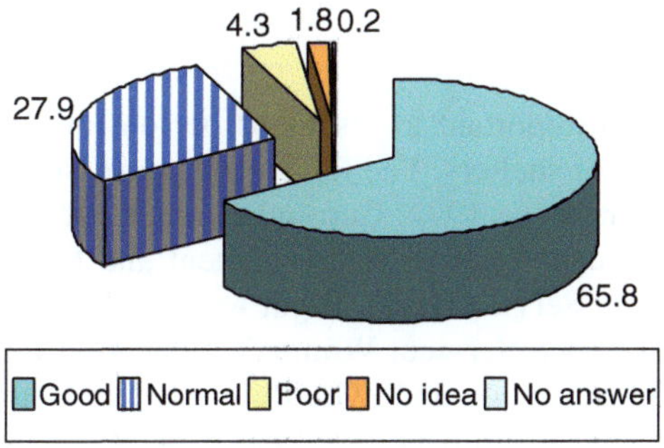

Fig. 4.9 Displaced persons opinion towards health care policy. *Source* The authors

length of time these temporary settlements have existed and the need for improvement. Many of the displaced persons have experienced traumatic events, including as victims of armed conflict. In addition, the long periods of confinement to the settlements endured by many of the displaced persons have eroded their self-esteem and abilities to be self-reliant, and can cause high levels of anxiety and stress. Another concern is about the shortage of health staff; many join the resettlement programme. The training and replacing of skilled health staff is a constant problem for NGOs. Secondary and tertiary health care is not readily available in the settlements and serious and complicated cases that need to be referred outside the settlements include obstetric complications and complex surgeries. Referrals outside the settlements are expensive and are covered by humanitarian organisations. In some cases, referrals may be delayed, or not happen at all, because of cost constraints.

Recommendations to integrate displaced persons health services within the Thai system (TBBC 2009a, b) will need many resources to increase the system capacity, regardless of the willingness of health personnel, as the services for local and migrant populations are already overwhelmed. Mae Sod Hospital, where displaced persons from Mae La shelter have been referred, employs 44 medical doctors to serve 122,059 local Thai and approximately 115,744 migrants, not including referred cases of the same number from nearby districts (Mae Sod Hospital Annual Report 2009). The limitation of local capacity is not only the budget for expanding services but the existing infrastructure and health personnel that need years of training; systems have not been designed to serve the huge increasing number of clients, if the displaced persons population is included (Interview MOPH Officer, 25/11/2010).

The RTG policy has responded to the displaced persons' basic needs for food, shelter and primary health care and the need to sustain good health. But there are some areas regarding the living environment that need to be improved. Data and information sharing in a prompt manner are needed to cooperate with local health authorities for better prevention and control the outbreak of infectious diseases.

4.2.4 Education

Education is considered important to displaced persons and schools have existed since the establishment of shelters. The RTG gave permission to NGOs to support education in the shelters since 1997. Currently, major agencies providing education in the shelters include Adventist Development and Relief Agency (ADRA), COEER, Jesuit Refugee Service (JRS), Right to Play, Shanti Volunteer Association, Taipei Overseas Peace Service, Women's Education for Advancement and Empowerment, World Education and ZOA Refugee Care Netherlands. The policy at first allowed education to primary level and expanded to secondary alongside education for Thai children. The education services gradually included other areas such as nursery, vocational training, special education, adult literacy, libraries and recreational services. The education services available are for all displaced persons' children, at least in seven shelters (ZOA 2010). In this survey, displaced persons highly value the education services provided to them, as two-thirds of respondents consider education is good, and only small number rate it poor. The positive opinion is shared by displaced persons of different registration status. But the number of non-registered displaced persons who have a negative opinion towards education policy is slightly higher than registered displaced persons, and the group of respondents aged 25–59 years want to see change in education most strongly (Figs. 4.10, 4.11).

Also, more than half of the respondents acknowledge the changes in education are significant during their living period in the shelters, and some see changes in vocational training, policy of employment and protection (Fig. 4.12).

Nevertheless, large numbers of children are not continuing their studies and number of drop-outs is quite large. According to an education survey by ZOA, the

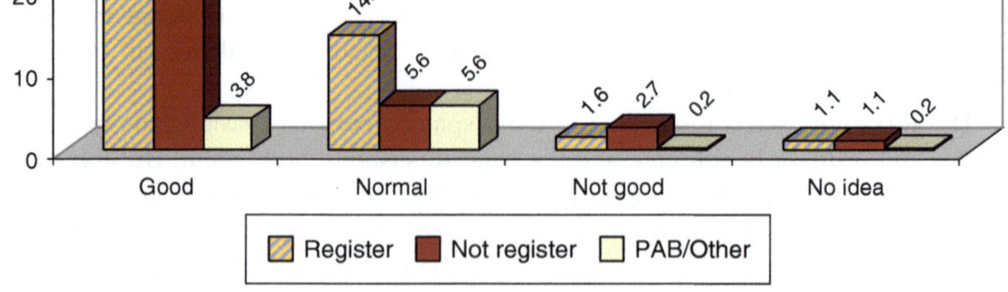

Fig. 4.10 Opinion towards education policy, by register status. *Source* The authors

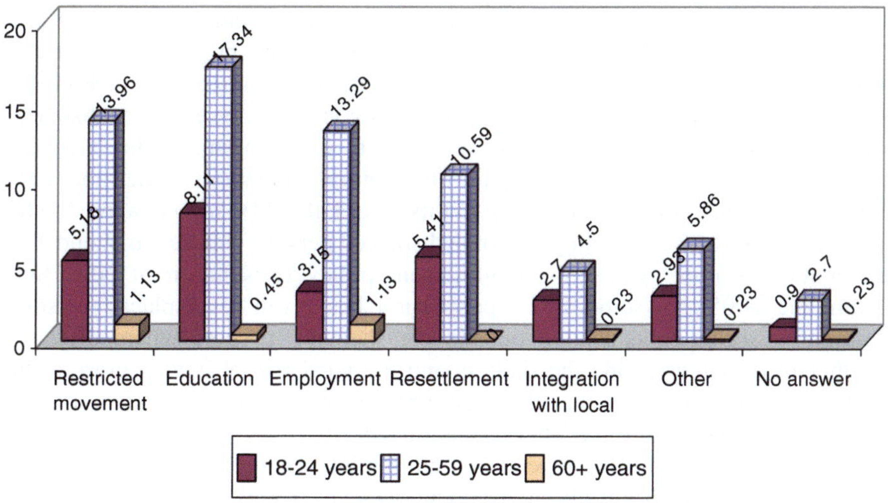

Fig. 4.11 Policy displaced persons want to change as first priority, by aged group. *Source* The authors

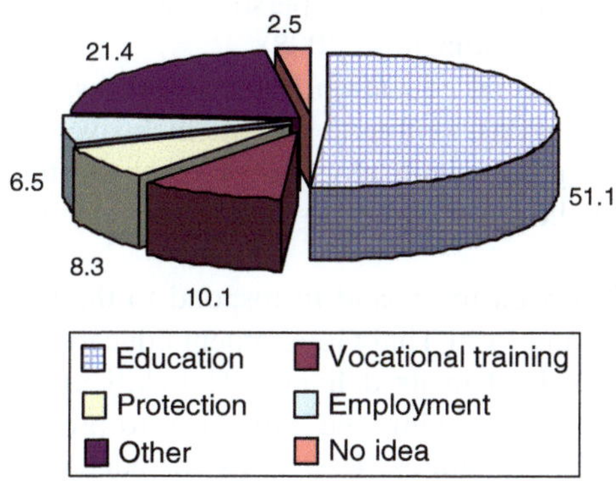

Fig. 4.12 Policies most significantly changed. *Source* The authors

number of displaced persons' children enrolling in secondary level in year 2008 was just slightly over half or 54 % of children enrolling in primary level, though the number of secondary students increased to 68 % of primary student in year 2010 (ZOA 2010). The same study indicates various major causes of education discontinuing such as getting married, difficulties in learning and assisting family work. The other causes that disrupt the education quality is the study environment, including from crowded and noisy classrooms (Interview school children, Mae La, 5/9/2010). This is the effect from the policy not allowing for school expansion.

In practice, the authority has supported education opportunity for all displaced persons children regardless of their registered status and is flexible enough to include children who are not eligible for displaced persons status but who enter the shelters for education purpose, as shown in the shelter population report (Karen Refugee Committee Newsletter, May 2010). The policy prohibits the attempt access to higher education outside the shelters, with the argument that the RTG has already supported education and other courses beyond basic level for the displaced persons. This matching to education provided to local children, who have free education to secondary level, is part of meeting obligations under the CRC (Interview MOSHS officer, 2/6/2010). In this regard, the RTG has not agreed to the attempts to put forward a policy for some displaced persons children to attend Thai universities as it is against the confinement policy (Resolution of NSC Sub-Committee 2005). In some areas, permission has given to displaced persons' children to access to education outside the shelters, in cases where there are insufficient resources inside the shelters and the local school is very close to the shelters, and on the basis that these children have sufficient language skills to follow the lessons within the Thai education system.

The integration of displaced persons' children into Thai education system needs language ability which not all children can achieve. In this current situation, the displaced persons children already have the challenge to acquire at least three to five languages: Karen, Burmese, English, Thai and Urdu for Muslim children (TBBC 2010a, b). According to an NGO study earlier, interest in learning Thai language was rather low among displaced persons though some accept the value of the knowledge (Purnell/Kengkunchorn 2008).

There is some basic special education for disabled displaced persons in some settlements (World Education), aiming to provide inclusive services for blind, deaf and other marginalised groups with physical or other disabilities. There are still some disabled people, however, who do not attend any form of education or support services.

The RTG policy has been to expand to respond to the need for skill training. There are many NGOs and local Thai Government education agencies, vocational colleges and so on, involved in its delivery. The skill trainings aim to provide income generation, such as weaving and carpentry, to prepare displaced persons for more self-reliance opportunities. Resources for educational provision in the settlements remain limited, and most classes are housed in temporary buildings where conditions require some improvement. Recently, permission was granted to build semi-permanent buildings. Internet access in the settlements currently remains prohibited by the RTG. The education in the settlements has been designed based on the Burmese curriculum; this has meant, for example, that instruction has been in the various ethnic group languages, rather than in Thai, though there are indications that this is another area where practice is changing. The education in the shelters does not gain accreditation from Myanmar. There has been an attempt to collaborate with MOE to solve this problem and adapt the curriculum to the Thai system but the result has not yet finalised (Thailand Education Forum 2009).

4.2.5 Individual Registration and Children's Rights

The registration of displaced persons has been formalised and individual ID cards have been issued to each displaced person since April, 2007 (UNHCR). The registration of displaced persons has been restrained after the non-functioning of PAB during 2006–2009. The pre-screening pilot in four shelters which aims to fill the procedure gap and screen out persons not eligible for displaced persons status seems to take longer. The challenge of individual registration is an important one, since Thailand is a signatory party to the CRC, which documents various areas of children's rights and, crucially, is intended to apply to all children within a country's borders, including refugee children. The RTG, however, retained two reservations to the CRC, on Articles 7 and 22. These articles, respectively, relate to birth registration and the right to nationality, and to specific rights of refugee children. The issue of birth registration has been a controversial one for the RTG, which maintained that its system of family registration, including children, was sufficient for recording who exactly resides within the settlements.

More recently, the practice of recording births more accurately, and providing formal birth certificates, has improved. From the RTG perspective, it is clear that children born to displaced persons from Myanmar are Myanmar citizens, and the issue of awarding Thai birth certificates would only complicate this idea. A practical issue, though, is that, should voluntary repatriation become feasible in the future, with no formal birth certificates the return of children to Myanmar, and especially the Burmese government's willingness to accept returnees, might be impaired by the lack of formal documentation of individuals. The Thai Cabinet has agreed to withdraw the reservation to CRC Articles 7 (Cabinet resolution, September 23, 2010) for birth registration of every child in the country. In practice, prior to this resolution, the registration of newborn children has already taken place in most shelters and recorded in family registration forms. According to the regulation, every parent has to report the birth of their child to the district office to obtain his or her birth certificate (Interview MOI Officer, 4/10/2010). This practice was applicable to displaced persons according to their status and confinement policy, and thus has left displaced persons' children without birth certificates. Since late 2009, the MOI has assigned camp commanders as authorised registration officers to issue birth certificates to newborn child. On a more general level, the RTG does seem to place a high premium on its signatory status of the CRC, and is diligent in its reporting (National report to CRC committee 2010).

4.2.6 Livelihoods, Economic Activity and Employment

According to existing policy, any displaced persons found outside the settlements are liable to arrest and deportation as illegal immigrants. This restriction has added to the sense of confinement in the camps, and to the sense of dependency felt by

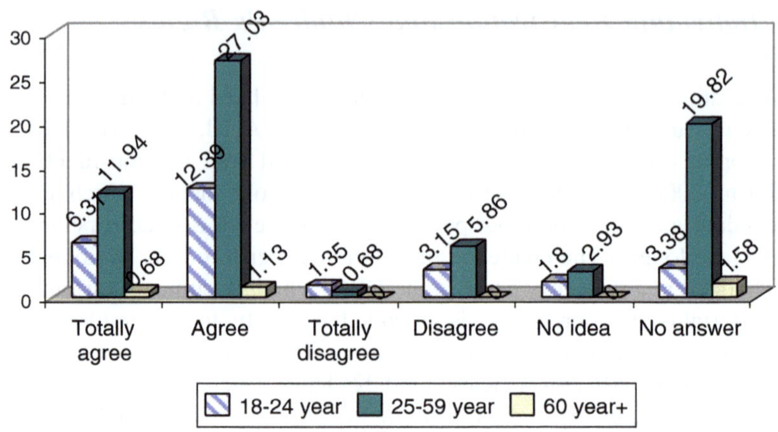

Fig. 4.13 Opinion towards policy allowing employment in the shelters. *Source* The authors

many of the displaced persons. It reinforces the need for all services and provisions to be provided to the displaced persons, from basics such as food and water to health and education. In practice, there does seem to be a level of tolerance of employment outside the settlements; but official policy remains much against it. While increasing education opportunity is the first priority policy where displaced persons would like to see more change, the restriction of movement comes second, followed by access to employment as the third (Fig. 4.13).

Some displaced persons admitted being engaged in income generating outside the shelters (FGD, Mae La, 5/9/2010). Seeking employment has been practiced by displaced persons in other shelters as well, according to a NGO report (IRC 2008).

In terms of livelihoods, there is no formal rejection from the RTG to the many activities related to the development of displaced persons life quality (Interview MOI, 7/8/10), including various skills training programmes, as long as these activities are performed within the settlement areas, though there are some restrictions: raising poultry is not allowed *especially when we have bird flu but we don't really stop them, we understand their need* (Interview MOI officer, 10/8/10). In part, the RTG is balancing the needs of its local population, who are in many cases already short of work. It is also remaining consistent with the idea that local integration is to be resisted; thereby ensuring the situation of the displaced persons is contained.

Plots of land have been rented in some instances with local officer's permission, because space is too limited in the shelters, so that displaced persons can grow their own food, and can sell any surplus to their communities and local. However, the problem is too little land has been allocated in most cases; and balancing the allocation of an already scarce resource to displaced persons against the needs of the local communities is a delicate act, and the RTG has unsurprisingly tended to put its own citizens first when conflict has arisen. There is some small-scale trading and barter activity in the settlements themselves, and this has enabled more entrepreneurial displaced persons to generate income through grocery stores, hairdressing and other activities, most of which include Thai traders from outside and operating inside the settlements, giving some benefit to local communities.

There are small income-generating projects set up within the settlements. There is some enthusiasm for this form of production to be permitted in the shelters as part of skill training, but there is a perception that investments from external investors would be necessary:

> *We're willing to consider if the activities take place inside shelters; the investment from foreign companies is needed but finally, they do not move further* (NSC officer, 14/10/10).

Local investors seem reluctant to expand their production units to the shelters, and some others do not support the hiring of displaced persons and consider that there is already a sufficient supply of migrant workers (Interview Tak Chamber of Commerce, 2/9/10).

It has already been pointed out that there is a curious anomaly here between the displaced persons and Burmese migrant workers. The latter usually enter the country illegally, but they have been allowed an exemption to work temporarily for 2 years with possible 2 years' extension. There is likely to be some overlap between the displaced persons and the migrant workers, and some have queried why people choose to be displaced persons when they know they will be confined and have rights such as freedom of movement curtailed. But what the migrant workers do not receive is the protection afforded by the settlements; and especially for the political activists amongst the displaced persons, this remains vital as long as the current regime in Myanmar pursues its current strategy towards the ethnic minorities.

4.2.7 Resettlement

The RTG has remained somewhat ambivalent about cooperating with resettlement solutions put forward by the international community. The reason for this is they do not want to create an attractive pull factor for new displaced persons, and possibly economic migrants, to cross the border into the settlements. However, having said that, more than 64,000 displaced persons have been resettled to third countries, mostly in 2005–2010. The policy to allow displaced persons to resettle has been perceived as the only solution they have (FGD, Mae La, 5/9/2010).

The RTG, along with NGOs, has made efforts to prepare those eligible for resettlement, through courses and vocational education, but problems remain. Surveys of the views of the displaced persons show that many find the policy of resettlement attractive, others favour remaining in Thailand, and some choose to repatriate when conditions improve. The breakup of families is one of the key factors against resettlement. Ironically, the skilled medical assistants and teachers within the settlements, by the nature of their work, make themselves the most attractive prospects for resettlement, creating an ongoing retraining issue within

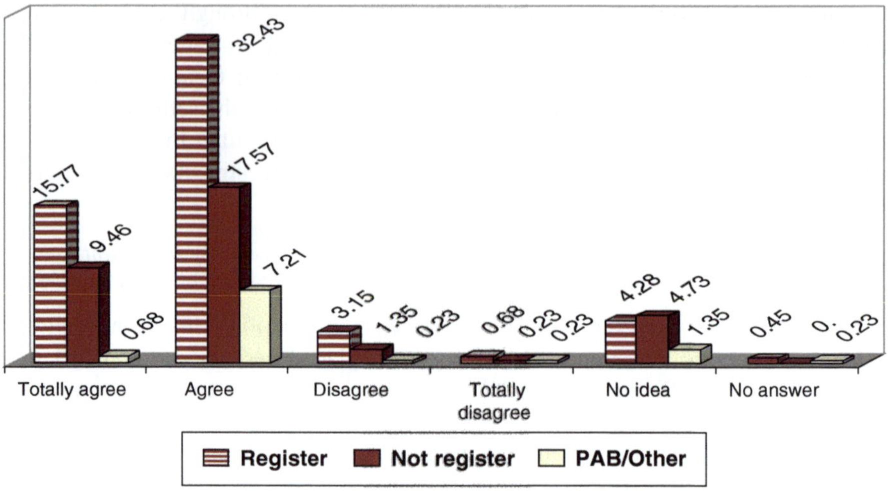

Fig. 4.14 Opinion towards policy of resettlement, by registration status. *Source* The authors

the settlements to keep going the schools and health centres which are run by displaced persons. It should be noted that the high percentage of respondents expressing a resettlement preference may come from the selected criteria to include displaced persons applicants for resettlement in the survey sampling (Fig. 4.14).

4.2.8 Local Integration

The access to work outside the settlements legally would undoubtedly benefit the displaced persons, and the confusion with the situation of Burmese migrant workers has already been noted. Work as an antidote for the feelings of indignity that can arise and have been documented in a situation of total dependency like that of the displaced persons is attractive in principle; but, again, the RTG has had to balance displaced persons needs with those of the local community with which they may well be competing for jobs and local resources. The issue of national security is also valid here for the RTG; the displaced persons are considered a target group for political attack, and allowing displaced persons to move freely in and out of the settlements will be a risk for them and also to local people (Interview MOI officer, 8/8/2010).

The wishes of the displaced persons population are less clear on this issue; some would undoubtedly like to move outside the settlements and to integrate fully with Thai society but, as has been stated, some displaced persons want to return to Myanmar. The situation of children and young people is especially

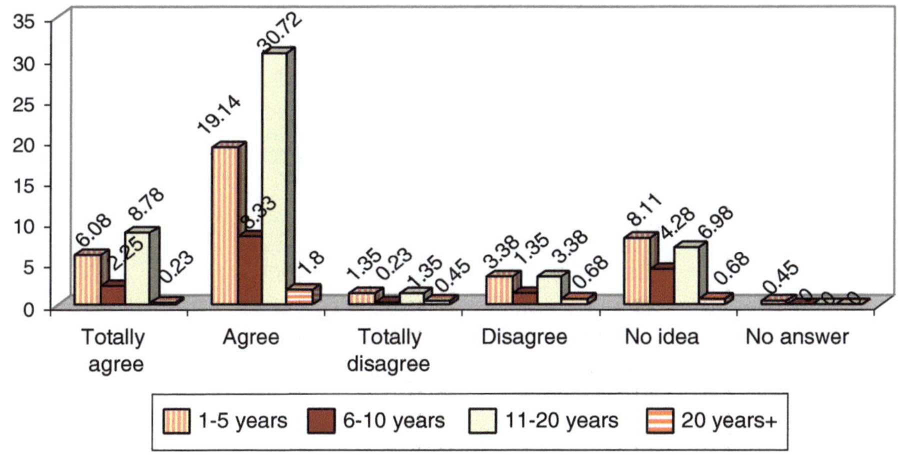

Fig. 4.15 Displaced persons opinion toward integration with local, by length of stay in the shelters. *Source* The authors

difficult to assess; many have lived their whole lives in exile in the settlements, and know neither Thailand nor Myanmar. As one NSC officer has said:

> *We don't permit them [the displaced persons] to go outside shelters to work because that will lead to potential to get permanent residency, and we're not ready for that* (Interview NSC officer, 22/10/10) (Fig. 4.15).

4.2.9 Preference for the Future

In this survey, almost half of the respondents chose to resettle in third countries if not staying in the shelters, while a smaller proportion wished to remain in Thailand and some prefer to go back to their hometown (Fig. 4.16).

It would appear that resettlement in another country and staying in Thailand is the desire for most of the displaced persons. But information gathered from several focus groups and interview of displaced persons key informants, which are conducted parallel to the baseline survey, convey other messages that need to be carefully considered. At the time when this study is taking place, resettlement is considered the only opportunity that can be offered to the displaced persons, as some of displaced persons who have been accepted for resettlement explain. It should be noted that the criteria for sampling selection include displaced persons applying for resettlement which can contribute to the high percentage of resettlement preference.

> *I've applied and will resettle soon, my family want to go, for the sake of my children we have no better choice* (Key informant, male 56 years, Tham Hin, July 14, 2010).

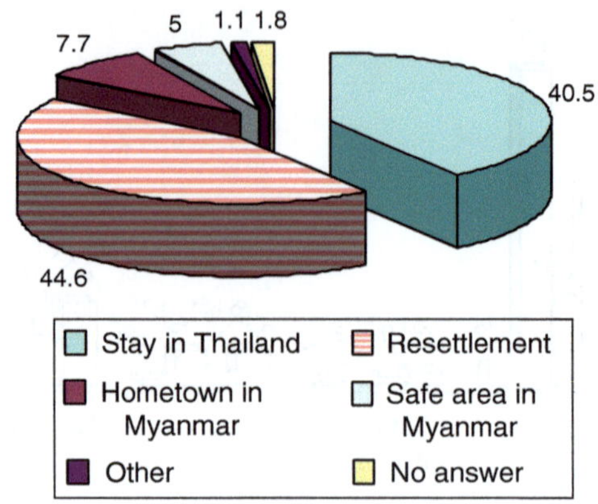

Fig. 4.16 The preferred place to stay after the settlement. *Source* The authors

> *I'm still thinking of going back home, but see no hope after so long, that's why I applied for resettlement* (Focus Group Interview, female, Mae La, September 3, 2010).

Some displaced persons choose to remain in Thailand because repatriation seems uncertain, and their fear of the unsafe situation that made them not desire to repatriate, although their thoughts of going back to their hometown still remain:

> *If it's safe, we prefer to go back, we're not sure for now the same to many of us* (Focus Group Interview, male Tham Hin, July 14, 2010).
>
> *We hope, one day we could go back home all of us would like to, when there is no more conflict* (Focus group interview, female, Mae La, September 2, 2010).
>
> *We don't have any choice now, stay here or resettle but many people living in the shelters, they prefer to going back, if possible* (Karenni key informant, female 50 years, Ban Mai Nai Soi, August 10, 2010).
>
> *I'd prefer to stay here, I'm afraid of the fighting and threatening* (Focus group interview, male, Tham Hin, July 13, 2010).

More than half of the respondents are looking for organisations to negotiate with Myanmar to make their safe repatriation possible (Fig. 4.17).

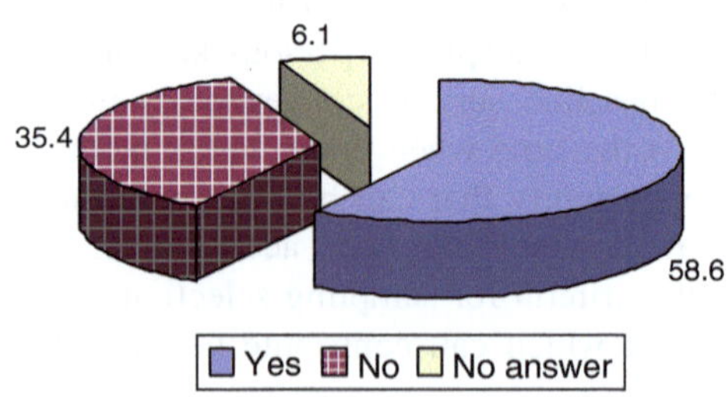

Fig. 4.17 Organisations displaced persons want to negotiate with Myanmar. *Source* The authors

4.3 Gaps in the RTG Policy Response to Displaced Persons' Needs and Existing Interventions

4.3.1 Protection

There are policy gaps in provision of services and other aspects of displaced persons needs. Protection is limited to the shelter areas because of the policy of confinement, for example, although there is flexibility for displaced persons to move between shelters. Permission has been given to the meetings between shelters, children's access to higher education levels in other shelters, vocational and capacity trainings. The protection needs of those seeking employment outside the shelters is limited. The prolonged screening procedure to grant displaced persons status has limited the protection towards non-registered displaced persons. The PAB process which only considers on a case by case basis is not only unsuitable for the real situation but also contributes to the increasing number of non- registered displaced persons which affects their eligibility to access the appropriate protection.

In order to respond to the situation and fill the gap of the status determination procedure, the pre-screening programme was launched in 2009, aiming to standardise the screening procedure before submitting the application to the PAB. The result will also screen out those not eligible for assistance. The programme will expand to cover another five shelters after the pilot programme in four shelters is completed. At the time of this research, the pre-screening result has not yet been released and the protection gap to displaced persons who need protection still remains.

4.3.2 Shelter Administration

Because the RTG policy has encouraged a high degree of self-management through the settlement committees, it has resulted in gender imbalances in the shelter management. In some shelters, over 80 % of committee membership is male, thus women's voices may not be heard and there may be a gender gap in provision of some services and facilities. It also means that the settlement administration tends to be conservative in outlook. RTG personnel, too, have included only a few female staff working in the shelters' offices, while all the corps members are male. All this helps create a largely male culture, and this is an area where the RTG could do better. Noticeably, the issue of gender imbalance is also reflected from MOI personnel at field level, where female security corps are not selected intentionally in some shelters:

> *We do not choose female security corps, male is more suitable to this kind of work* (Interviewed MOI officer, Tham Hin 6/8/10).

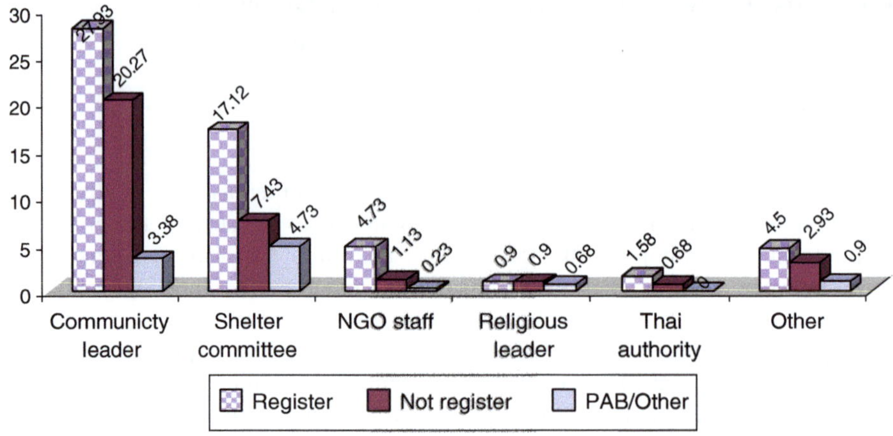

Fig. 4.18 The persons displaced persons first seek for help. *Source* The authors

The reasons for not choosing female corps are the concern about the tough work and heavy responsibility to oversee security issues but this practice also reflects the lack of gender sensitivity among RTG officers.

The other factor that may result in shelter administration is the relationship between displaced persons and the authorities. There was some relations gap between displaced persons and Thai authority indicated in the displaced persons response in this survey. In spite of their answer about having good relationships with authority, most displaced persons will first seek help from people acquainted to them. The majority prefer to go to community leaders for help, or the shelter committee; a smaller number go to NGO staff, their religious leaders and Thai authorities. The answers from different status groups are similar (Fig. 4.18).

When they needed help from the Thai authorities only 15.8 % would have direct contact but the majority would contact through other persons: almost half would contact through shelters committee, 24.1 % would contact through other shelter members, 4 % would contact through NGOs staff and 8.8 % stated that they had no contact.

The relationship gap could cause some problems for displaced persons stress, and may come from the communication challenges; only a small number of displaced persons were able to communicate in Thai and many Thai officers and voluntary guards did not speak the displaced persons' languages.

4.3.3 Accreditation and Access to Higher Education Level

Education is the main area where displaced persons feel positive changes could and should be made. The RTG has supported children's access to basic education at the same level as local children, but the limited space has made classrooms too noisy and crowded due to the policy that limits school expansion. The policy has made the study environment inappropriate and not effective or conducive to quality education.

Accreditation is another area that needs to be improved, since certification within the Thai system has been another difficult area. The MOE has responded to solve the problem of accreditation by collaboration with ZOA, one of the main responsible organisations in education in seven shelters with the support from UNICEF (ZOA), to adapt the curriculum in the shelter to the Thai system. The MOE at local and national levels collaborating and supporting on this issue should fill in the gap of gaining accreditation for the displaced persons' children. The Thai language will soon be included as a second language from primary level in shelter curriculums and will help to improve their communication skills in order to communicate better with locals and authorities.

Higher education, though it is provided in other forms such as *post-10* level and business courses, is not real tertiary education; and access to this level of education has not been encouraged. RTG policy restricts education at higher levels because it is beyond the basic level required by law for all local children. A few trial cases that have been proposed to tertiary education could be useful to increase the capacity and capabilities of displaced persons to take forward the development of their community, as well as making them more value-added citizens when they repatriate to Myanmar. The number of children reaching this level will be small, but they can become a new generation of community leaders. Access to tertiary education is still a gap that RTG policy does not respond to positively.

The RTG policy has been to expand to respond to the need for skill training. There are many NGOs and local Thai Government education agencies, vocational colleges and others, involved in its delivery. The skills trainings aim to encourage income generation, such as weaving and carpentry, to prepare displaced persons for more self-reliance opportunities. Resources for educational provision in the settlements remain limited, and most classes are housed in temporary buildings where conditions require some improvement. Recently, permission was granted to build semi-permanent buildings. Internet access in the settlements currently remains prohibited by the RTG. The education in the settlements has been designed based on the Burmese curriculum; this has meant, for example, that instruction has been in the various ethnic group languages, rather than in Thai, though there are indications that this is another area where practice is changing.

4.3.4 Confinement Policy and Income Generation Activities

The confinement policy, supposedly temporary, has lasted too long. The policy is not practically successful as many displaced persons, driven by other needs than basic food, have managed to seek employment outside the shelters.

The wishes of the displaced persons population are less clear on this issue; some would undoubtedly like to move outside the settlements and to integrate fully with Thai society but, as has been stated, some displaced persons want to return to Myanmar. The situation of children and young people is especially difficult to assess; many have lived their whole lives in exile in the settlements, and know neither Thailand nor Myanmar.

RTG policy on confinement of displaced persons to settlements has led to the situation where many of the displaced persons are unemployed. There are some jobs available within the camps, such as administrators, nurses and teachers; but these are limited. The RTG has permitted several vocational training courses in the settlements. These training courses are geared towards future income-generating activities; but, under current RTG policy, these activities have little potential to provide the displaced persons with income at present but are envisaged to take place back in Myanmar after repatriation becomes possible.

There have been projects planned to set up real income-generating activities, such as food production and small trading, within the settlements, linked to vocational training and making use of the ready supply of labour. It is unclear what affect this would have on the displaced persons; it would depend on how wages were calculated and distributed, what voice the workers would have in the activities, and other factors. However, thus far it has proved too difficult logistically to set up a manufacturing or other operation which would involve bringing in the raw materials from outside the settlements, and then exporting the finished products back into Thailand. There is some enthusiasm for this form of production to be permitted in the shelters as part of skill training, but there is a perception that foreign investments would be necessary.

4.3.5 Resettlement

The permission for a resettlement programme has served as one solution to the protracted situation of the displaced persons from Myanmar. The gap is the failing of PAB process that does not speed up the status determination. During 2005–2009, with the inactive PAB process in some provinces, applicants for displaced persons status were mostly rejected, and pre-screening pilot programme has affected some displaced persons who waited to determine their status. As the application for resettlement is only open for registered displaced persons, the delay in registration process has thus limited the number and need of displaced persons who may be eligible to the programme. The reconsidering of granting displaced persons status is necessary in order to make resettlement a durable solution. On the other hand, the proper screening process will effectively screen out those who are not eligible to the status.

4.4 RTG Contribution to the Displaced Persons' Situation

The RTG has faced difficult problems with the displaced persons from Myanmar, for many of the reasons noted earlier in this report. The displaced persons have been provided protection, basic needs, sustenance, shelter, education and health care; and also a degree of self-administration. In the views of the displaced persons themselves, they largely feel safe, and believe their education and health care provision are at a certain level satisfactory. The RTG has made clear it is not open to local integration, and has stuck to this line. Its initial opposition to resettlement was not helpful; nor the inadequacies in the registration and screening processes, though these have largely been fixed.

The areas that have used for shelters are mostly reserved forest and water resources which have to be shared with local communities surrounding the shelters. In many cases, especially in the dry season, the displaced persons consume water and do not release enough water for local use (Interview Local Administration Officer). Some land was being used by other government sectors prior to the establishment of shelters and they have had to move out to let the displaced persons use those lands. In most areas, there is conflict or complaints from local people over the competition for land use and natural resources.

Thailand has had to deploy considerable people resources to provide safe areas for the displaced persons, including security personnel to safeguard the shelters. In order to ensure that, RTG has used its own limited budget and employees from local areas, with the Territorial Volunteer Security Corps (TVSC) assigned to the task under the management of deputy district officers. There are now 447 TVSC on duty, who cooperate with displaced persons volunteers to manage shelter safety. The TVSC takes on duties for external security and border control using RTG government budget. In all shelters, one deputy district officer is assigned to be responsible for the administration of the shelter as camp commander. In large shelters, the camp commander has to spend 70–80 % of the time on shelter matters. There are small numbers of government employees to assist camp commanders, plus one UNHCR support assistant to every shelter. The RTG contributes more officers of relevant government sectors at central level. At local level, government personnel that contribute to displaced persons welfare and protection are provincial officers such as governors, deputy governors, border petrol police officers, military forces, local health personnel and others. Part of their responsibility, and budget for their salaries, is for responsibility on the displaced persons issue. Approximately 40 million baht has been used annually for only TSDC salaries. The in-kind contribution is lands used for settlement areas, sharing of natural resources and shouldering of environmental degradation surround the shelters.

Considering that Thailand has not signed the UN refugee convention, its policy and practice on the basics of hosting refugees, the *displaced persons* of official RTG language, have largely been according to international standards in some respects.

Undoubtedly, the RTG has contributed to the protracted nature of the issue. However, this has not just been down to RTG intransigence. There are strong indications that the RTG did not believe this issue would continue so long, and did not give it a high priority, or at least not as high as the UN agencies and the international community would have liked. In part, it is quite clear that the RTG's opposition to local integration as a durable solution is because of its limited capacity to cope with new arrivals and the many more IDPs who could cross over to Thailand if the more flexible policy is introduced. The RTG has also had higher priority policy issues to deal with, notably the ongoing internal political turmoil within Thailand, and the 2 million migrant workers from Myanmar, as opposed to the relatively small number of displaced persons, that has provided a huge management challenge.

The RTG has not had very much success in engaging constructively with Myanmar to deal with the root cause of the displaced persons issue. But it has hardly been alone in this, and Thailand has the added complication that Myanmar is its nearest neighbour. Nevertheless, formal relations do exist, and contacts are happening, giving some hope for the future, especially if ASEAN's recent interest in developing Myanmar is maintained.

Overall, the displaced persons seem satisfied that they have been treated well in Thailand under difficult circumstances. What the displaced persons actually want, in some cases, is safe voluntary return and repatriation; and this is not something the RTG can achieve by itself. Data from our survey shows that large numbers of displaced persons prefer to go back to their homeland, if the situation allows them to do so, either to their original areas or to safe areas. Thailand, too, considers repatriation the best choice for displaced persons: *We believe repatriation is the best solution, because research and informal interviews indicates that some of them still want to go back to their country* (NSC officer, 23/11/10). This belief, however, should not overlook the fact that a lot of effort and collaboration from all stakeholders including the Myanmar government are needed to make it real. In the meantime, other solutions should be considered, as many displaced persons are struggling for their survival out of the shelters. The reasons why they risk being arrested and deported are clear: they do not want to live without hope and dignity. The ability to look after themselves should not be discouraged. The flexible opportunity for them to become more self-reliant, while waiting to settle, either in a third country, their homeland or even locally, will at least increase their share of taking care of themselves and make them less burden to all stakeholders.

References

CSDPT, 2006: *2006 Annual Health Information Short Report* (TBBC).
TBBC, 2009a: *Programme Report, January–June 2009* (Bangkok: TBBC).
TBBC, 2009b: *Programme Report, July–December 2009* (Bangkok: TBBC).
TBBC, 2010a: *Programme Report, January–June 2010* (Bangkok: TBBC).

TBBC, 2010b: *Programme Report, July–December 2010* (Bangkok: TBBC).

UNHCR, 2006: "Protracted Refugee Situations: The Search for Practical Solutions", in: *The State of the World's Refugees 2006: Human Displacement in the New Millennium*; at: http://www.unhcr.org/publ/PUBL/4444afcb0.pdf.

Vungsiriphisal, P., 2010: "The Challenge of Education Policy for Migrant Children in Thailand from Security Standpoints", Paper presented at the workshop on "Human Security in Migrant Population for the Reconciliation of Society; A Case Study of Unskilled Migrant Workers and Refugees", Kyoto University, Kyoto, Japan, 18–19 January.

Chapter 5
Solutions and Policy Options

Premjai Vungsiriphisal, Graham Bennett, Chanarat Poomkacha, Waranya Jitpong and Kamonwan Reungsamran

Abstract Various approaches, options and solutions are examined to the protracted situation on the Thai–Myanmar border, looking at the issue from the different perspective of the displaced persons, the RTG, and various other stakeholders in the international and donor community. Improvements in practice have happened over time, such as the greater provision of vocational training, which could increase the self-reliance of displaced persons and prepare them for local integration or eventual repatriation. A combination of policy options is suggested, including the one that many international agencies ignore; repatriation to Myanmar. The option of building on recent change in Myanmar, with the ultimate aim of making it a safe place of return for the displaced people, is seen as one that needs to be explored.

Keywords Durable solutions · Repatriation · Local integration · Resettlement · Self-reliance · Livelihoods · Confinement · Policy flexibility

---

P. Vungsiriphisal (✉) · G. Bennett · C. Poomkacha · W. Jitpong · K. Reungsamran
Asian Research Center for Migration, Institute of Asian Studies, Chulalongkorn University, 3rd floor, Prachadhipok Rambhai-Barni Building, Bangkok 10330, Thailand
e-mail: premjai.v@chula.ac.th

G. Bennett
e-mail: grahambennett777@hotmail.co.uk

C. Poomkacha
e-mail: cpoomkacha@abeam.com

W. Jitpong
e-mail: wec135@hotmail.com

K. Reungsamran
e-mail: kamonwan24@yahoo.com

P. Vungsiriphisal et al. (eds.), *Humanitarian Assistance for Displaced Persons from Myanmar*, SpringerBriefs in Environment, Security, Development and Peace 17,
DOI: 10.1007/978-3-319-02795-1_5,

5.1 Introduction

The first displaced persons from Myanmar began arriving on Thai territory in significant numbers in the early 1980s. Now, more than 25 years on, a significant number remain. Registered and feeding figures vary from 98,644 to 141,076 (TBBC 2010a, b), giving the scale of the issue. The impasse on the Thai–Myanmar border is one of the world's most protracted refugee situations, and there is no consensus about which, if any, of the standard durable solutions, resettlement, repatriation or local integration, offers the best outcome for all the various stakeholders, including the RTG, the Myanmar government, international agencies and the international community. Most of all, a solution remains elusive for the displaced persons themselves, some of whom have spent their whole lives inside the temporary settlements on the border.

The RTG policy has provided protection to displaced persons and assistance for basic services. However, the root cause of the flow of displaced persons has not been successfully addressed: human rights violations, including military attacks in the ethnic areas, continue to be reported. While the RTG does not intend to include local integration for the displaced persons from Myanmar in its policy, it has tried to pursue policies of education and vocational training which create self-reliance skills that in theory are equipping the displaced persons for voluntary repatriation to Myanmar when it is safe, or for resettlement. But the protracted nature of the issue and the insistence on confinement in settlements as a key part of its policy has created a dependency amongst the displaced persons which is far from self-reliance. Most of the displaced persons still rely on basic rations from the various NGOs that operate in the settlements, though the NGOs are now cutting back their budgets. The confinement has led to huge frustration for the displaced persons; local Thai officials are overlooking breaches of strict confinement, which puts them in a difficult position, and can risk the opportunity for bribery in the settlements. Resettlement, where it has taken place, has tended to take away the more talented displaced persons, weakening the remaining community.

The long road to democracy in Myanmar was signified by the November 2010 elections and the release of the opposition leader Aung San Su Kyi. However, these will only be important in the longer term if the opportunity is grasped internally in Myanmar, and is supported politically and economically by key elements in the international community. Reports, post-election, from Myanmar are not encouraging; the regime appears to have stepped up fighting with the armed ethnic armies, evidenced and reported in November 2010. Ongoing fighting is not going to make Myanmar a safer place for voluntary repatriation and it would seem the flow of displaced persons across the border has again increased since the election, adding to the problem that already exists.

For the RTG, this poses a problem. It may be that the government has to some extent tried to keep the problem of the displaced persons in the settlements at the edge, primarily because of its relationship with the Myanmar government and other pressing security issues. However, more displaced persons arriving will ramp up public pressure, both local and international, to put more effort into finding a suitable durable solution. For example, the pressure on existing land, and the resentment of local Thai communities, could increase, making the issue a priority. The reporting of the incident in late December 2010, when Thai border forces were alleged to have forcibly returned some Burmese displaced persons to their side of the border, whether accurately reported or not, is a taste of what negative publicity may come. So this may be the right time for the RTG to give the issue of the displaced persons a higher priority than it has done.

The international community is also going to have to play its part in a more proactive way. Local integration is not part of RTG policy towards displaced persons, whether its reasons are legitimate or not. However, by seeming to support this solution above others, as pointed in the Five-Years Strategy Plan (CCSDPT/UNHCR 2007), the international community is risking alienating the RTG, and making a lasting and durable solution favourable to the displaced persons ever more unlikely. The international agencies have their humanitarian mandate towards their key stakeholders, the displaced persons, and integration to the local system is seen as an effective way to define a useful and satisfactory future for the displaced persons, especially as the current state of Myanmar remains so grim. However, the plan to integrate services provided to displaced persons to Thai system (TBBC 2010a, b) suggested in the 5-year strategy has not been agreed by the RTG. There is, therefore, a lack of agreement on approach between the RTG and other stakeholders.

The RTG has been careful to avoid creating *pull factors* for the displaced persons, one of the key reasons why it has opposed any strategies that might make local integration more feasible, and why initially there was opposition also to resettlement. However, previous surveys (Nukul 2002) and interviews (TBBC 2004), including those for this study, suggest voluntary repatriation to Myanmar remains one favoured option for some displaced persons. The data from this study show that resettlement is favoured by many displaced persons; but when questioned more closely, return to Myanmar would be the choice if it was possible, and should not be forgotten as one of a durable solution among others.

5.2 Admission to the Settlement and Status Determination

Formal admission to shelters is permissible after the PAB procedure has been completed but in practice there are numbers of displaced persons residing in the shelters before application to PAB have been made, as observed from the feeding figure which is higher than the registered one. It may be argued that the non-registered displaced persons result from the lack of screening procedure and status determination, the PAB. The current practice of PAB to consider only on case basis (Interview MOI, 12/11/10) is certainly unable to cope with the influx of new arrivals which continues to come every month. In addition, the approximately 50,000 non-registered displaced persons may include not only genuine asylum seekers but others who seek to be in the settlements for other purposes. The Pre-screening programme, which has operated since 2009 to screen out those not eligible for PAB, has not yet proved effective. The high numbers of non-recognised population in the shelters have led to many problems, including determining food rations to meet the needs of the displaced persons and offer opportunity for registered cases.

The first step of status determination is to finalise the result of pre-screening programmes in a timely manner, and to resume PAB functioning as it is the only formal mechanism to screen out the non-eligible populations. At the same time, effective measures to manage the rejected cases must be enforced. The rejected cases should be deported from the shelters. The authority, NGO and shelter committee should work together to set up the prevention measures to provide assistance more effectively. The prevention of non-eligible new arrivals is necessary to make the screening procedure more effective and useful to the most vulnerable ones.

5.3 Improved Situation

The practice of registering the displaced persons has improved following the individual registration in the settlements in 2007, and now the newborn babies are being added to these. It has been speculated that the previous approach was intended to reduce the likelihood that at some point in the future there might be increased pressure on the RTG to grant the right to remain in Thailand to all individuals in the settlements. It is also likely that any resettlement process would be made more complex; and lack of individual ID would be a possible reason for Myanmar to refuse to take people back if the conditions are right for safe voluntary repatriation. Whatever the reason, individuals, including new born infants, are issued now with personal ID cards. The issuing of ID cards is one of the policy shifts that the RTG has made to improve the situation for the displaced persons. However, UNHCR expectation to use the ID card as a protection mechanism if displaced persons are allowed to work outside the shelter may not be what the RTG envisions.

Another improvement is the provision of enhanced education, going beyond the basic primary and secondary education to *post 10* further education and various forms of vocational education, such as computer training. However, this expansion and improvement of education has not been explicitly placed within a clear future aim; adapting to the Thai curriculum for education in the shelters, which is underway, aiming to access accreditation and guarantee time spending in schooling, should not be interpreted too broadly.

Previously, justice systems have not been linked to the Thai system, but have rather been based on a mixture of systems, including the prevailing customary law of the dominant ethnic group of any particular settlement. The initiative to ask IRC to set up LACs in the settlements has meant that access to justice has in principle improved for the displaced persons, making it possible for serious crimes such as sexual assault and murder to be prosecuted, notwithstanding the cultural and other barriers that remain.

These policy shifts have improved the conditions of displaced persons, but they have not brought a durable solution closer. The policy of the RTG in not wanting to formalise local integration, or anything that makes it more likely or possible, is consistent with the hope that voluntary repatriation will become possible. Considering the flow of new arrivals and high numbers of IDPs inside eastern Myanmar, the pull factor is a real risk in the RTG's perception, one that could place an overload burden on its resources.

The lack of a formal refugee policy is at least partly to blame for the illegal status of the displaced persons and the use of the Immigration Law to deal with them; though the RTG may be using this ambiguity deliberately as a basis for non-action. So in the absence of a formal asylum act, the other legal policy making is a complex process involving many actors.

5.4 The Openness of RTG's Policy Towards a Durable Solution

It appears that the RTG is adopting a passive policy towards the displaced persons, with little action to search for solutions. By resisting local integration as a durable solution, the RTG allows the status quo to continue; though the current events in Myanmar make this position more difficult to maintain. In contrast, international agencies and parts of the international community see the issue as a priority in the region, not least because of the costs involved in maintaining the settlements. There has been talk of donor fatigue; and there certainly seem to be signs of frustration that there is little or no progress in addressing the displaced persons issue. As noted, there have been some policy shifts by the RTG that have made aspects of settlement life and administration acceptable to some displaced persons. Yet the principle of confinement policy remains unchanged. To facilitate the displaced persons capacity for self-reliance can be done in some ways that do not necessarily lead to full local integration. The RTG had, in the past, started to consider the proposal for employment outside the shelter, as reported in the meeting between RTG, private sector, and civil society in Tak in 2005 (MOI). Though that was considered the exercise of the RTG leader at that time, this idea should be aired.

The RTG does not reject the possibility of displaced persons working inside the shelters (Interview MOI and NSC officers). Also, the approach to increase displaced persons' self-reliance is acceptable. It needs good planning and consulting with the authorities. Working under a training scheme may be one of the possibilities, as well as a sub-contracting work. To equip displaced persons with better skills does not always lead to a threat of local integration; it can be preparation for displaced persons to be productive human resources if and when repatriation will occur in the future.

The RTG's point that granting formal rights to local integration will act as a pull factor is difficult to argue against, given the continued unrest in Myanmar and the estimated half a million IDPs in eastern Myanmar (TBBC 2009a, b). Thailand could not cope with so many displaced persons. The number of potential displaced persons does, then, add validity to the RTG government concerns about resource allocations, especially land for agriculture, manufacturing and housing. Transporting integrated displaced persons to other parts of Thailand in large numbers would trigger more local conflict, a situation made worse by the RTG's lack of a formal, transparent policy and its failure to have the displaced persons issue debated openly in public through the media or in other ways.

However, the RTG has allowed the situation with the Burmese migrant workers to become intertwined with that of the displaced persons, partly through lack of formal, written asylum policy. It is harder to argue against local integration of the displaced persons when up to two million migrant workers are living and have been *integrated* in Thailand, even if many of them live in poor conditions and are employed in menial jobs. But the working contract that allows a certain period of employment has given the RTG some relief, while the displaced persons issue is different.

In turn, the international community has made a positive contribution in terms of providing care and protection for so long, in cooperation with the RTG, and in working to bring about some of the shifts in practice by the RTG that have made life easier for the displaced persons. Where there has been little progress is engaging with repatriation, the most difficult issue. A significant omission in the recent CCSDPT/UNHCR 5-year plan was any mention of Myanmar, and repatriation is not seen as part of the plan. Though many of the measures in the plan will improve the lives of the displaced persons if enacted, the root cause of the displaced persons issue will not be tackled. A coordinated diplomacy and rethink about Myanmar's status and position, and what inducements and penalties can be used to bring Myanmar into the international community, must accompany improvements in the conditions for the displaced persons. The RTG is far more likely to allow greater integration if it can see that doing so within an overall framework is about creating the right conditions for at least limited return of the displaced persons. Crucially, too, both the RTG and all other stakeholders will need a durable solution that removes the factors that forced displaced persons into Thailand in the first place.

To solve the problem and bring a durable solution to the protracted situation of displaced persons from Myanmar will need collaboration from all stakeholders which carry their own mandate and agenda. From what Loescher/Milner (2007a, b) have stated in their paper, a durable solution needs to be based upon the collaboration of all stakeholders which need to have a common ground to agree upon. Then the comprehensive plan should include all possible solutions; each may become possible at different periods of time. The possibility for the RTG to adapt its policy towards a durable solution is open; the willingness to share this responsibility together will only work well in a friendly atmosphere of equal partnership.

5.4.1 Increased Opportunity for Resettlement

The RTG formally resisted resettlement as an option until the mid 1990s. Again, in practice, this changed, and over 64,000 displaced persons have been resettled, the majority to the USA. However, resettlement has not led to the significant decline in displaced persons numbers that was expected, because of new arrivals. However, the resettlement programme has made a significant contribution as one durable solution for certain sections of the displaced persons community, and large numbers have been resettled. The RTG appears committed to supporting this solution, though there are signs that third countries may be growing weary of it. The timely status determination procedure should be implemented for group status to support the programme. The MOI should facilitate a transparent process screening for resettlement and support for more flexible criteria and status determination. For example, the fast track determination for family members of resettled displaced persons should be considered.

5.4.2 Increasing Displaced Persons' Self-Reliance

Assimilation or settlement in one form or another, which is not favoured by the RTG, may need to be reconsidered. In theory, local integration (Kuhlman 1994) includes legal process to grant the displaced persons wider rights and entitlement, enables them to keep their own identity, guarantees no discrimination or other forms of violation by host country, and grants increasing degrees of self-reliance. The negative impacts of local integration, losing control over the movement of people across the border and risking the good relationship with Myanmar, will make the RTG not willing to deliver the full package but partly at some level it can be applied. This may be explained by Jacobson's conclusion (Jacobsen 2001) that local integration must be acceptable to at least the host country, the local community and the displaced persons. The activities that lead to local integration, including access or integration of displaced persons services to Thai systems, will place a threat to the RTG that the burden may be shifted to its shoulders.

The possibility of increasing displaced persons' self-reliance is not totally closed and can lead to some kind of settlement wherever possible in the future. The principle of encampment in RTG policy, though, has been carried to the present day but increasing permission for skill trainings has been considered. There has been flexibility at the practical and local level. It may be that limited local integration, as part of a broader strategy that includes repatriation, will form part of an ultimate durable solution.

There is also some evidence that the *closed* status of the settlements is not strictly adhered to in practice, but individual displaced persons have reportedly been arrested seeking work outside the settlements. This practice is borne out of the need to seek employment, and a desire for self-reliance. The strict legal position may need to be flexible for displaced persons to work in certain areas adjacent to the shelters or designated areas under the authority supervision.

However, in common with many other countries, the local population has developed a mostly negative attitude to their displaced persons neighbours in the settlements, partly based on resentment about the perceived benefits received by the displaced persons, including basic provisions and healthcare. One of the challenges for the RTG has been to balance the displaced persons condition with local communities, a factor for NGOs and UNHCR also. More development programmes that cover local communities as well as displaced persons will bridge the gap and reduce the negative attitude of the local people.

5.4.3 Planning for Voluntary and Safe Repatriation

Since voluntary repatriation is the favoured durable solution of the RTG and some displaced persons, it is useful to assess what efforts it has made to promote the right conditions for this and other solutions. This study proposes an integrated strategy which includes actions over short, medium and long-term, and which is based on the ultimate goal of voluntary repatriation when conditions are right in 5–10 years. The time frame at least sets a limit to concentrate minds and resources; but may well be accelerated by circumstances, especially the rate of political change in Myanmar, which is unpredictable but which may well increase in the context of events in the Middle East in particular.

The international and national NGOs, for their part, will have an agreed framework within which to design and deliver their services, and a fixed timeframe within which to manage costs and funding. The international agencies, in particular, will have a role to play in Myanmar in aiding resettlement back into the host country, with its practical and political aspects, and including linking and capacity building of national Myanmar structures and organisations.

The RTG has tried to build and maintain contact with the Myanmar government at national, regional and local levels, including cooperation on border issues. The Joint Commission meeting (MOD) and the Ministers discussion in the recent ASEAN meeting have included the issue of the displaced persons and their eventual return to Myanmar in their talks, and the Myanmar side has moved from a basic position that the displaced persons are terrorists to one where it accepts some responsibility for them as citizens of Myanmar, and that at some point they will need to return. However, unless the root cause that drives people to flee from Myanmar has been solved, clearly not the case with incidents of recent fighting, then safe return will not be possible. It will require input not only from Thailand but from the international community, to be more engaged and supportive to make Myanmar a peaceful country to live.

The RTG needs to consider investment in Myanmar, though not any mega project that poses a threat to or allows violations to take place in the ethnic areas. The Thai government or government enterprises must not consider collaboration with Myanmar in such projects that will lead to a huge relocation of people and which may finally end up causing further displacement into Thailand. The same should be considered by other Asian countries. Cooperation among Asian countries may be needed to engage with other investor countries such as China, Japan, Singapore and India to work towards non-abusive enterprises and real development in Myanmar.

In seeking a lasting, durable solution, it is necessary, therefore, to think beyond local integration, resettlement and repatriation, and look at the core problems that make displaced persons flow. This is where the international community, maybe through the UN Security Council, or peace-keeping forces, or regional dialogue, or trade, can act to stabilise and put pressure on countries of origin and the factions within them. This, of course, is the hardest task. As was the case in Liberia, when refugees began to return before the underlying issues were resolved and politics stabilised, then the refugees will flee again. Refugee problems have chronic underlying political causes; unless these are resolved, the refugee problem will remain, and will become protracted. This is the case with Myanmar.

References

CCSDPT/UNHCR, 2007: *Comprehensive Plan 2007/8: A Comprehensive Plan Addressing the Needs of Displaced Persons on the Thailand/Myanmar (Burma) Border* (Bangkok: UNHCR/ CCSDPT).

Loescher, G.; Milner, J., 2005a: *Protracted Refugee Situations: Domestic and International Security Implications* (London: International Institute for Strategic Studies).

Loescher, G.; Milner, J., 2005b: *Security and Forced Migration: Developing DFID's Policy Approach to Refugees and Internally Displaced Persons* (Oxford: Refugee Studies Centre).

Loescher, G.; Milner, J., 2006: "Protracted Refugee Situation in Thailand: Towards Solutions", Presentation to the Foreign Correspondents' Club of Thailand.

Loescher, G.; Milner, J., 2007a: "Protracted Refugee Situations: Causes, Consequences, and Trends", Paper presented at the RSC 25th Anniversary Conference.

Loescher, G.; Milner, J., 2007b: "Protracted Refugee Situations: Towards a New Research Agenda", Paper presented at the RSC 25th Anniversary Conference.

Jacobsen, K., 2001: "The forgotten solution: local integration for refugees in developing countries", in: *New issues in refugee research, Working Paper No. 45.* (Geneva: UNHCR).

Nukul, A., 2002: "The problem of controlling Karen Displaced Persons in the temporary shelter in Tak Province" (Master Thesis, Chiang Mai: Chiang Mai University, Graduate Institute).

TBBC, 2004: *Between Worlds: Twenty Years on the Border*; at: http://www.tbbc.org/resources/ 2004-between-worlds.zip.

TBBC, 2009a: *Programme Report, January-June 2009* (Bangkok: TBBC).

TBBC, 2009b: *Programme Report, July-December 2009* (Bangkok: TBBC).

TBBC, 2010a: *Programme Report, January-June 2010* (Bangkok: TBBC).

TBBC, 2010b: *Programme Report, July-December 2010* (Bangkok: TBBC).

Chapter 6
Conclusions and Recommendations

Premjai Vungsiriphisal, Graham Bennett, Chanarat Poomkacha, Waranya Jitpong and Kamonwan Reungsamran

Abstract The issue of displaced persons in Thailand cannot be viewed, after 25 years, as *temporary*; it is one of the world's most protracted refugee situations. In order to find a solution for the huge numbers of people exiled from Myanmar, and to prevent further flows, cooperation is needed from the various stakeholders on a coordinated plan of action which will see voluntary repatriation to a safe and conflict-free Myanmar as its long-term aim. In the meantime, greater flexibility and support is needed by the RTG and others, including international agencies moving from an emergency approach to a developmental one, to build greater self-reliance amongst the displaced persons, restoring their dignity and preparing them for a mixture of repatriation, resettlement and local integration while ensuring they have greater autonomy in the interim.

Keywords Recommendations · Thai government · NGOs · Displaced persons · International community · Aid donors · Resettlement · Local integration · Myanmar · Repatriation

P. Vungsiriphisal (✉) · G. Bennett · C. Poomkacha · W. Jitpong · K. Reungsamran
Asian Research Center for Migration, Institute of Asian Studies, Chulalongkorn University, 3rd floor, Prachadhipok Rambhai-Barni Building, Bangkok 10330, Thailand
e-mail: premjai.v@chula.ac.th

G. Bennett
e-mail: grahambennett777@hotmail.co.uk

C. Poomkacha
e-mail: cpoomkacha@abeam.com

W. Jitpong
e-mail: wec135@hotmail.com

K. Reungsamran
e-mail: kamonwan24@yahoo.com

P. Vungsiriphisal et al. (eds.), *Humanitarian Assistance for Displaced Persons from Myanmar*, SpringerBriefs in Environment, Security, Development and Peace 17, DOI: 10.1007/978-3-319-02795-1_6,

6.1 Characteristics of RTG's Policy and Practice

The RTG's policy towards displaced persons from Myanmar does not appear in a formal asylum policy, but is shaped in various Cabinet resolution, Ministry announcements and regulations. The situation of the displaced persons is seen first and foremost as a security issue rather than a humanitarian one. The leading roles to administer the issue have been assigned to security sectors including the National Security Council (NSC) and the Ministry of the Interior (MOI) which set up ad hoc subcommittees that include members from various other sectors. The initiative of new programmes, and the changing or improving of some regulations and guidelines, have been done with the participation of these subcommittees. The three principles of the policy for displaced persons management have included confinement of the displaced persons to the settlements, reducing the burden on the RTG of providing sanctuary and services, and addressing the root causes of the displaced persons issue. These principles have been carried through to the present day, though there have been some changes and shifts in the implementation of the policy.

The whole approach has been based on the traditional paradigm that prioritises national security. National security has shaped the issue because the displaced persons are seen as illegal entrants into the country against the immigration laws, because of the possible destabilising effect in the face of growing public hostility and communities adjacent to the settlements, and the delicate nature of the relationship with Myanmar. Thailand does not abide with the UN convention on the status of the refugees and uses its own definition of *displaced persons* with a higher threshold for those seeking protection.

The RTG has permitted humanitarian organisations to provide basic assistance to displaced persons from the time when the nine current shelters were set up by consolidating the many smaller resettlements. Since 1998, UNHCR has been invited to provide protection and started formal registration with the establishment of Provincial Admission Board (PAB) as a status screening and confirmation. The registration process has slowed down from group determination to case basis after 2005, while new arrivals continued and contributed to a high non-registered population in the shelters. These non-registered displaced persons are not eligible for the resettlement programme that has taken place since 2005.

The RTG policy can be seen as rigid in its principles that have remained unchanged for almost 30 years, though there have been many shifts in the implementation and some approaches. The areas of improvement have included education, health and vocational training that equip some displaced persons with skills to earn their living. However, the increasing number of displaced persons under the confinement and strict regulation has made the shelters crowded areas with unhealthy environmental problems. Though the conditions are acceptable to the majority of displaced persons, compared to the worse situation in Myanmar, improvement in living conditions is needed. The confinement policy has proved ineffective because many displaced persons have managed to find jobs outside the shelters. Some were arrested and deported, but managed to come back to the shelters. The shortage of funding, accompanied with the donor strategy to reduce the care and assistance approach programme, has limited the assistance to the displaced persons, while the need for cash to buy some extra food, clothes and other items is obvious. The limited demand inside the shelters cannot absorb the oversupply labour of displaced persons.

6.2 Factors Influencing the Current RTG's Approach to Displaced Persons

The RTG policy is considered to be a passive one towards the displaced persons and will not lead to durable solutions. There are many factors that influence the policy formulation. The internal factors include RTG's concern for security of its sovereignty, resulting from the attacks of the Burmese army and DKBA army on the shelters. The radical political activity of some displaced persons has also contributed to the more restricted policy. Arguably, the policy of confinement has been the principle of the RTG from the beginning, in addition to minimising the population and Thailand's burden. The policy implementation changed from a flexible approach in the early period, when displaced persons served as the cheap labour to the local labour market, to a more restricted approach when Thailand was able to bring in migrant labour from three neighbouring countries including Myanmar.

The experience from long hosting Indochinese refugees, and local resistance, are among factors that have contributed to the current policy of the RTG of keeping displaced persons from Myanmar far from public knowledge. Thai national law, notably the Immigration Act 1979, clarifies the classification of displaced persons as *illegal immigrants*. Section 17 of the Act does allow for decisions by the RTG Cabinet to overrule the Act in special cases, and this was used in some cases in the 1970s and 1980s for some Indochinese refugees, but it has been little used more recently and does not apply to the displaced persons residing in the shelters. The Constitution of Thailand, in principle covering all who reside in the country, Thai and non-Thai, ought to offer some protection to the Burmese displaced persons, since it mentions human rights and human dignity; in practice, though, it applies only to citizens, and displaced persons are classified as non-Thai citizens. It has not been tested in the Courts.

Thailand's problems include management of its migrant workers, internal conflict, the coup in 2006, short-lived governments since 2006 and many recent changes of Prime Minister and ministers. Even external stakeholders concede the RTG has had competing priorities, meaning the issue of displaced persons is not an urgent issue to the RTG. The migrant workers issue remains difficult to resolve, and it is hard to envisage that the RTG will devote much time and effort to solving the displaced persons issue until other priorities are dealt with.

The relationship with Myanmar remains, therefore, the key factor affecting Thai policy. Thailand and Myanmar have a long and mixed history of conflict, trade and exchange; something that is often overlooked by Western governments that have too often assumed that the RTG will follow closely the line of the USA, EU and other Western liberal powers. Myanmar is a source of migrant labourers for Thailand, is an increasing trade partner, and has rich deposits of oil and gas. For the RTG, the relationship with Myanmar is vital, and it will make great efforts to keep it open and cordial. The only factor which might grab the attention of the RTG is if many more displaced persons start crossing the border into Thailand. Though there have been mixed reports, this may well be happening following an upsurge in fighting after the November 2010 election in Myanmar.

Thailand's commitment to various international conventions and presence in the international arena has also influenced the RTG to apply those conventions and improve practice towards displaced persons; the CRC leading to displaced persons children being provided with birth certificates is the latest example.

6.3 RTG Policy Towards Durable Solution

The RTG policy does not consider local integration as it will become a pull factor for many IDPs already near the border. In spite of absorbing the early wave of displaced persons to local communities, reports show that the greater number and competition over resources contribute to the hostility from local people around the settlements to displaced persons. The negative attitude among public Thai is reflected in a national survey linked to incidents performed by some displaced persons and POCs in 1998. Self settlement was a natural process in the early stages of the displaced persons issue, especially since there are some ethnic links which extend on both sides of the Thailand–Myanmar border. It was only after the numbers became much greater that the RTG was forced to formalise the settlements, and then to consolidate the camps that had grown up into the nine formal settlements that exist now. The integration into local communities becomes difficult in terms of population size, the availability of land, resources and other factors.

The international community has cooperated with the RTG to bring about some shifts in RTG policy including the resettlement programme which has contributed to durable solution for certain sections of the displaced persons community. Repatriation has remained the most difficult and there has been little progress. The recent CCSDPT/UNHCR 5-year plan does not mention repatriation to Myanmar, and the root cause of the displaced persons issue is not tackled. Coordinated diplomacy and a rethink about Myanmar's status and position, and what inducements and penalties can be used to bring Myanmar into the international community, must accompany improvements in the conditions for the displaced persons. Crucially, too, both the RTG and all other stakeholders will need a durable solution that removes the factors that forced displaced persons into Thailand in the first place.

The Myanmar government is not easy to work with but more engagement is needed to make a difference and deal with the protracted status of the Burmese displaced persons issue which needs careful and creative thinking to work with Myanmar and its leaders.

A short-term, medium-term and long-term plan of action to work with Myanmar, as with the Somalia CPA, may help in making at least part of Myanmar safe for voluntary repatriation. This may be the most practical approach.

6.4 The Way Forward: Self-Reliance and Plan of Action Towards Myanmar

The main lessons from other protracted refugee situations for finding a solution to the situation of Burmese displaced persons in Thailand are that it will take time, and that a wider political engagement will be needed, not just because of the opposition by the RTG to local integration, one of the key durable solutions. It is clear that no protracted situation can be finally solved without addressing the root causes for the displacement of large numbers of civilians. By explicitly adopting the framework for all other activities relating to the management and support of the displaced persons from Myanmar, all stakeholders could feel they are working towards the same end to the durable solution in the context of voluntary repatriation and resettlement, and possible local integration. The RTG will be willing to increase self reliance opportunities in the context of all durable solution based on the ultimate goal of voluntary repatriation with right conditions. The international organisations will also deliver their services towards development in Myanmar in aiding repatriation and to Myanmar structures and organisations.

6.5 Recommendations

6.5.1 To the Royal Thai Government

- Promote the human security principle which is claimed to balance with the traditional security paradigm of the National Security Policy since 2003 to cover the issue of displaced persons from Myanmar, since they are a group of people with permission to reside in Thailand, no matter what status they are. This principle should be applied to the regulation for approving services providing to displaced persons, allow more activities relating to improvement of their livelihood as well as to allow more flexibility for employment opportunity.

- Regulate timely screening process and status determination and applying a broader definition *fleeing from persecution* to screen out people not eligible to settlement and enforce the measures to deport the rejected cases with or without the assistance from UN agencies.
- Consider a long-term plan or strategy focusing on irregular displacement in the country, including displaced persons from Myanmar. This strategy should be accompanied with foreign policy approaches to Myanmar which should also support the solution to the root cause of the problem. The strategy should be drafted, based on updated situation data and information from relevant stakeholders related to displaced persons, including civil societies and local communities.
- Play the leading role to initiate the dialogue platform with UN and donors to work for possible collaboration towards solutions for displaced persons in Thailand which includes all possible solutions: increased self-reliance of displaced persons and acceptable forms of integration, increase more flexible criteria and countries for resettlement opportunity and plan for future safe voluntary repatriation.
- Reconsider collaboration with the Myanmar Government, as well as the private sectors, to develop any mega projects that may lead to relocation or exploitation of the ethnic areas which will drive more displacement to Thailand.
- Collaborate with other Asian countries that host displaced persons from Myanmar, Malaysia, Indonesia and China, to more closely dialogue with Myanmar to eliminate the conditions that contribute more displacement.
- Collaborate with ASEAN and other investment countries such as China, Japan and India to use a flexible engagement approach with Myanmar towards reconciliation with ethnic groups and improvement of people's living conditions.

6.5.2 To the Donors and UN Agencies

- Collaborate and dialogue with the RTG towards the solutions for displacement from Myanmar with equal consideration of all possible resolutions.
- Initiate supporting strategy instead of funding strategy to encourage shifting of policy, and provide technical support and collaboration where necessary.
- Provide more support to improve the conditions in the affected areas surrounding the shelters to reduce the negative attitude of local communities towards displaced persons.
- Collaborate with more countries and allow more flexible criteria to increase resettlement opportunity.
- Initiate long-term dialogue with the Myanmar government to improve the conditions in ethnic areas and initiate development for safe repatriation.
- Collaborate and support organisations working for sustainable development in ethnic areas.
- Start planning for possible voluntary repatriation.

6.5.3 To Non-Governmental Organisations

- Collaborate with the RTG and shelter committees not to provide assistance to screened out people, to reduce the non eligible population in the shelters.
- Promote a reduced expense approach along with the approach to increase employment opportunity.
- Initiate a pilot sufficiency economic programme to improve the livelihood of displaced persons.
- Initiate more programmes to secure food producing using appropriate technologies.

6.5.4 To Displaced Persons

- Avoid breaking the regulations and laws to reduce the risk of being deported.
- Avoid taking Thai community resources to reduce the negative feelings.
- Engage in more skill trainings to prepare for all possible options and opportunities.
- Construct good relationships with local communities to reduce tensions and conflict.

Part II
Analysis of the Royal Thai Government Policy and of Donor, INGO/NGO and UN Agency Delivery of Humanitarian Assistance for Displaced Persons from Myanmar

Chapter 7
Introduction

Dares Chusri, Tarina Rubin, Ma. Esmeralda Silva, Jason D. Theede, Sunanta Wongchalee and Patcharin Chansawang

Abstract The key actors whose policy and actions impact on displaced persons in Thailand are outlined, including the Royal Thai Government (RTG), UN agencies, donors and international Non-Government Organisations (NGOs). The research approach is outlined, including questions to be asked, and the study framework is presented. The methodology employed, including how displaced person respondents were sampled in the three settlements studied, is also detailed, along with possible limitations of the approach and ethical considerations.

Keywords Displaced persons · Burmese refugees · Aid donors · UNHCR · NGOs · International community · Research objectives · Research methodology

7.1 Study Background

The current displacement of people from Myanmar to the Thai–Myanmar border began in 1984 when approximately 9,000 Karen displaced persons seeking refuge in Tak province reported attacks from military government forces. The Ministry of Interior (MOI) invited the Committee for Coordination of Services to Displaced Persons in Thailand (CCSDPT), then working with Indochinese displaced persons in Thailand, to provide emergency assistance to them. It was expected that the situation would be temporary but the displaced persons were unable to return to their country during the rainy season and attacks on Karen communities continued

D. Chusri (✉) · T. Rubin · Ma. E. Silva · J. D. Theede · S. Wongchalee · P. Chansawang
Asian Research Center for Migration, Institute of Asian Studies, Chulalongkorn University, 3rd floor, Prachadhipok Rambhai-Barni Building, Bangkok 10330, Thailand
e-mail: dares_c@hotmail.com

T. Rubin
e-mail: tarina.Rubin@gmail.com

P. Vungsiriphisal et al. (eds.), *Humanitarian Assistance for Displaced Persons from Myanmar*, SpringerBriefs in Environment, Security, Development and Peace 17,
DOI: 10.1007/978-3-319-02795-1_7,

in the years that followed. This resulted in an ongoing flow of displaced persons into Thailand. As of December 2010, according to UNHCR, there are an estimated 98,644 displaced persons in nine camps along the Thai–Myanmar border (TBBC 2010a, b).

Displaced persons living in the temporary shelters in Thailand are forced to subsist on external humanitarian assistance provided by NGOs and international donors. This continued reliance on external assistance has created a significant degree of aid-dependency for those living in the shelters. It has also raised the question among donors of how the current model of assistance can be made more sustainable and solutions-oriented. Alternative approaches that provide displaced persons with greater opportunities for self-sufficiency, self-reliance and independence, such as increased educational and livelihood opportunities, have been proposed and implemented as pilot projects. However, for the most part, these projects have yet to be scaled up to a level where they have made a significant impact.

There are at least three major actors who have an influential role in humanitarian actions toward the displaced persons from Myanmar along Thai–Myanmar border: the Royal Thai Government (RTG), donors and implementing organisations, including International Non-Government Organisations (INGOs)[1] and Non-Government Organisations (NGOs). A number of INGOs and NGOs, including UNHCR, have been active partners with the RTG. Funding for each NGO is dependent on donor contributions. However, donor fatigue has increasingly become an issue, with some donors stating it will not be possible to continually increase support for displaced persons from Myanmar and others suggesting it is time to look for an *exit strategy* (CCSDPT/UNHCR Comprehensive Plan 2007/8).

Although some donors have yet to confirm their funding intentions, the projected income for 2010 is 1,083 million baht, 5 % lower than in 2009. This will result in a shortfall of 149 million baht for the year (TBBC 2009a, b). To respond to this challenge it is necessary to develop more comprehensive solutions by shifting from the current *care and maintenance* approach to a more *solution-oriented* approach. The comprehensive concerns of host countries and the limitations on their willingness to host displaced persons must also be taken into account (Loescher/Milner 2007).

This study, supported by the United Nations Development Programme (UNDP), is one of six-related studies by the Asian Research Centre for Migration (ARCM) to seek sustainable solutions to the Displaced People situation along the

---

[1] Generally INGO means non-profit, non-partisan organisations which have a main/head office abroad and a field office in Thailand. NGO refers to non-profit, non-partisan organisations which are locally based. However, in this study INGOs and NGOs refer to implementing agencies which provide services to displaced persons or the local community. INGO and NGO terms will be used interchangeably.

Thai–Myanmar Border. In particular, this study analyses the role of donors, international organisations and non-government organisations, their policies and implementation of these over the years, and their relations with the Royal Thai Government (RTG) and the agencies they support.

The outcome of the study is expected to serve as a basis for policy dialogue with decision-makers and those in a position to influence them; to facilitate the design of an improved strategy to implement policy, to advocate for a change in policy towards sustainable and long-term solutions that will be beneficial and agreeable both for the uprooted population as well as their host country. These groups comprise first of all the RTG, in particular the MOI, as well as a number of line ministries whose functions and services are relevant in this context. The donor community, NGOs, international organisations and displaced persons committees will equally benefit from and be involved in this research. Networking consortiums such as the Thai–Burma Border Consortium (TBBC) and the CCSDPT will also benefit greatly from this work.

7.2 Study Framework, Objectives, Research Questions

7.2.1 Study Framework

A variety of humanitarian actors are working to develop sustainable and ultimately durable solutions for displaced persons in the temporary shelters in Thailand. The displaced persons' situation in the temporary shelters in Thailand is quite unique in that the provision of humanitarian assistance is supervised by the RTG, implemented by NGOs, supported financially by donors and the UN, and motivated by the now protracted duration of encampment for the displaced. As the displaced persons have been living in the camps for over two decades, the donors' policies for supporting this model of assistance are currently being reconsidered. There is the possibility that some donors may discontinue or reduce their support for these displaced persons if progress towards a more sustainable and solutions-oriented model of aid is not achieved.

By undertaking an analysis of donor policies and motivations, as well as the interventions of NGOs and international organisations, this study will gather evidence that can be used to determine the extent to which current policies and strategies constitute a sustainable and solutions-oriented approach to the situation. These findings will provide the evidence base for the development of alternative policy options in the policy synthesis phase of this project (Fig. 7.1).

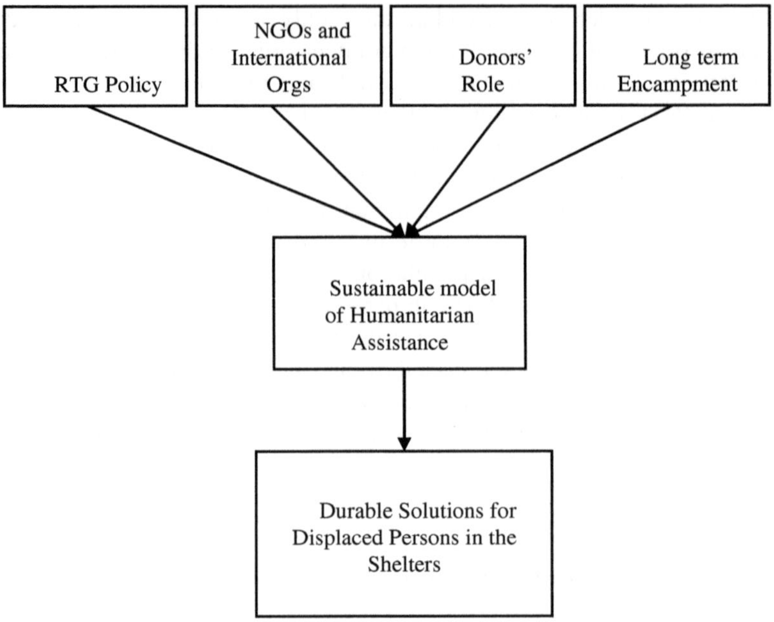

Fig. 7.1 Study framework. *Source* The authors

7.2.2 Goal

The goal of this study is to provide an analysis of the roles, existing policies and implementation processes behind the current rationale for intervention by donors, international organisations, NGOs and UN agencies to provide humanitarian assistance to the displaced persons along the Thailand–Myanmar border through a community-based camp management structure.

7.2.3 Research Objectives

1. To analyse the current rationale behind the international intervention along the Thai–Burma border by different stakeholders.
2. To examine the historical role of donors, UN agencies, international and local non-government organisations providing humanitarian assistance to the displaced persons along the Thailand–Burma border.
3. To analyse the funding policies of donors, the specific mandate of each organisation towards displaced persons, the project implementation strategies by different organisations and their cooperative strategies with the Royal Thai Government.

4. To identify the dynamics, needs and constraints of different stakeholders in engagement with the displaced persons.
5. To analyse the positive and negative impacts of existing intervention mechanisms, including gender-related aspects.
6. To identify the limitations and constraints on effective intervention mechanisms that exist as a result of current RTG policies towards displaced persons.

7.2.4 Research Questions

1. What is the nature and extent of current and future strategies of humanitarian aid agencies toward displaced persons along the Thai–Burma border camp? Are strategies the same as or different from the past? Why?
2. What are the current and future funding policy directions of donors? What strategies do stakeholders apply to work with the RTG?
3. What strategies or mechanisms will be combined or integrated to develop an intervention programme for durable solutions for displaced persons? Do the donors, INGOs and NGOs have any plans to fund or implement the strategies further along the continuum from emergency response to sustainable development? If so, how?
4. What are the strengths, limitations and impacts of current intervention policies? What are the remaining challenges for effective intervention mechanisms?
5. What are the dynamics, needs and constraints of different stakeholders in engagement with the displaced persons?
6. What are the perceptions of humanitarian aid organisations regarding the displaced persons and their needs?

7.3 Methodology

7.3.1 Research Design

Qualitative and quantitative approaches are applied in this research. A combination of these methods was used in order to gain the perspective of all target audiences. The purpose of the quantitative research is to describe and explain the perceptions and needs of displaced persons for humanitarian aid. The purpose of qualitative research is to understand the policies, mandates and strategies defining the nature of humanitarian aid. Relevant archives and documents were reviewed, relating to the experience of other regions and that of donors, UN agencies, NGOs and host countries relating to protection and durable solutions for displaced persons.

7.3.2 Study Area and Study Population

7.3.2.1 Study Area

Three temporary shelters with a diversity of culture, ethnicity and population were purposively selected for this study: Tham Hin, Ban Mai Nai Soi and Mae La. Tham Hin is predominantly Karen ethnicity and forms the southernmost camp in Thailand, located in Suan Phung District, Ratchaburi Province. It is the camp with the most cramped living conditions. The vast majority of the population has likely limited experience with modern public transportation or other modern conveniences. Mae La camp is the largest camp, located in Tha song yang district, Tak province. The area features clay earth and a stream. The majority of the population is Karen ethnicity whereas the camp population in Ban Mai Nai Soi in Mae Hong Son province is majority Karenni.

7.3.2.2 Study Population

Four main groups were the focus of this study; donor staff, international organisation staff, RTG officials and displaced persons.

Donors

Although members of the donor group are the primary research target of this study, access to them was neither easy nor a given and it took time to schedule interviews depending on their availability and interest. The research team was persistent, sometimes sending three or four follow-up emails before receiving a response from some donors. However, the majority of donors were helpful and offered suggestions or assistance in soliciting the participation of others. During the interviews themselves, the research team found all donor representatives to be friendly and willing to share information and opinions, even within the limited time available. The research team approached 12 donors for interview, of which nine participated. Of those that declined to participate, two had been declined funding for displaced persons from Myanmar in the shelters along the Thai–Myanmar border, while the third had expended funds for these displaced persons and were not available due to a heavy travel schedule during the 3 months of the interview period. As an observation, requesting responses through email is not easy or always appropriate for donors due to the sensitive nature of some issues. A total of 12 people representing donors participated in this study, most of them are senior or high-level officers directly responsible for the areas of displaced persons and cross-border funding.

Royal Thai Government

Interviews with RTG officials were conducted in conjunction with other parts of the overall study to reduce the burden on each interviewee. The RTG study population comprised of senior, high or officer level representatives of the MOI and the NSC, Office of the Prime Minister in Bangkok. District governors of the three targeted temporary shelters were also included in this study.

International Non-Government Organisations and UN agencies

The third study population was recruited from relevant international NGOs (INGOs) and UN agencies from July to November 2010. The research team contacted INGOs directly to request their participation in this study, while meetings with UN agencies such as UNHCR and WHO were coordinated through the UNDP. All six INGOs contacted participated, including 16 staff in Bangkok, three Thai field staff, seven displaced persons field workers and one network (CCSDPT). Of the four UN agencies contacted, five representatives of three agencies participated. The fourth indicated that his organisation does not operate in Thailand.

Displaced Persons

The research team requested that the camp committee and leaders publicly announce this study and invite displaced persons from all living zones to participate. The survey respondents were recruited on the basis of certain inclusion criteria: age 18 and over, residing in shelter at least 1 year, informed consent, willing and voluntary participation to answer the questionnaire, and matched to gender and ethnicity balance and registration status within the shelters.

7.4 Data Collection and Tools

7.4.1 Administration and Coordination

The Asian Research Centre for Migration (ARCM) team was responsible for the policy study as well as the overall coordination of the six studies, and led the preparation of the approach paper and coordination with the UNDP. ARCM contacted MOI for permission to access temporary shelters and conduct the study; contacted international consultants for advice, feedback and consultative workshops as well as carrying out other coordinating functions.

ARCM invited representatives from the NSC, MOI, Ministry of Foreign Affairs (MOFA) and the Army Department of Border Affairs to be members of the advisory committee as the study addresses the RTG asylum policy and the role of various offices in charge of displaced persons affairs. In addition, the chairperson of the National Human Rights Commission (NHRC) and two academics from Chulalongkorn University, including Professor Vithit Muntarbhorn, joined the committee, which provided advice to the research teams on the direction of the study as well as on policy options.

7.4.2 Research Team

A data collection and a research team contributed to this study. The data collection team was responsible for fieldwork: the baseline survey, focus group discussions, key informant interviews and other key aspects. The research team was responsible for data analysis and report writing. It should be noted that each member of the research team also participated in fieldwork and data collection. The team leader is knowledgeable in this field and has extensive experience in working with displaced persons populations in temporary shelters.

7.4.3 Data Collection

The data collection tools used in this study were designed in accordance with quantitative and qualitative research methods (Table 7.1).

7.4.3.1 Data Collection for Baseline Survey

Two teams were formed for field data collection; Team A comprised of the subsection studies on the labour market, social welfare and environment, while Team B comprised of RTG policy, role of donor, international organisations, NGOs and UN agencies and resettlement groups. Each questionnaire took approximately 30–40 min per displaced persons interviewee; a reasonable length of time. The teams visited the shelters using different questionnaires. A gift, canned fish or a raincoat, was given to all respondents as a token of appreciation for their cooperation. In order to specify the samplings size, each team applied Taro Yamane formula as followed:

$$n = \frac{N}{1 + e^2 N}$$

Table 7.1 Research methods and tools

Method	Target group	Tool
Baseline survey	Displaced persons in 3 selected shelters (Tham Hin, Mae La, Mae Hong Son)	Face-to-face interview, using structured questionnaire
FGD	Displaced persons in 3 selected shelters	Face-to-face interview, using interview guide
IDI	Displaced persons in 3 selected shelters	Face-to-face interview, using interview guide
KII	Donor, UN agencies, INGOs	Face-to-face interview, using interview guide

Source The authors

where N = Element of population, in this study was 145,786, e = Error of sampling, in this study was 5 % or 0.05 proportion, n = sample size

$$n = \frac{145{,}786}{1 + 145{,}786(0.05)^2}$$

Substitution for this formula: = 400 displaced persons for each team.

Therefore, the two teams collected information from 800 displaced persons. A total sampling of 800 respondents from the three temporary shelters were randomly selected to answer the questionnaire. (See Table 7.2 for breakdown and locations). The sampling herein covered all variations in terms of gender, ethnicity, legal status within the shelter (registered, non-registered and others), resettlement intentions and status and age group.

Team B initially planned a total sampling of 400 respondents from the three temporary shelters, though this was inflated to an actual number of 444 respondents to prevent incomplete responses. However, it was found that all interview questionnaires could be used for data analysis. All respondents were randomly selected to answer the questionnaire. The sample covered all variations in terms of gender, ethnicity, legal status within the shelter, resettlement intentions and status and age group (Table 7.3).

Teams A and B consulted each other continuously during data collection. We also shared preliminary findings and discussed issues as they occurred in the field. Such close management of communications ensured that beneficiaries were not confused or overwhelmed by the visits of the research teams.

The quantitative study took the form of a baseline survey, based on 3-week-long research trips to interview 444 displaced persons between July and September 2010. The survey used a face-to-face interview structured questionnaire in three

Table 7.2 Sampling site by location and research team

Temporary shelters	Team A	Team B	Total
Tham Hin	100	100	200
Ban Mai Nai Soi	100	100	200
Mae La	200	200	400
Total	400	400	800

Source The authors

Table 7.3 Sampling site by location of team B

Temporary shelters	Initial plan	Actual number
Tham Hin	100	113
Mae La	200	218
Ban Mai Nai Soi	100	113
Total	400	444

Source The authors

targeted temporary shelters. The baseline survey questionnaire consolidated the questions of the two other research teams in order to prevent interviewee fatigue and solicit further cooperation. The questionnaire consisted of four parts: demographic data; RTG policy; perceptions on the role of donors, INGOs, UN and the RTG, and finally, resettlement. The interview procedure was guided by ethical concerns such as informed consent, voluntary participation and confidentiality.

7.4.3.2 Displaced Persons Respondent Characteristics

As mentioned above, 444 displaced persons respondents in three targeted temporary shelters were recruited in this study. Females made up 55.4 % of all respondents. Mae La shelter hosts half of all respondents, with a further 25 % living in both Tham Hin and Ban Mai Nai Soi. The majority of respondents, 68 %, are aged 25–59 years and 70 % are married. Only half of respondents are registered as displaced persons. Karen/S'gaw is the largest ethnic group at 48 %. Many, some 41 %, have lived in the shelters between 11 and 20 years. Half of them are Christian and 31 % are Buddhist. Some 75 % of respondents were literate and, of these, 68 % had graduated studies in Myanmar rather than within the temporary shelter. Of the literate respondents who had graduated from Myanmar, 50.7 % reached middle school level. Around half of the respondents reported the current number of people in their household to be five to eight persons. Only 52 % of respondents are employed and 48.1 % earn between 501 and 1,500 baht per month. In 37.4 % of interviews, Thai–Karen language was used.

7.4.3.3 Qualitative Method

Apart from the baseline survey, focus group discussions (FGD) and in-depth interviews (IDI) were also conducted according to the same interview guide with some displaced persons in the three targeted temporary shelters. It was planned that key informant interviews (KII) would take place from July to September 2010 with donors, UN agencies, NGOs and relevant RTG agencies. Key informants (KI) were purposively selected based on their knowledge or experience in work related to displaced persons, or those who provide services to displaced persons, and their willingness to share their opinions, knowledge and experiences. KI comprised donor government staff, UN staff, INGOs staff, displaced persons who serve as INGO field workers and residents of temporary shelters. Individual interview and group interviews used a semi-structured interview guideline and structured questionnaires were used in the baseline survey to obtain the required information from temporary shelter residents. The qualitative study consumed more time than expected due to the limited availability of interviewees, taking 7 months from June 2010 to January 2011.

A total of 16 FGDs were conducted with 80 displaced persons: 40 female and 40 male in three selected temporary shelters from July to September 2010. IDIs were also conducted with 18 displaced persons: nine female and nine male in the three targeted temporary shelters.

7.5 Data Analysis

Quantitative data from the baseline survey conducted by the RTG policy team, the donor, INGO and UN agency team and the resettlement team were analysed together using the SPSS programme. Data were stratified by gender to see how various situations in the temporary shelters, such as an assessment of needs for self-sufficiency, cover both women and men adequately and equally.

Qualitative data from interviews and focus groups were analysed by using the content analysis technique, and then integrated into the quantitative data to give more depth to understanding of the various impacts on displaced persons people, policy formulation processes and influencing factors, and possibilities for policy shift given the evidence revealed by the study. The baseline survey also includes policy recommendations, based on the responses of all beneficiaries.

7.6 Ethical Considerations

The study identifies displaced persons as the major stakeholders. Data collected in this sample will be kept confidential and anonymous in accordance with Chulalongkorn University Ethical Guidelines for Research on Vulnerable Groups. These guidelines focus on the principles of respect for person, minimising harm and justice.

The same principles are applied to other target groups, including key informants inside and outside of the holding centres, officials from the RTG government, members of INGOs, the UN and the embassies. The research team is aware of the sensitivities in the perceptions and criticism of various stakeholders on RTG asylum policy in Thailand. Researchers thus ensure that different opinions will not put informants into conflicting or dangerous situations during or after the study. Informed consent and confidentiality concerns have been discussed as a priority with all participants.

In terms of displaced persons' expectations, the study did not mislead them into thinking that it can provide them with new status or a new future through the study's findings and recommendations. The objectives and the outcomes of the study were clarified with the displaced persons during the data collection period.

7.7 Study Limitations

There are several factors which served as obstacles throughout the various stages this study. Study dimension agreements between ARCM and UNDP were finalised only after work had commenced, took almost 2 months and resulted in initial uncertainty and hesitation among the team on how best to proceed. This led to a delay in the study and also affected the time available for the study process, including management. A study period of only 6 months was restrictive for the conduct of both quantitative and qualitative research. As such, time constraints affected the data collecting process and consequently, some important data were not captured. Considerable time was required to complete data collection in each temporary shelter and with all stakeholders. The tight schedule also limited opportunities to cross check information gathered from shelters, RTG, donors and INGO staff.

The qualitative study consumed more time than expected due to the unavailability of interviewees and their busy schedules. It therefore took 7 months, from June 2010 to January 2011, to complete the qualitative interviews and this also affected the timeline for data analysis.

Additionally, significant components of the data collected from stakeholders such as donors, INGOs and the RTG, were confidential; funding figures and financial and meeting reports, for example. Although many stakeholders were open to sharing this confidential information with the research team, this meant it was ultimately necessary to analyse and interpret this data at a general, overview level only. Also, the analysis relies on data shared voluntarily by interviewees and cannot identify donors individually, in accordance with the study's respect of confidentiality guidelines for key informants.

Most of the displaced persons interviews were conducted in their own native language, whether Karen, Karenni or Burmese, and it was necessary for the research team to employ the services of an interpreter. Although the interpreters were of a very high skill level and measures were taken to overcome language barriers, some bias may have been introduced by the presence of foreigners, whether Thai or expatriate, in the temporary shelters.

Considerable turnover among key informants and respondents inevitably results in a loss in institutional memory, making it at times difficult to gather information.

Selection of temporary shelter respondents was based on a convenience sample of who were available and may have been biassed against those who are more active. This may affect the quality of the data.

References

CCSDPT/UNHCR, 2007: *Comprehensive Plan 2007/8: A Comprehensive Plan Addressing the Needs of Displaced Persons on the Thailand/Myanmar (Burma) Border* (Bangkok: UNHCR/CCSDPT).

CCSDPT/UNHCR, 2009: *Five-Year Strategic Plan* (Bangkok: CCSDPT/UNHCR).

Loescher, G.; Milner, J., 2007: "Protracted Refugee Situations: Causes, Consequences, and Trends", Paper for the RSC 25th Anniversary Conference.
TBBC, 2009a: *Programme Report, January–June 2009* (Bangkok: TBBC).
TBBC, 2009b: *Programme Report, July–December 2009* (Bangkok: TBBC).
TBBC, 2010a: *Programme Report, January–June 2010* (Bangkok: TBBC).
TBBC, 2010b: *Programme Report, July–December 2010* (Bangkok: TBBC).

Chapter 8
Literature Review

Dares Chusri, Tarina Rubin, Ma. Esmeralda Silva, Jason D. Theede, Sunanta Wongchalee and Patcharin Chansawang

Abstract The role and contribution of key actors to supporting the displaced persons is detailed, including changes that have taken place over time. The role of the RTG, and its various ministries and departments, in developing policy and practice, and managing the camps, is examined, including how this has evolved in practice. Each of the other actors is looked at in details, including UN agencies such as United Nations High Commission for Refugees (UNHCR), and the NGO bodies such as Thailand Burma Border Consortium (TBBC) and CCSDPT. The role of donor countries, including the EU, UK and USA, is also examined, including the funding they have brought, and how this is currently under threat as donors and other actors grow weary of the protracted nature of the displaced persons situation. The move from humanitarian relief to self-reliant development is discussed.

Keywords Humanitarian assistance · Burmese refugees · Displaced persons · Refugee camps · NGOs · Aid donors

D. Chusri (✉) · T. Rubin · Ma. E. Silva · J. D. Theede · S. Wongchalee · P. Chansawang
Asian Research Center for Migration, Institute of Asian Studies, Chulalongkorn University, 3rd floor, Prachadhipok Rambhai-Barni Building, Bangkok 10330, Thailand
e-mail: dares_c@hotmail.com

T. Rubin
e-mail: tarina.Rubin@gmail.com

P. Vungsiriphisal et al. (eds.), *Humanitarian Assistance for Displaced Persons from Myanmar*, SpringerBriefs in Environment, Security, Development and Peace 17,
DOI: 10.1007/978-3-319-02795-1_8,

8.1 The Historical Role of Stakeholders Providing Humanitarian Assistance to the Displaced Persons

In response to the first Karen people crossing the border in 1984, the Ministry of Interior (MOI) invited International Non-Governmental Organisations (INGO) working with refugees[1] in Thailand to provide emergency assistance to those fleeing the fighting. It was expected that the situation would be temporary, but attacks on Karen communities by the Burmese army did not stop, resulting in continued flows of refugees fleeing into Thailand (TBBC 2009a, b). Over the decades, more and more refugees have crossed the border and the fighting has now escalated into *one of the longest running civil wars in modern history* (DFID 2008).

Despite the fact that minimum basic needs are provided to displaced people in the shelters, they live in conditions of hardship. They have no access to telephones and limited access to information. With shelters heavily protected, displaced people are not allowed to go outside shelters to work and can be subject to detention or deportation by Thai authorities. They have become dependent on assistance from humanitarian aid agencies, often resulting in the loss of their sense of self-esteem and dignity, the chance to solve their own problems, to defend their rights and to become self-reliant. This also increases the likelihood of their becoming an economic and social burden for the host nation and related stakeholders, as many displaced people end up living in these camps for many years.

Current distributions of *humanitarian aid* tend not to be allocated impartially, but rather are concentrated on the visible emergencies in which Western donors play a prominent military and political role. For example, between 1996 and 1999, the top five recipients of bilateral humanitarian aid were all political hotspots: Bosnia, Serbia and Montenegro in the Former Yugoslavia, Iraq and Israel, which together accounted for £2,725 million (Macrae et al. 2002, 2004). In 1990–2000, official humanitarian aid flows doubled from $2.1 to 5.9 billion. Bilateral donations from donors, aid given by one country directly to another, accounted for over 90 % of official humanitarian aid spending. This trend is continuously moving away from multilateral methods of disbursing assistance in favour of bilateral channels, a trend that is highly criticised in term of effectiveness. Multilateral aid refers only to funds that are not earmarked aid, and is channelled through multilateral institutions such as the UN and the World Bank.

The balance between bilateral and multilateral channels for aid has changed over the years, with the trend now pointing towards the *bilateralisation* of multilateral aid. Donor countries began to use multilateral institutions in the mid-

[1] Thailand is not a signatory to the 1951 UN Convention on the Status of Refugees or to the 1967 protocol that classifies these displaced people as 'illegal immigrants'. Thailand has, however, provided protection to this population and designated them as 'displaced persons'. For the purposes of this document, the terms 'Displaced persons' and 'temporary shelter' will be preferred to the terms 'refugee' and 'camp', respectively. The document occasionally uses the terms 'refugee' and 'temporary shelter' when directly quoting the literature.

1980s to manage their own bilateral aid programmes, primarily by establishing trust funds and co-financing projects. This has reduced the amount of *core* resources available to multilateral institutions, increased the proportion of *non-core* resources provided by donor countries for specific purposes, and led to hidden subsidies, as donors rarely pay the full administrative costs associated with the use of non-core resources (Sagasti 2005).

All other aid, including earmarked assistance to the UN, NGOs and funds spent by governments themselves, is technically *bilateral aid.* Most of the funds supporting the United Nations High Commission for Refugees (UNHCR) are earmarked, with the exception of Northern European donor countries. This places UN agencies in a difficult position, struggling between accountability and protection of universal human rights.

Humanitarian aid decision-making is becoming more complex and sensitive and the framework for measuring donor performance is weak, affecting the accountability and the trust necessary for positive relations between donors and their partners (Macrae et al. 2002, 2004). Indeed, humanitarian aid should be impartial and neutral, while humanitarian donors need to be accountable. But while there has been much talk of *accountability* over the last decade, the role of official donors in the humanitarian arena has attracted little examination. There has been also little discussion as to what constitutes a good humanitarian donor. A critical analysis of humanitarian aid, though, has been put under trial to test the real effectiveness of aid and the lack of accountability. Indeed, the years 2004–2005 constituted a window of change in the international *aid architecture*, as the UN Special Assembly began to assess the progress of the Millennium Development Goals, leading in March 2005 to the signing of the Paris Declaration on Aid Effectiveness.

The need for humanitarian aid has increased over the last few years due to a combination of factors: a rise in the number of refugees and displaced persons due to often protracted conflicts; and a rise in the number of natural disasters attributable to climate change and the impact of the most recent economic crisis (EC 2010). After several decades of housing the Burmese in these *temporary shelters*, a different type of response and assistance is now required. Donors tend to agree that it is imperative to move from relief and providing handouts, to a more long-term and sustainable solution, which includes livelihood alternatives. This transition is particularly important because the displaced populations have become totally dependent on aid after nearly three decades (EC 2010).

8.2 Temporary Shelter-Based Stakeholders and Services

Aside from the displaced persons themselves, donors, INGOs, NGOs and UN agencies are the major stakeholders in the Thai–Myanmar displaced persons situation. The MOI is responsible for the overall governance of the shelters while the humanitarian aid agencies, most organised through the CCSDPT and joined by

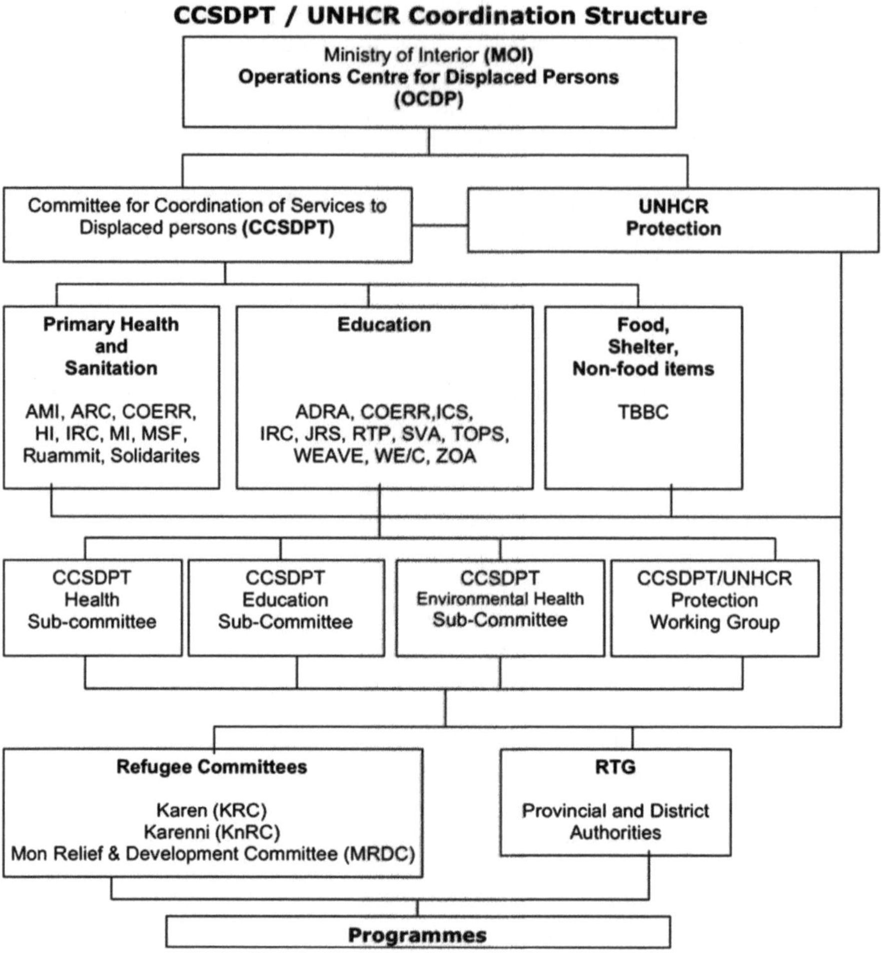

Fig. 8.1 MOI&CCSDPT/UNHCR Coordination Structure. *Source* CCSDPT/UNHCR

UNHCR, each play a specific and collaborative role advocating and supporting basic services and humanitarian needs, in what UNHCR describes as *one of the most protracted refugees situations* (UNHCR 2010a, b) (Fig. 8.1).

8.2.1 Committee for Coordination of Services to Displaced Persons in Thailand

The CCSDPT was established in 1975 as a communications network for INGOs who met on a regular monthly basis to exchange information and discuss their work. CCSDPT coordinated their efforts and assisted in representing the members'

Table 8.1 CCSDPT Members

ADRA	Adventist Development and Relief Agency	NCA	Norwegian Church Aid
AMI	Aide Medical International	RF	Ruammit Foundation
ARC	American Refugee Committee	RTP	Right To Play
COERR	Catholic Office for Emergency Relief and Refugees	Sol	Solidarities
HI	Handicap International	SVA	Shanti Volunteer Association
ICS-ASIA	International Child Support—Asia	TOPS	Taipei Overseas Peace Service
IRC	International Rescue Committee	TBBC	Thailand Burma Border Consortium
JRS	Jesuit Refugee Service	WEAVE	Women's Education for Advancement and Empowerment
MI	Malteser International	WE/C	World Education/Consortium
MSF-F	Médecins Sans Frontières-France	ZOA	ZOA Refugee Care Netherlands

Source CCSDPT/UNHCR Comprehensive Plan 2007/8 (2007)

interests to the RTG through the MOI. There are other NGOs in the camps who are not part of CCSDPT, though the committee acts as the main forum for NGOs to communicate and coordinate with the RTG through the MOI. Currently there are 20 member NGOs implementing 29 projects within the CCSDPT which provide humanitarian services to address the needs of the population (Tables 8.1 and 8.2).

8.2.2 Thailand Burma Border Consortium

Under the CCSDPT umbrella, Thailand Burma Border Consortium (TBBC) works in cooperation with the RTG and in accordance with regulations of the MOI. TBBC has the largest programme mandate of all the CCSDPT member organisations and is itself a consortium of 12 stakeholders working to provide food, shelter, non-food items and capacity-building support to Burmese displaced persons inside the shelters. Established formally in 1996, the head office is in Bangkok with field offices in Mae Sot and Mae Sariang, Mae Hong Son and Sangkhlaburi, with a sub-office in Chiang Mai for displacement research (TBBC 2009a, b).

The five core objectives of the TBBC for 2009–2013 are: pursue change leading to durable solutions while ensuring a protective environment for displaced people of Burma; increase self-reliance and reduce aid dependency by promoting and supporting livelihood opportunities; ensure continued access to adequate and appropriate food, shelter and non-food items, prioritising support for the most vulnerable; support mutually accountable community-based management which ensures equity, diversity and gender balance and develop TBBC organisational structure and resources to anticipate and respond to changes, challenges and opportunities.

Table 8.2 CCSDPT Camp Projects

Project	Implementing organisation
Sexual abuse and exploitation prevention project	IRC
Expansion of basic protection training	UNHCR
GBV prevalence survey	IRC
Promoting the rule of law in refugee camps	Burma Lawyer's Council
Addiction programme for Karenni camps	RF
Training of new addiction workers	RF
Border-wide training of medics	IRC
Strengthening mental health intervention	ARC
Awareness raising on mental health disorders	AMI
Income generation and relapse prevention	RF
Child and adolescent health (Umpiem, Nu Po and BDY)	ARC
Health messenger child magazine	AMI
CCSDPT health information systems programme	CCSDPT
Provision of compensation for refugee teachers	ZOA
School building construction	ZOA
Provision of school supplies	ZOA
Materials for school buildings	ICS-ASIA
KWO nursery schools—MRML camp	Karen Women's organisation
Expansion of school libraries	ZOA
Care and education for disabled refugee youth and children	Karen Women's Organisation
Support to post-10 education	ZOA
Technical support to livelihoods programme	UNHCR
Micro-enterprise development	ARC
Research and application of appropriate technology	UNHCR/ILO
Strengthen demand-driven skills development	UNHCR
Agricultural activities inside camps	*N/A*
Pilot agricultural sites for income generation beside refugee camps	ZOA
Support self-reliance of disabled refugees	UNHCR
Waged employment service	UNHCR/ILO

Source CCSDPT/UNHCR Comprehensive Plan 2007/8 (2007)

TBBC's programmes are implemented through partnerships with camp committees, community-based organisations (CBOs) and local groups employing a community-based management system that is in line with international humanitarian best practice. Camp residents take an active role in daily operations and provision of basic services, lead by the Community Elders Advisory Boards (CEAB), providing overall guidance and advice on internal matters, and the Refugee Committees for camp coordination and Camp Committees (CC) as an operational body, as the primary representatives of the camp population. These committees liaise with the MOI, UNHCR, CCSDPT and other relevant stakeholders (Loescher/Milner 2006). Through this model they deliver timely, quality services to the camp populations to maximise their participation in all programme matters (TBBC 2009a, b).

8.2.3 United Nations High Commission for Refugees

The UNHCR is the only global organisation with a specific mandate to ensure the protection of displaced people and to find solutions to their plight. It pursues its mandate linking with a wide range of other actors like donors, governments hosting displaced populations, other UN agencies and NGOs. UNHCR is dependent on voluntary contributions from donor states, along with these states' interests and priorities, which play a significant role in the work and evolution of the agency. UNHCR is responsible for the monitoring and protection mandates of their populations through coordination, representation to the RTG and protection of asylum seekers (DFID 2008). UNHCR in Thailand became operational in 1998 and currently has three field offices in Mae Hong Son, Mae Sot and Kanchanaburi that coordinate and act through key camp partners.

Principally the UNHCR will (UNHCR 2010a, b):

- Consolidate protection activities through improvement of national screening mechanism for asylum seekers. These activities will be enhanced through advocacy and intervention with key authorities and partners.
- Continually engage in policy discussion with the RTG, donors and relevant actors aimed at finding durable solutions and increasing the protection space. In the absence of a national mechanism to process the claims of non-Myanmarese asylum seekers, UNHCR will continue to register and conduct refugee status determination (RSD) for urban refugees, with the exception of those from Myanmar, for whom a camp-based, Government-led procedure is in place.
- Engage relevant actors, including governments and donors, in discussions to support policy changes.
- Monitor the rights and well-being of people of concern, intervening with the national authorities on their behalf and striving to meet their basic needs, including medical care and educational support.
- Continue its advocacy efforts aimed at sensitising the Government to statelessness issues and will explore joint programming opportunities with other UN agencies.

8.3 Funding Policy and Use of Funds

Providing humanitarian aid to displaced people of Myanmar should not be seen only as emergency relief and assistance as the need for aid has persisted for years. The displaced people are now so dependent on external assistance that any sudden decision to reduce aid or stop it altogether would only exacerbate their situation. Within the temporary shelters it is clear that the risks of pulling out altogether are high enough to warrant donors' continued involvement. Present overall levels of funding for the shelters allow for the provision of adequate levels of food, shelter, health and education, barring shocks such as the recent sharp rise in rice prices.

The rationale behind donor provision of funds is not easy to analyse or judge. Based on available information, the following section will discuss the funding policies of the EU, USA and UK, and the use of those funds by shelter implementers.

8.3.1 International Level

8.3.1.1 The European Union

The European Union (EU) is an economic and political union of 27 member states. It was established by the Treaty of Maastricht in 1993 upon the foundations of the European Community. The EU traces its origins from the European Coal and Steel Community formed among six countries in 1951 and the Treaty of Rome formed in 1957 by the same states. Since then, it has grown in size and in power through the addition of policy areas. The last amendment to the constitution of the EU, the Lisbon Treaty, came into force in 2009 by virtue of which the Charter of Fundamental Rights of the European Union was elevated to legally binding status. The process of European cooperation began shortly after the Second World War in order to prevent any future war, as several European leaders became convinced that lasting peace could only be secured through economic and political integration.

The EU is one of the world's biggest donors of humanitarian aid, based on the humanitarian principles of humanity, impartiality, independence and neutrality, and promoting the respect of international humanitarian law, a set of rules which seeks to limit the effects of armed conflict on civilians, humanitarian issues, human rights and refugees. The European Commission's (EC) humanitarian assistance, through the European Commission Humanitarian Aid department (ECHO), alone represents between 30 and 40 % of the total EU humanitarian funding, reflecting the EU's solidarity with the victims of natural and man-made disasters. ECHO is the EC's department for overseas humanitarian aid from the EU to developing countries.

In 2009 funding was distributed among ECHO's partners as follows: NGOS 47 %, UN agencies 39 % and international organisations 14 % (EC 2010). It implements its mission by funding community humanitarian action through NGOs and international organisation partners who agree to sign the Framework Partnership Agreement (FPA), such as the Red Cross family, or the Financial and Administrative Framework Agreement (FAFA) for UN agencies, mainly UNICEF, UNHCR and WFP (EC 2007). ECHO assistance aims at facilitating, together with other aid instruments, the return of populations to self-sufficiency wherever and whenever possible, and to permit the phasing out of ECHO funding if conditions are favourable. In this perspective, ECHO is actively engaged in implementing a linkage strategy among relief, rehabilitation and development, and in developing stronger cooperation with other Commission services or donors (EC 2007).

In 2001, the EC undertook a wide-ranging internal and external consultation on Linking Relief, Rehabilitation and Development (LRRD), to fill the gap that exists between relief, or short-term humanitarian aid, and development aid, which is long-term. The priority of LRRD was a desire to improve the coordination of international efforts. The results of the consultative process provided a broad view of the problems involved in assisting those in need, taking account the various types of crises, other international actors and the risk of structural dependence. By focusing on the interdependence of the two policies, the EC emphasised that better development could reduce the need for relief, that better relief could contribute to development, and that the transition between the two is facilitated by rehabilitation.

As the international context in which humanitarian aid takes place began to change and the EU's aid was being criticised for being inefficient, incorrectly targeted and linked to economic objectives, the three EU institutions, European Parliament, Council and EC, signed the European Consensus on Humanitarian Aid in December 2007, recognising the increasingly challenging environment for humanitarian response and driving forward a more efficient and coordinated approach. This consensus was followed up in 2008 by an Action Plan representing the concrete and operational translation of the numerous political commitments contained in the Consensus (EC 2007). The principle of *one instrument per policy area* established by the EC to improve the efficiency of action, together with the EC's communication on the financial perspectives 2007–2013, transferred the responsibility for the management of humanitarian food aid to ECHO with effect from 1 January 2007 (EC 2007).

The EU is unique in clearly differentiating humanitarian aid from other forms of external assistance. ECHO is the only publicly financed department in the world solely devoted to funding the delivery of humanitarian aid. Through ECHO, the EC spends on average €640 million per year on humanitarian aid. Since 1995 the EC, through ECHO, has been one of the major donors assisting those living in the shelters on the Thai–Burmese border. Since the beginning of the crisis ECHO has provided some €95 million in humanitarian aid to these displaced people (EC 2010). All the shelters are dependent on large-scale funding by international donors. In 2010 alone, ECHO provided €8 million to help cover the basic needs of the displaced population for food aid, health assistance, clean water and sanitation in six out of the nine temporary shelters, bringing the total EU funding since 1995 to over €140 million (Eick n.d.). The funding is channelled through a number of INGOs such as ICCO, AMI and Malteser, in addition to the International Red Cross (EC 2010).

8.3.1.2 Assistance to Uprooted People

Providing support for uprooted people in post-crisis situations and fragile states is a priority for EC regional programming. The priority is to bridge short-term humanitarian aid and long-term development assistance by providing funds to help improve the living conditions of displaced people, and to facilitate their reintegration into their home country or their integration elsewhere. The beneficiaries also include host communities in the resettlement areas. The aim of this programme is to ensure the link among relief, rehabilitation and development in crises involving uprooted people; to find durable solutions; to promote peace-building and reconciliation; to protect of uprooted people and to address the needs of demobilised former combatants and child soldiers (European Commission, Multi-annual Indicative Programme for Asia 2007–2010). Cooperation in this area is intended to assist refugees, internally displaced persons, and returnees as well as demobilised former soldiers and other combatants, including child soldiers, to return to and settle in their country of origin or in a third country. The objective is to reintegrate them into the socio-economic fabric of the relevant country and to provide support to local communities and resettlement areas that are hosts to such integration. A regional approach is justified because, in many cases, crises involve several countries, for example the Burmese crisis covers Myanmar, Thailand and Bangladesh.

Activities will be closely coordinated with operations carried out by the Humanitarian Aid department of ECHO and with those carried out in the context of country programmes. As crises involving uprooted people are often highly political, it will be necessary to ensure strong links with the activities carried out at bilateral level. In implementing the uprooted people programme, the EC will thus try, whenever possible, to work with local partners, in order to progressively build up local partnership and development capacity. (EC Regional Programming for Asia Strategy Document 2007–2013).

This change of funding strategy change took effect in 2007 and earmarked €112 million to be spent over the 4 years between 2007 and 2010. The EU-Asia Regional Strategy Paper for 2007–2013 continues to present support to uprooted people as a key funding area. Implementation will occur mainly through calls for proposals for each of the uprooted people crises, as well as in some cases direct agreements with certain organisations. UNHCR is likely to remain the EC's main partner in the implementation of operations to aid uprooted people, given its mandate for the protection of refugees and displaced persons and advocacy activities.

Aid will support existing as well as new crisis profiles. There is a need to ensure the continuum of assistance in countries still greatly affected by uprooted people issues. Especially in protracted refugee situations, support will aim at promoting the search for long-term solutions. Whenever possible in the prevailing political environment, the focus will be on fostering medium- and long-term activities aimed at the self-sufficiency and integration or reintegration of uprooted people, ensuring that an integrated and consistent approach among humanitarian aid, rehabilitation and development cooperation is pursued. (EC Multi-annual Indicative Programme for Asia, 2007–2010).

8.3.1.3 United States

The United States (U.S.) has been the most generous donor for decades. The US government provides assistance to refugees through the Bureau of Populations, Refugees and Migration (PRM). PRM has primary responsibility within the US Government for formulating policies on population, refugees and migration, and for administering US refugee assistance and admissions programmes. In Fiscal Year 2009, the PRM programmed over $1.7 billion in support of humanitarian activities. Its mission is to provide protection, life-sustaining relief and durable solutions for refugees and conflict victims, working through the multilateral humanitarian system to achieve the best results for refugees and conflict victims.

The Bureau does not operate refugee camps, or otherwise give aid directly to refugees. There primary activities support the efforts of key multilateral humanitarian organisations including the UNHCR, the International Committee of the Red Cross (ICRC), and the International Organisation for Migration (IOM). In fact roughly 90 % of Bureau-managed funds are allocated to international organisations. The Bureau collaborates closely with the US Agency for International Development (USAID) and funds NGO programmes that are coordinated with the multilateral system and help fill critical gaps (US Bureau of Population, Refugees and Migration 2009).

The US government through the Bureau of Populations, Refugees and Migration has programmed over $37 million in East Asia, a portion of which was used to assist refugees, returnees and other conflict victims in South-East Asia. Of this total, $24.2 million was contributed to the UNHCR and the ICRC. Over $12.5 million was provided to NGOs and the IOM for assistance to Burmese (US Bureau of Population, Refugees and Migration 2010). NGOs that receive money from the Bureau are obligated to align with the Bureau's mission to provide protection and life-sustaining relief such as food, water, sanitation, education and medical care to refugees and victims of conflict.

8.3.1.4 United Kingdom

The Department for International Development (DFID) is the UK Government agency responsible for promoting development and reducing poverty overseas (DFID 2007). DFID funds work with both internally displaced persons (IDPs) in Burma and refugees in Thailand. The UK provides assistance to Burma in line with the EU Common Position, which states that non-humanitarian aid or development aid should be suspended, with exceptions made for: human rights, democracy, good governance, conflict prevention and building the capacity of civil society; health and education, poverty alleviation and in particular the provision of basic needs and livelihoods for the poorest and most vulnerable populations; environmental protection, and in particular programmes addressing the problem of non-sustainable, excessive logging resulting in deforestation (Council of the Europe 2006).

In 2007, DFID supported displaced people with a grant to TBBC of £1.8 million over 3 years, via Christian Aid. The UK contributes around the same amount again as its share of EU funding to TBBC. Following an internal review in 2007, DFID announced that it was removing the restriction on the use of funds for assistance to displaced people, so that they can be used for either cross-border or assistance for the displaced, as need and funding dictates. Having a 3 year, rather than an annual, funding agreement is seen by Christian Aid as a positive step because it adheres to Good Humanitarian Donorship initiative principles of predictable and accountable financing. Channelling DFID funding through this organisation saved TBBC, a small organisation with 14–15 bilateral donors, valuable time according to Christian Aid officials. No major donors fund TBBC directly; for instance, the EC funds through the Dutch agency ICCO and other NGO members of the consortium. Although this is the status quo, funding indirectly through a third party has proved problematic with oversight and engagement problems by DFID. To alleviate these issues the parliamentary commission believes that funding TBBC directly might improve communication and encourage stronger engagement on DFID's behalf. Facilitation of this approach was made easier as TBBC was registered as a UK charity in 2005, which would allow for a more straightforward manner in which to receive direct funding.

DFID funding to TBBC has increased annually over the past few years, from £535,000 in 2005 to £611,050 in 2006 to £672,155 in 2007. This represents about 4 % of TBBC total budget.

8.3.2 National Level and Use of Funds

In 2007/8 the 20 CCSDPT member agencies and UNHCR shared their current budgetary expectations. In total CCSDPT/UNHCR expected to raise and spend THB 2,082 million on services in 2007, equivalent to US Dollars 59 million or Euros 45 million, plus an additional THB 237 million on resettlement processing, US Dollars 7 million, Euros 5 million (Table 8.3).

Notes:

- Some agencies did not separately identify administration costs and these are included in the service sectors.
- In addition to services provided direct to host communities, many local Thai villagers use health and education facilities in the camps.
- Allocations to community services, camp management, administration and Thai support are not consistent for some agencies between years.

Some 15 governments fund the refugee services in Thailand, plus the EU. Bilateral government grants account for 72 % of the total service expenditures. UNHCR expends an additional THB 187 million of its own funds and UNICEF supports the NGOs with THB 15 million, bringing the total contribution by

Table 8.3 Combined CCSDPT/UNHCR budget statement 2007–2009

Sector amounts in millions	2007 THB	% 2007	2008 THB	% 2008	2009 THB	% 2009
Protection	87	4	84	4	110	6
Community services	93	5	66	4	37	2
Camp management	61	3	75	4	66	3
Food, shelter, non-food	1,017	50	1,006	53	960	49
Camp infrastructure	19	1	8	0	2	0
Water, sanitation	35	2	44	2	49	3
Health	291	14	193	10	251	11
Education	200	10	115	6	135	7
Skills training, inc gen	39	2	35	2	38	2
Other	11	1	19	1	12	1
Administration	147	7	207	11	258	14
Local Thai community support	25	1	30	2	14	1
Local Thai authority support	6	0	8	0	9	0
Subtotal	2,032	100	1,892	100	1,942	100
Resettlement processing						
Total	2,269		2,128		2,256	

Source

Governments and the UN to THB 1,704 or 82 % of all expenditures for 2007/8. The EU with 22 % and the US with 20 % are the largest sources of funding. Resettlement processing will account for another THB 237 million in 2007, supported by US and UNHCR funds.

Governments tend to channel their resources to particular service sectors, although there is an awareness of what others are doing, all grants are negotiated bilaterally and there is no coordination mechanism or overall funding strategy shared by governments. Whilst Governments and the UN provide the vast majority of funding for Burmese refugees in Thailand, a significant amount, THB 377 million, 18 % of total funds, come from other sources such as individual donations, NGO own fund-raising, churches, charities and businesses in the private sector.

8.3.2.1 Funding Specifics for UNHCR

The Executive Committee (ExCom) of the UNHCR consists of 72 member states meeting annually to decide the budget and projects needing funds. Countries in need of funding for refugees submit for proposals, from which the biggest donor nations decide where and who will get support according to their differing political agendas. The agency depends almost exclusively on voluntary contributions to carry out its programmes. Each year the ExCom makes its appeal in December and donors commit to fund activities. As the process is year by year, this makes multiyear planning very difficult as UNHCR cannot predict from year to year what funds it will have available. As such, engagement in areas that require multiyear

Table 8.4 2010 UNHCR budget for Thailand

Rights groups and objectives	Refugee programme pillar 1	Stateless programme pillar 2	Total
Total (US Dollars)	20,523,091	240,858	20,763,949
Favourable protection of the environment			
Prevention of statelessness	0	178,755	178,755
Cooperation with partners	298,816	0	298,816
Access to territory	49,184	0	49,184
Non-refoulement	658,264	0	658,264
Subtotal:	1,006,264	178,755	1,185,019
Fair protection processes and documentation			
Registration and profiling	566,482	0	566,482
Access to asylum procedures	84,139	0	84,139
Fair and efficient status determination	950,409	0	950,409
Family reunification	26,662	0	26,662
Civil status documentation	252,974	0	252,974
Subtotal	1,880,666	0	1,880,666
Security from violence and exploitation			
Law enforcement	47,618	0	47,618
Community security management system	24,336	0	24,336
Gender-based violence	842,710	0	842,710
Protection of children	1,354,165	0	1,354,165
Non-arbitrary detention	99,865	0	99,865
Access to legal remedies	2,358,757	0	2,358,757
Subtotal	4,727,451	0	4,727,451
Basic needs and essential services			
Nutrition	38,516	0	38,516
Shelter and other infrastructure	156,867	0	156,867
Basic domestic and hygiene items	1,411,514	0	1,411,514
Primary health care	488,808	0	488,808
HIV and AIDS	175,616	0	175,616
Education	933,415	0	933,415
Sanitation services	86,867	0	86,867
Services for groups with specific needs	663,417	0	663,417
Subtotal	3,955,020	0	3,955,020
Community participation and self-management			
Participatory assessment and community mobilisation	122,272	0	122,272
Self-reliance and livelihoods	1,806,136	0	1,806,136
Subtotal	1,928,408	0	1,928,408
Durable solutions			
Durable solutions strategy	291,297	0	291,297
Voluntary return	137,477	0	137,477
Resettlement	1,671,263	0	1,671,263
Subtotal	2,100,037	0	2,100,037
External relations			

(continued)

Table 8.4 (continued)

Rights groups and objectives	Refugee programme pillar 1	Stateless programme pillar 2	Total
Public information	521,450	0	521,450
Subtotal	521,450	0	521,450
Logistics and operations support			
Supply chain and logistics	977,275	0	977,275
Programme management, coordination and support	2,074,276	62,103	2,136,379
Subtotal	3,051,551	62,103	3,113,654
Headquarters and regional support			
Global strategic direction and management	139,575	0	139,575
Protection advice and support	459,575	0	459,575
External affairs	159,575	0	159,575
Fund-raising and resource mobilisation	119,575	0	119,575
Media relations and public affairs	314,369	0	314,369
Capacity-building, skill development and knowledge management	159,575	0	159,575
Subtotal	1,352,244	0	1,352,244

Source UNHCR (2010a, b)

commitments, such as development and rehabilitation for returning refugee populations, are very difficult (Loescher/Milner 2006; UNHCR 2007).

Funds come from a limited range of donors, with three quarters of the total amount coming from the United States with 30 %, and the EC, followed by Japan, Sweden, Spain, Germany, Denmark, UK, Norway and Netherlands. The problem is that 80 % of the funds are tightly or lightly earmarked for specific countries and activities, leaving only a 20 % with no restriction. Some states earmark more than others, like the U.S., EU and Japan, while north-EU countries are more flexible (UNHCR 2010a, b).

The Thai operation budget has grown steadily over the past 5 years (Table 8.4).

8.3.2.2 Thai–Burma Border Consortium

The Thai–Burma Border Consortium (TBBC), as part of the CCSDPT working on health, education, community services and protection, is provided around half of the total annual budget for the work in the temporary shelters, which hovers around US $30 million. Ninety-three percent of TBBC funding comes from a core set of Government donors: ECHO, Australia, Canada, Czech Republic, Denmark, Great Britain, Ireland, New Zealand, Norway, Poland, Spain, Sweden, Switzerland, Taiwan, The Netherlands and USA (TBBC 2009a, b).

8.4 Current Funding Commitments

The US policy statement revealed that along with their own interest in increasing aid, the UK, EC and Australia are already moving to significantly ramp up their assistance (NGO Statement on US IDPs Policy 2008). The CCSDPT has also projected but not confirmed increases from Denmark and Australia. Only three government donors, Sweden, the Netherlands and Taipei have so far formally committed to grant amounts for 2010, although some others have given strong indications (TBBC 2009a, b). The Canadian International Development Agency (CIDA) has committed $15.9 million over 5 years.

8.5 Directions of Current Donors' Policy and Possible Long-Term Solutions and an Exit Strategy

Donor fatigue has become an increasing problem due to the global financial crisis. Some have stated that it will not be possible to continually increase support for Burmese refugees while others have suggested it is time to look for an *exit strategy*. To confront such issues and avoid compounding problems found within the temporary shelters and among the resident population, stakeholders have made positive strides at trying to address conflicts and policy gaps in the hope of finding plausible long-term solutions.

8.5.1 European Union Policy

In 2009, the concept of linking relief, rehabilitation and development (LRRD) was refined to follow previous development in EU policies and instruments, such as policies on fragility and security in development, the establishment of instrument for stability, and reorganisation of cooperation instruments. The LRRD approach is not limited to the notion of exit strategies for humanitarian aid, particularly in situations where humanitarian and development actors are present for a long period. LRRD challenges are tackled by applying a policy mix of humanitarian, stabilisation and development interventions which ensure the coherence of European interventions programmed and implemented simultaneously or successively in a country (EC 2010).

However, one of the current main challenges facing EU's humanitarian aid is the difficulty in linking short-term humanitarian aid to long-term development cooperation activities (EC 2010). Donors, including ECHO, are supporting the CCSDPT and the UNHCR in their efforts to implement a 5-year Strategic Plan to find durable solutions to expand the displaced persons' self-reliance. Pilot projects have already started in most camps, including vocational training, livelihood opportunities, health care integration and others. In Mae La camp, for example, agricultural projects introducing small-scale intensive farming, including fish ponds, help supplement the diets of the participating refugee families (Eick n.d.).

At the national level, much has been published regarding the policy stance of the RTG towards camp-based IDPs. In 2009, CCSDPT and UNHCR coordinated in the creation of a 5-year Strategic Plan for coordination of all service sectors aimed at increasing refugee self-reliance and, where possible, integrating refugee services within the Thai system. Presented in late 2009, the RTG has provided little indication that its policy direction will change any time soon (TBBC 2009a, b). However, the plan marks a significant step forward in this process. It will provide a good basis for dialogue with the RTG on finding sustainable solutions for the refugees by providing them with an alternative to increase their self-reliance (EC 2010).

In 2009, the EC started scaling down the EU contribution to the Burmese refugee camps in Thailand, a total of €8.75 million, just slightly lower than the 2008 figure of €9.5 million. The EC's strategy has been coordinated with other EU instruments and donors, and is searching for the most effective way to accompany early implementation of the 5-year strategic plan of the CCSDPT and UNHCR (EC 2010).

8.5.2 United States

Current indications state that US policy towards Burma is set to change as there is new hope within a new administration that intends to provide overall leadership on the humanitarian reform efforts of the UN and be a stronger advocate for discovering solutions for IDPs. The US admits to traditionally targeting the government and not the plight of the millions of people in and outside of Burma (NGO Statement on US IDP Policy 2008). The PRM is the State Department's *functional* bureau, which focuses on a particular issue wherever it arises around the world. The PRM focus is on refugees, other migrants and victims of conflict, with the goal of protecting these people, often living in quite dangerous conditions.

In 2010 the US government's policy objectives for Burmese refugees in Thailand include: maintaining life-saving assistance to Burmese refugees in the official camps; reinvigorating Thai government protection and screening for new arrivals, especially in the run-up to the 2010 elections in Burma and possible refugee outflows to neighbouring Thailand and China; and advocating for livelihood opportunities and freedom of movement in the Burmese border camps.

8.5.3 United Kingdom

It is well documented that the refugee situation on the border has continuously been mired in policy. Although the RTG has the final say on all camp-based matters, and has made great effort over the years to ease restrictions and change contentious policy, donors continuously strive to push for camp-based policy that provides for greater freedoms and full participation of the camp population.

Though this is a fractious issue, the UK Government indicated its desire to cooperate closely with the UNHCR to encourage the Thai authorities to take all practical steps, consistent with their resources and interests, to offer refugees as full a life as is possible. Donors are working with TBBC, UNHCR and the RTG to develop a medium-term strategy that will address the sustainability of support to the refugee camps. Without a strong appeal and engagement by the international community to resolve these issues, donors may risk funding the status quo (DFID n.d.). A parliamentary commission tasked with a review of the displaced people situation recommended that DFID must undertake a strategic reassessment of the appropriate mechanism for dealing with the long-term interests of refugees, as a clear delineation is needed between TBBC and other NGOs' work in providing food and basic services to refugees on the one hand, and the UNHCR, RTG and third country governments' sustainable solutions for the refugee crisis, including employment and resettlement on the other (DFID n.d.).

8.5.4 National Level

NGOs have continually been at the forefront, encouraging donor governments to increase humanitarian assistance to alleviate suffering, strengthen civil society and encourage dialogue between the international community and the Burmese government. Since the 2005 Plan, progress has been made in the establishment of large-scale resettlement to third countries; more protection programmes were initiated; education opportunities were expanded, including Thai language education; permission was provided to expand vocational training and income generating activities, and ID cards were issued to refugees as a step towards providing a documentation basis for increased mobility (CCSDPT/UNHCR 2009).

To build on the success of the 2005 plan, the CCSDPT in collaboration with UNHCR has in 2009 drafted a new 5-year strategic plan that will attempt to move from a relief effort to a developmental model. The plan envisages sustainable solutions allowing for significantly expanded refugee self-reliance and contributions to the Thai economy and society. The strategy has five sectors and two cross-cutting themes (CCSDPT/UNHCR 2009).

8.5.5 Key Strategy Objectives of CCSDPT Plan by Sector and Cross-Cutting Theme

- Protection—A fair, efficient and transparent PAB system in line with relevant international standards; supportive policies for a form or legal migrant status for refugees; as well as refugees having access to the Thai judicial system.

- Health: sustainable, integrated, comprehensive health services for refugees and nearby Thai populations, managed by the Thai Ministry of Public Health, assisted by international and Thai NGOs, at a standard of service comparable to that provided to Thai citizens and migrant workers in Thailand.
- Environmental Health and Infrastructure: sustained refugee management of camp-based environmental health and infrastructure activities and increased cooperation with local Thai communities as well as Thai NGOs and RTG line-ministries to ensure access and effective management of sites, surrounding land, forest and water resources.
- Education: sustainable, integrated education services for refugees, managed by the Thai Ministry of Education in cooperation with international and Thai NGOs, at the same standard as that envisioned for migrant workers in Thailand.
- Food and Shelter: increased self-reliance and reduced aid dependency, targeting assistance to the most vulnerable.
- Livelihoods: increased self-reliance with the creation of sustainable livelihoods for refugees and local host communities facilitated through improved direct access to resources and capital, markets and infrastructure, legitimised by supportive policy frameworks.
- Camp Management: broaden focus from delivery of basic services towards strengthening the governance of the communities and managing the needs of an increasingly diverse group of people through democratic processes. Pay particular attention to the needs of the most vulnerable and under-represented groups, ensuring their equitable access to services, including justice.

8.6 Resettlement Issues of Donors

According to the UNHCR, *resettlement is a vital instrument of protection and solution for refugees, and in this situation resettlement may be the only durable solution* (UNHCR 2010a, b). Resettlement offers a future for the displaced people who have been in exile for more than two decades, and as such, resettlement activities should prioritise those refugees identified as eligible for resettlement according to UNHCR criteria (Sciortino/Punpuing 2009). Though all displaced people are considered, resettlement countries, NGOs and UNHCR have highlighted eight particular types of refugees who are given priority for resettlement (Loescher/Milner 2006):

1. Refugees with legal and physical protection problems in the country of asylum.
2. Women at risk, especially female-headed households who do not benefit from traditional community support structures.
3. Survivors of violence and torture.
4. Medically vulnerable cases.
5. Unaccompanied minors.

6. Elderly refugees.
7. Refugees with family members abroad.
8. Refugees with no local integration prospects in their country of first asylum.

A consequence of resettlement has been the depletion of skilled individuals engaged in camp management, service provision or working with shelter-based NGO activities. If not managed efficiently, the number of highly educated and more skilled residents being accepted for resettlement could affect the overall organisation of the camps, not to mention the implementers who rely on their knowledge and position within the population (DFID 2008).

A UK Commission recommended the Government to take steps to ensure that resettlement of refugees through the UK Home Office's Gateway Protection Programme does not create a sudden diminution in capacity amongst the camp populations and leave camps with gaps in their skilled workforce. The UK Government has been charged to advocate on this issue in coordination with other governments, particularly the US (International Development Committee 2007).

The UK Government considers for resettlement up to 150 Burmese refugees from Thailand each year under the Gateway Protection Programme. The UK's criteria for considering cases are based on protection need rather than skill sets. They consider that all refugees with a need for protection should have equal access to the ability to apply for resettlement and are committed to providing protection to those who need it as identified by UNHCR.

Current programmes are underway to work with other donors and resettlement countries to minimise the impact of the resettlement programme on the skill sets in the temporary shelters through targeted training programmes to replace those selected. Such initiatives should be supported and therefore a further recommendation for donors may be to work closely with the NGOs in the development and implementation of capacity-building strategies (International Development Committee 2007).

The majority of host countries require a mandatory medical check-up, including chest X-rays, and some, Canada, Australia, the U.S. and New Zealand, ask for HIV testing prior to departure. As 5 years have now passed since the first displaced persons left the temporary shelters, current information however has indicated that several host countries have begun examining such policy as the HIV and AIDS screening amongst other *stumbling blocks*.

Other important host policy changes have been made in the past, such as the United States issuing waivers for provisions in the Patriot and Real ID Acts for Karen National Union (KNU) and other groups fighting the Myanmar military as the current policy excluded everyone who had provided *material support* to armed groups (Sciortino/Punpuing 2009).

References

CCSDPT/UNHCR, 2007: *Comprehensive Plan 2007/8: A Comprehensive Plan Addressing the Needs of Displaced Persons on the Thailand/Myanmar (Burma) Border* (Bangkok: UNHCR/ CCSDPT).

CCSDPT/UNHCR, 2009: *Five-year Strategic Plan working draft: Aid to Uprooted People Programme (AUP) Thailand 2009/2010* (Bangkok: UNHCR/CCSDPT).

Council of the European Union, 2006: "Council Common Position 2006/318/CFSP of 27 April 2006; Renewing Restrictive Measures against Burma/Myanmar: Article 3", in: *Official Journal of the European Union*; at: http://eurlex.europa.eu/LexUriServ/site/en/oj/2006/l_116/ l_11620060429en00770097.pdf.

DFID, 2007: *Humanitarian Funding Guidelines for NGOs* (London: DFID).

DFID, 2008: *Review of Aid to Refugees and Internally Displaced People on the Thailand–Burma Border* (London: DFID).

DFID, n.d.: *DFID's Assistance to Burmese Refugees on the Thai-Burma Border*; at: http:// www.publications.parliament.uk/pa/cm200607/cmselect/cmintdev/645/64511.htm#a27.

Eick, M., n.d.: *Thailand—World Refugee Day 20 June 2010: Refugees in Thailand: Another 25 years in limbo?*; at: http://ec.europa.eu/echo/aid/stories/asia30_en.htm.

European Commission, 2007: *Annual Report on Humanitarian Aid Policy in 2007*.Brussels: European Commission; at: http://ec.europa.eu/echo/files/media/publications/annual_report/ annual_report_2007.pdf.

European Commission, 2010: *Aid in action—Thailand*; at: http://ec.europa.eu/echo/aid/asia/ thailand_en.htm.

International Development Committee, 2007: *DFID Assistance to Burmese Internally Displaced People and Refugees on the Thai–Burma Border: Responses to the Committee's Tenth Report of Session 2006–07: Eleventh Special Report of Session 2006–07* (London: International Development Committee/HMSO).

Loescher, G.; Milner, J., 2006: *Protracted Refugee Situation in Thailand: Towards Solutions*. Presentation to the Foreign Correspondents' Club of Thailand.

Macrae, J. et al., 2002: Uncertain Power: the Changing Role of Official Donors in Humanitarian Action. *HPG Report 12 December*; at: http://www.odi.org.uk/resources/download/279.pdf.

Macrae, J. et al., 2004: Redefining the Official Humanitarian Aid Agenda. *OPINIONS,* 1-2, February, *1–2*; at: http://www.odi.org.uk/opinions.

Refugees International, 2008: *NGO Statement on US IDP Policy*; at: http://www.Refugees.international.org.

Sagasti, F., 2005: *Official Development Assistance: Background, Context, Issues and Prospects*; at: http://www.l20.org/publications/Phase%20III/ODA/ODA%20Sagasti.pdf.

Sciortino, R.; Punpuing, S., 2009: *International Migration in Thailand 2009* (Bangkok: IOM).

TBBC, 2009a: *Programme Report, January–June 2009* (Bangkok: TBBC).

TBBC, 2009b: *Programme Report, July–December 2009* (Bangkok: TBBC).

TBBC, 2010a: *Programme Report, January–June 2010* (Bangkok: TBBC).

TBBC, 2010b: *Programme Report, July–December 2010* (Bangkok: TBBC).

UNHCR, 2007: *Handbook for Emergencies: The Emergency Preparedness and Response Section* (Geneva: UNHCR); at: http://www.reliefweb.int/rw/lib.nsf/db900sid/AMMF-75TFLQ/$file/ unhcr-feb2007pdf?openelement.

UNHCR, 2010a: *Backgrounder: The State of the International Refugee Crisis*; at: http:// thebluekey.org/dev/press/Backgrounder%20International%20Refugee%20Crisis.pdf.

UNHCR, 2010b: *2010 UNHCR country operations profile—Thailand working environment*; at: http://www.unhcr.org/cgi-bin/texis/vtx/page?page=49e489646.

US Department of State, Bureau of Population, Refugees and Migration, 2009: *FY 2010 General NGO Guidelines for Overseas Assistance*; at: http://www.state.gov/g/prm/130740.htm#policy.

US Department of State, Bureau of Population, Refugees and Migration, 2010: *Southeast Asia*; at: http://www.state.gov/p/sca/index.htm.

References

Chapter 9
Funding Policy, Project Implementation Strategies and Cooperation Strategies with the RTG

Dares Chusri, Tarina Rubin, Ma. Esmeralda Silva, Jason D. Theede, Sunanta Wongchalee and Patcharin Chansawang

Abstract The funding of the humanitarian and developmental programmes with the displaced people is examined in more detail, including how bodies such as UNHCR receive their funding. The relationship between the RTG and international actors is explored, looking in particular at the different perspectives that exist and how these have made joined-up policy and practice more difficult. The relationship between NGOs and other actors is also reviewed, and between them and the RTG, showing that communication has been a weakness. The 5-year strategic plan of CCSDPT/UNHCR is evaluated in terms of its scope and likelihood of success; it fails to put forward a solution based on a combination of the durable solutions. The relationship of actors with the RTG remains a barrier, in terms of culture and understanding of each others' perspectives.

Keywords Donor cooperation · Humanitarian aid · Funding levels · Refugee

This chapter reveals the results of key informant interviews, analysed and integrated into the qualitative data. It discusses current rationale for funding through analysis of organisational philosophies, funding policies and trends. Results of the baseline survey are also included to better understand the perceptions of displaced persons in this regard.

D. Chusri (✉) · T. Rubin · Ma. E. Silva · J. D. Theede · S. Wongchalee · P. Chansawang
Asian Research Center for Migration, Institute of Asian Studies, Chulalongkorn University, 3rd floor, Prachadhipok Rambhai-Barni Building, Bangkok 10330, Thailand
e-mail: dares_c@hotmail.com

T. Rubin
e-mail: tarina.Rubin@gmail.com

P. Vungsiriphisal et al. (eds.), *Humanitarian Assistance for Displaced Persons from Myanmar*, SpringerBriefs in Environment, Security, Development and Peace 17,
DOI: 10.1007/978-3-319-02795-1_9,

9.1 Current Rationale for Funding: Working Philosophy

Donor countries, INGOs and local NGOs involved in the Thai–Myanmar border camps all operate under a humanitarian philosophy. These organisations are driven by their commitment to addressing the needs of refugees, people *at risk* or the most vulnerable. The engagement of some organisations is targeted towards specific subgroups, such as extremely vulnerable individuals (EVIs). As some respondents shared, as long as there are refugees along the Thai–Myanmar border, their organisations will continue supporting the humanitarian efforts to provide them with assistance.

Efforts in the camps are largely driven by the perception that the situation is still an *emergency*. Almost all implementing organisations believe that this will continue to be an emergency situation as long as there are refugees crossing the border to flee persecution and violence in Myanmar, whether the influx is large-scale or not. Interestingly, one respondent indicated that it is the protracted nature of the situation that makes it a *humanitarian crisis*.

But there are also those, particularly some donors, who are slowly shifting from an emergency and humanitarian response to a more developmental perspective. This transition is strongly linked to the push for more sustainable or durable solutions on the ground.

9.2 Current Funding Policy and Trends

The long-term nature of settlements on the Thai–Myanmar border, some in existence since 1984, has resulted in increased frustration among both donors and CCSDPT at the static nature of the current humanitarian response. Donors especially, would like to see some or even slight change towards the development of self-sufficiency among refugees.

Funding from donor countries is bilateral in nature. Included in this are European donor countries that are also members of the EU. These countries direct funding bilaterally, separate to their European Commission EC contributions which are channelled through the ECHO and Aid to Uprooted People (AUP) mechanisms within the EU structure. A significant proportion of overall donor contributions are channelled through the TBBC to support their operations. Beyond this, other NGOs receive donor funds to support projects related to health, education and capacity building. These NGOs also source funds from private foundations and organisations.

Most of the stakeholders interviewed indicated that funding has been in decline over the past 3 years, the impact of which has been felt particularly in the past two. This has been driven largely by effects of the global recession in donor countries. This has directly affected NGOs working with the refugees in Thailand by limiting their day-to-day operations and, subsequently, the projects and interventions that

Table 9.1 Trends in future funding

Organisation	Declining	Steady	Unpredictable	Increasing
Donor countries	2	–	6	1
International organisation	1	–	–	–
Total	3	–	6	1

Source The Authors

these organisations have the capacity to implement. But despite this trend, most respondents do not foresee any complete phase-out of funding in the immediate future. Although respondents from donor countries indicated that funding streams will continue, this remains unpredictable, subject to policy and funding decisions of home-base donor governments (Table 9.1).

In line with its shift in working philosophy to address the situation along the border, the EU is gradually transferring its focus from humanitarian relief to a more developmental approach. This is reflected in their reallocation of funds from ECHO to AUP in recent years. Funding through ECHO, emergency relief and humanitarian in nature, has declined over the past year or so. On the other hand, funds through AUP, which supports developmental cooperation, have increased and are expected to continuously increase over the coming years. This shift has been noted by other donor countries and NGOs because its impact is very significant, affecting the scale and reach of NGO operations, as well as the nature of projects and their ability to provide basic needs and services.

Interviews with donors revealed a shared sense that we are now at juncture in this protracted situation to instigate necessary change in the way camps deliver assistance to displaced persons. The provision of humanitarian relief has been ongoing for more than 25 years and there is frustration that shelter populations have not diminished, despite the relative success of the resettlement programme so far. There is strong sentiment that all stakeholders, donors, INGOs and the RTG, need to better collaborate to affect change.

To improve cooperation, a more widely understood notion of *shared responsibility* is necessary. To date, processes of responsibility sharing have clearly been at play, evidenced by the ongoing financial support of international organisations and donor governments to implementing agencies for refugee emergency relief, rehabilitation and development phases over the last two decades. While the RTG has also been involved in the refugee emergency since the beginning by providing temporary shelters, security and human resources, expenditure on refugee protection has not been publicly disclosed.

Although no stakeholders have articulated a desire to phase-out funds to the temporary shelters, a more clearly defined system of shared responsibility among stakeholders may help prevent this in the future. Awarding stakeholders particular jurisdictions within a coordinated response could better ensure service gaps are filled and duplications avoided.

9.2.1 Cross-Border Aid

Apart from providing funds to camp-based displaced persons, some donors also fund cross-border activities. Of those interviewed, the USA, Norway, Canada, Denmark and the UK are currently supporting cross-border aid programmes to IDPs in Yangon and ethnic communities in eastern Myanmar. These funds are directed to CBOs and their own national NGOs, rather than the Myanmar government. Some donors believe that development assistance to people in need internally in Myanmar will not only provide relief but can also prevent the movement of new asylum seekers across the Thai–Myanmar border. At the same time, others give aid for purely humanitarian reasons only; the potential benefits outweighing any risks of operating inside Myanmar. The majority of funds go to health and education programmes, medical and education supplies, and target childhood and maternal mortality and combating infectious diseases. The amount of funding support for IDPs persons in Myanmar is actually greater than that allocated to displaced persons in the shelters in Thailand.

Several donors have no interest in funding cross-border programmes due to a lack of adequate monitoring and evaluation mechanisms. Some also stressed that it is imperative their funding be impartial in accordance with their humanitarian mandate, in conflict with the opinion that that CBOs delivering cross-border services may have a political agenda.

9.3 The CCSDPT/UNHCR Strategic Framework: The Effort in Linking Relief, Rehabilitation and Development

An effort to short-term and long-term assistance, Linking Relief, Rehabilitation and Development (LRRD) is well underway. The efforts thus far in LRRD by implementing agencies can be seen through their initial policy advocacy towards the RTG and their work in developing the 5-year strategic plan.

In April 2005 CCSDPT/UNHCR wrote a joint letter to the RTG, advocating a comprehensive policy approach which would allow refugees greater access to education and skills training and engage them in productive activities which would better equip them for the future, wherever that might be (TBBC 2005). Moreover, the UNHCR/ILO led a consultancy on livelihoods in 2006/7 and a household survey on *Livelihood Vulnerability Analysis* was conducted in four camps in 2009, at Mae La, Nu Po, Site1 and Tham Hin. Community Agriculture and Nutrition (CAN) is another project which supports self-reliance, initiated by members of the Karenni Refugee Committee in 1999.

TBBC's latest initiative has been to encourage the community to work together to nurture the environment and expand the green zone around the camps by planting six selected species of bamboo as a pilot. Bamboo plantations not only provide building materials but also protect the land from soil erosion and provide nutritious bamboo shoots for consumption. The project will be expanded in 2011. Other LRRD projects are being implemented by NGOs such as COEER, IRC, ZOA and WEAVE.

9.3.1 Is the 5-Year Strategic Plan a Comprehensive Solution?

UNHCR and CCSDPT have developed a 5-year strategic plan as a platform for discussion among partners involved in providing protection and assistance to refugees along the Thai–Myanmar border by linking refugee assistance with development policy. The purpose of developing this 5-year strategic plan was to form the basis of discussion with and active participation of the RTG. However, the question remains as to the extent to which RTG decision makers buy into the direction of the plan.

As the plan states, *There is a pressing need to develop comprehensive solutions which acknowledge that third country resettlement is an option for only a portion of the population and voluntary repatriation remains a distant possibility* (CCSDPT/UNHCR 2009a, b). A comprehensive plan can only be effective if all parties believe in its common interest and objectives. Moreover, a factor in the success of any comprehensive strategy is the formulation process which almost certainly requires the commitment of all relevant parties, in particular the host country. The successful implementation of durable solutions will rely on all interested parties, including the countries concerned and UNHCR, working in partnership (UNHCR 2005a, b).

Having a plan in place is an important step for stakeholders' direction and resource allocation. The CCSDPT and UNHCR focused efforts on the development of this plan at the request of donors with the expectation of full funding to support its implementation. However, only selected grants have been allocated to respond to some strategies put forward by this plan. It should be noted that the plan is ambitious in its timeframe of 5 years. Development activities by nature require more time than this. The current plan also lacks a specified action plan or clear indicators. Specifying those agencies responsible is a critical concern, as is identifying financial support. To have a plan in place is better than none at all. But it is also critical that the strategies are actionable and can translate to policies and programmes on the ground. This is where the need for a clear action plan is vital.

It could be said that this plan is a comprehensive plan for the purpose of local integration, rather than a comprehensive plan which encompasses all options for durable solutions. UNHCR defines *local integration* as a process which ultimately leads to the permanent settlement of refugees in the country where they sought asylum (UNHCR 2005a, b). Likely a factor of donor interests, the focus of this strategic plan is on *local integration* as a solution only, while there is little or no discussion of the other two options, resettlement and repatriation. Nor is there an indication of future management directions following the initial 5-year period. Local integration is a broad phrase, its meaning, purpose and extent understood differently by different stakeholders. It unclear whether the purpose of local integration as a solution here is the means to, or the end result of, a transition from humanitarian aid to development aid.

There are three options for durable solutions: voluntary repatriation, local integration and resettlement (UNHCR 2005a, b). A sound and truly comprehensive plan should incorporate all three durable solutions. Exclusion of repatriation and resettlement would indicate that the plan directly targets a change in policy from the host country only, leading to the apparent difficulty for the RTG to endorse the plan. This may cause the RTG to misinterpret what is intended as *burden-sharing* among stakeholders to be *burden-shifting* to Thailand.

It is possible that the RTG is wary of all responsibility falling to it as the host country, in line with the view that integration of displaced persons into local communities would not only create a huge burden for Thailand but also contradict RTG policy, based on temporary accommodation and repatriation of displaced persons. Moreover, the plan clearly states the need for *greater ability for refugees to move outside the camps particularly for educational and livelihood-related purposes*, despite acknowledgement of the unlikelihood of change to RTG policy on restriction of movement.

Although still in development at the time of writing, the revised strategy, which is no longer a *plan*, according to key informants, must engage the RTG in dialogue or consultation before the strategy formulation workshop stage so that no assumptions are made in relation to RTG policy. It is clear that comprehensive durable solutions demand the commitment from the highest levels of the RTG, as this is the essential factor which will facilitate the enactment of this strategy and precipitate its success. Unfortunately, it would appear that until now only medium level officers from the RTG have attended the strategic workshops.

9.3.2 Alignment of Funding Support for Implementation of Strategy

Although the process of developing the 5-year plan was based on discussion and participation amongst the RTG, donor community, UNHCR and CCSDPT to move from an emergency relief to a development model (CCSDPT/UNHCR Comprehensive Plan 2007/8), the funding allocation to pursue these strategies has to date been insufficient. While funding for individual NGOs is dependent on donor contributions and donor funding is unsustainable in the long run, an initial outlay for a defined period is needed for funding security during the transition period to LRRD. This will help ensure a continuum of services and change.

Table 9.2 Perceptions of INGOs, NGOs and donor respondents on whether the situation is a humanitarian crisis/emergency

Responses	INGOs	NGOs	Donor countries
Still a humanitarian emergency	1	3	4
Need a development approach	–	–	2

Source The Authors

This process has largely been driven by disconnect between the perceptions of the different stakeholders and, ultimately, their mandates (Table 9.2).

It can be seen that most of the stakeholders still perceive the situation to be a humanitarian emergency. For NGOs, this has implications for the way their organisations are set up as well as the types of projects they engage in and the expertise of the staff they employ. For donor countries, the status of the emergency is directly related to their ability to source funding as well as the types of projects they support.

9.4 NGO Strategies for Cooperation with the RTG

The cornerstone of the strategies employed by NGOs in dealing with the RTG is the need to build and maintain good interpersonal relationships with RTG counterparts at the camp, local, district and national levels. The nature of the relationship between the organisation and the RTG is largely driven by the strength of personal relationships with individual officials.

A strategy that NGOs emphasised during the course of the study was the importance of continuous engagement with the RTG. One approach they have instituted is to *learn to follow the rules first*. That is, careful adherence to the processes and guidelines set forth by the RTG in implementing its policies on the ground.

Another strategy that local implementers have adopted is to ensure the open flow of information between the organisation and their counterparts at the camp, local and district levels. Although this flow has largely been vertical, it has been helpful for the NGOs to keep the communication lines open. These strategies have not always been easy follow, especially in light of changes to policies themselves, as well as the turnover of staff with whom NGOs work in the RTG. Essentially, a change in RTG staff means NGOs must commit new efforts to develop good relationships with officials.

However, in terms of influencing policy change, local NGOs have little influence. Most of the NGOs interviewed interacted with the RTG predominantly at the local level. For larger NGOs and donor countries, they find engaging with RTG at the national level to be difficult at best. One big challenge is the difficulty in engaging the RTG in open and meaningful dialogue on how to progress the current situation in the temporary shelters. This has been attributed to a number of factors, such as differences in culture and approach as well as the reserved response of the RTG in discussions on this issue. Another challenge cited is the slow, bureaucratic process within the RTG when it comes to gaining approval for large-scale projects. One example cited was the experience in setting up Legal Assistance Centres (LACs) in the camps. The process of obtaining approval for the pilot phase of the LAC took a significant amount of time and the roll-out phase for this project has been in the pipeline for more than a year now. These challenges have serious implications on the ability of stakeholders to advocate and implement durable solutions in the future.

9.5 RTG Policy on Displaced Persons

RTG concern with human rights is evident in the National Security Policy A.D. 2007–2011, which focuses on human rights in the restoration of national reconciliation policy to promote patriotism and unity among the national population. It states: *3.4 Enhance understanding of government officials and the public to focus on human rights principles including human dignity and the protection of fundamental rights of the people who live in Thailand that will lead to a fair management to populations equally and without discrimination. So that these people can predict their future and it will lead to the prevention of negative behaviours that affect social stability.* However, in reality greater efforts are needed to translate policy to implementation, especially for the displaced persons group. Displaced persons have lived in Thailand *temporarily* for more than 25 years, their dignity corroding as a result of their status as displaced persons and their self-esteem decreasing due a lack of opportunities for self-reliance, especially in terms of working opportunity. Displaced persons further suffer from a lack of RTG strategy to promote their human dignity.

Displaced persons' situations may be perceived as a threat to the security of recipient countries and their national interest. RTG policy and its restrictive access to self-reliance are interlinked with this. In the case of displaced persons from Myanmar, Thailand has practiced *The Management Strategy for the problem of the status and rights of individuals*, issued as a Cabinet Resolution on 18th January 2005 to come into effect in 2011 (The office of National Security Council n.d.). The strategy is concerned with the balancing human rights principles, human security and national security and is relevant to Thailand within its obligations under international law. The RTG will only determine the status of an individual recognised by Thai law or in accordance with its obligations under binding international law. In this way it overlooks the protection of the human rights of those who do not have any such status. In relation to the displaced persons from Myanmar, by referring only to *Displaced Persons Fleeing from Fighting*, the RTG is able to strategically restrict eligibility for anything more than temporary protection.

It should be noted that both the national security policy and the *Management Strategy for the Problem of the Status and Rights of Individuals* have a similar focus on encouraging cooperation with neighbouring countries and international organisations to develop the quality of life, public health, education and vocational training of people who live along both sides of the border This serves to prevent migration and illegal migration to Thailand, for whom good relations with neighbouring countries is important. It is apparent that the RTG has no development plans for displaced persons; its intension is for them to wait in temporary shelter until a time when repatriation is possible. Individual government officials must comply with these measures to support government policy.

References

CCSDPT/UNHCR, 2007: *A Comprehensive Plan Addressing the Needs of Displaced Persons on the Thailand/Myanmar (Burma) Border in 2007/2008* (Bangkok: CCSDPT/UNHCR).

TBBC, 2005: *Programme Report, July–December 2005 including emergency funding appeal for 2006* (Bangkok: TBBC).

UNHCR, 2005a: *Handbook for Planning and Implementing Development Assistance for Refugees (DAR) Programmes: Overview of Part I: Main Concepts and Issues, Module One and Two*; at: http://www.unhcr.org/44c4854b2.html.

UNHCR, 2005b: *Handbook for Self-reliance: Book 1—Why self-reliance?* at: http://www.unhcr.org/44bf3e252.html.

CCSDPT/UNHCR, 2009a: *Five-year Strategic Plan working draft: Aid to Uprooted People Programme (AUP) Thailand 2009/2010* (Bangkok: UNHCR/CCSDPT).

CCSDPT/UNHCR, 2009b: *Five-Year Strategic Plan* (Bangkok: CCSDPT/UNHCR).

National Security Council (n.d.). *The Management Strategy: the problem of the status and rights of individuals*; at: http://www.nsc.go.th/index.php?option=com_content&task=view&id=571&Itemid=63.

Chapter 10
The Dynamics, Needs and Constraints of Stakeholders

Dares Chusri, Tarina Rubin, Ma. Esmeralda Silva, Jason D. Theede, Sunanta Wongchalee and Patcharin Chansawang

Abstract The current situation is looked at from the perspectives of the different actors, in terms of commitment to finding a solution and to carrying on funding when change appears distant. The attitude of the different actors to the standard durable solutions is examined; international humanitarian agencies have long favoured local integration as a sustainable solution, one which the Royal Thai Government (RTG) implacably opposes. Resettlement has had some effect, but there is a question mark over its continued operation, and it has not reduced camp size, because new arrivals have replaced those who have gone. Gradually, there is an acceptance among most actors, including long-term donors, that voluntary repatriation must be at the heart of any sustainable solution; the challenge remains how to make Myanmar feel like a safe place of return for those who have fled, and for those born in the camps who have no memory of Myanmar.

Keywords Aid donors · NGOs · Repatriation · Resettlement · Thai refugee policy · Local integration · Funding shortages

Finding durable solutions for refugees are much more complex than simply providing emergency relief assistance. It is about obtaining agreement and cooperation from all relevant stakeholders. It is about recognising the human rights of all displaced persons and their right to protection. It is about collective management in the provision of both technical and funding support. These are the fundamental tasks that lie ahead for donors, NGOs, Royal Thai Government (RTG) and displaced persons representatives who must work and plan together to

---

D. Chusri (✉) · T. Rubin · Ma. E. Silva · J. D. Theede · S. Wongchalee · P. Chansawang
Asian Research Center for Migration, Institute of Asian Studies, Chulalongkorn University, 3rd floor, Prachadhipok Rambhai-Barni Building, Bangkok 10330, Thailand
e-mail: dares_c@hotmail.com

T. Rubin
e-mail: tarina.Rubin@gmail.com

P. Vungsiriphisal et al. (eds.), *Humanitarian Assistance for Displaced Persons from Myanmar*, SpringerBriefs in Environment, Security, Development and Peace 17,
DOI: 10.1007/978-3-319-02795-1_10,

ensure the successful realisation of their common goals, objectives and activities (UNHCR 2000). However, each of these stakeholders has a different role, responsibility and, in particular, capacity to influence the realisation of durable solutions for refugees. This chapter will discuss the dynamics, needs and constraints of stakeholders in identifying appropriate durable solutions for displaced persons in Thailand.

10.1 The Different Roles of Stakeholders

Actors in the displaced people situation along the Thai–Myanmar border generally fall into four main groups: donors, international organisations (including NGOs), the RTG and the displaced people themselves. Each actor has a particular role, as governed by organisational policy or regulation and based on organisational culture and working philosophy.

10.1.1 Donors

The principal role of donors is to allocate funds to implementing agencies, whether international agencies or NGOs. Donors provide funding in order to assist people in need or vulnerable people for humanitarian reasons. Emergency funding aims to immediately alleviate people's suffering within a certain, short period of time. Some donor governments provide financial support solely for emergency relief programmes. This means that if the approach to the situation shifts from emergency relief to development, the interest and involvement of some donors may be impacted as it no longer aligns with their funding priorities.

Donors are involved in the border camps on the basis of good humanitarian *donorship*, a shared sense of responsibility and a global commitment to providing humanitarian assistance to refugees. The majority of donors direct their funds bilaterally through NGOs and International Non-Government Organisations (INGOs) who implement policies and programmes in the border camps. While many programmes are NGO-driven, some donors are more directive, earmarking funds for particular activities. Current policy trends reveal a divide in donor perspective: some donors are focused on continuing the humanitarian relief effort to sustain the border camps and provide ongoing basic needs services to refugees; a few are pushing strongly to shift the focus to a developmental approach which links LRRD for camp populations; while others are seeking to quell push factors by targeting sustainable, long-term development inside Myanmar itself.

In a protracted refugee situation of 25 years, there is a strong sense among donors that the status quo is inadequate. All agree that sustainable solutions which offer opportunity for increased self-reliance are needed and that the RTG needs to be more engaged in identifying real and practicable durable solutions.

Differences in opinion appear in the way donor groups prioritise projects and influence assistance efforts through their grants processes.

However, it should be noted that, together, donors have paid relatively little attention to how they themselves are held accountable for the impact of their decisions. It would appear there has been minimal consideration as to what constitutes a good humanitarian donor. Establishing such agreement would be timely. Humanitarian aid flows are increasing, humanitarian decision-making is becoming more complex and sensitive and the framework for measuring donor performance is so far weak, undermining accountability and development of the trust necessary for positive relations between donors and their partners (Macrae 2002).

10.1.1.1 International Non-Government Organisations

INGOs engaged in the border situation are mandated to go where there is need and deliver humanitarian assistance to refugees and vulnerable individuals. INGOs are responsible for the implementation of relief and development programmes in the border camps, supplying residents with food, shelter, health services, education and vocational training. The quality of service provision is relatively high in this particular refugee situation, with many INGOs having been involved from the outset.

INGOs working on the Thai–Myanmar border are interestingly situated between the dual pressures of meeting donor funding requirements and priorities while contending with RTG policy and regulations to secure ongoing access to the camps each year. The roles of various stakeholders are closely interwoven and demand a collaborative effort in finding sustainable solutions to this protracted refugee situation.

10.1.1.2 Royal Thai Government: Roles and Responsibilities

The RTG has been involved in the refugee emergency from the outset by providing temporary shelters and human resources for refugee protection. Although the RTG has not publicly disclosed its expenditure, there are a number of agencies involved in many aspects of the displaced persons' situation. The Ministry of Interior (MOI), through provincial and district authorities, enforces refugee policy and controls the day-to-day running of the camps in collaboration with refugee and camp committees.

The MOI is the primary civilian institution within the government responsible for the policy implementation process. It oversees the authorities working on the ground, including the Police Department, which includes Border Patrol Police, the Immigration Authority, provincial governors and district level officers. The MOI has direct security and administrative responsibilities over the camps that are located at least 3 km from the border and coordinates with other responsible organisations on policy changes such as relocation of camps. The activities of the

CCSDPT and its constituent NGOs also fall under the direct authority of the MOI (Lang 2002). Various other government agencies, including the Royal Thai Army Paramilitary Rangers and the Border Patrol Police also assist in implementing policy and providing security. Usually an MOI local District Officer, *Palat,* is assigned as the Camp Commander in each camp, with Territorial Defence Volunteer Corps, *Or Sor,* personnel providing internal security under his jurisdiction (TBBC).

However, despite these contributions, refugee issues are likely to remain low on the national agenda and Thailand's refugee policy will continue to be shaped by security concerns and bilateral considerations. The overall protection environment in Thailand is set to remain uncertain, marked by detentions and a shrinking of the asylum space for urban refugees and asylum seekers. The policy of confinement to camps has resulted in the slow progress of the promotion of refugee self-reliance (TBBC 2010a, b).

The international community for the last several years has been increasingly focused on skills training and educational opportunities, as well as income generation projects and employment to supplement the resettlement solution as evidenced by the CCSDPT/UNHCR Comprehensive Plan (CCSDPT/UNHCR 2007). Despite this, it has proved difficult to make real progress towards refugee self-reliance on the ground. This is at least in part related to discontinuity in the RTG policy process caused by multiple regime changes since the 2006 military coup. The CCSDPT/UNHCR 5-year Strategic Plan once again focuses on shifting away from the *care and maintenance* model and towards increased refugee self-reliance as well as integration of refugee services with the health and educational institutions of the Thai system (CCSDPT/UNHCR 2009).

However, in contrast, the RTG policy environment to date has created a situation of almost absolute dependence of the displaced people on humanitarian assistance. Restrictive RTG policies place vast limitations on each of the durable solutions, though it should be noted that during this last 5 years there has been some easing of the RTG policy stance in relation to education, health and labour opportunities.

10.1.1.3 Provincial Admissions Board: Refugee Status Determination

The first formal registration of the border population was undertaken by the MOI and the United Nations High Commissioner for Refugees (UNHCR). In 1999, the Provincial Admission Board (PAB) was set up as a mechanism to determine the status of any subsequent new arrivals (TBBC 2009a, b). The UNHCR had a minimal role in the outcomes of the PAB decisions, given observer status and allowed to submit names of new arrivals to the provincial and local authorities. Unfortunately, the PAB was never fully functional and had unclear decision-making guidelines. This is partly due to the fear that accepting the current caseload would create a pull factor for more arrivals from Myanmar (Lee/Glaister 2005).

The decline in the willingness of states to provide asylum is a major challenge for people fleeing their countries in search of safety and for organisations attempting to assist them (UNHCR 2000). In this case, the absence of a PAB mechanism to screen asylum seekers means they are caught in an assistance limbo, a political vacuum and a no-man's land of human and legal rights. Status determination for asylum is needed to prevent both human rights violations and the insecurity faced living illegally in Thailand. Moreover, a screening process will be useful for allowing services and protections to be provided to those who are really in need and to differentiate between real refugee who flee from persecution and those who are not. For refugees this is the first step in a durable solution for the problems they face (IRC/JRS 2005).

Refugee status determination (RSD) is a precondition for applications for resettlement, a durable solution for refugees. Moreover, the determination of PAB status is a guarantee against forced return, or *refoulement,* to their original country (UNHCR 2005b). The RTG has prohibited UNHCR from registering any Burmese since January 2004. On 15 September 2007, UNHCR reopened registration for all those arriving in Thailand after this date for reasons related to the protests in Yangon. However, as with the previous batch of holders, the new registration slips offer no legal status in Thailand and do not grant any rights. Slips are only proof of their registration with UNHCR and merely represent a request to the Thai authorities not to arrest or deport the bearers.

In the last few years, international organisations, including the Jesuit Refugee Service (JRS), have been advocating for slipholders and non-slipholders alike to undergo national screening for refugee status and admission into the nine official camps along the border. Recommendations have been made to the Thai Government to allow registered Burmese asylum seekers to stay temporarily in Thailand and for assistance to be provided to them by UN and other relief agencies. So far, advocacy efforts by UNHCR and a handful of international organisations have met with limited success (Lee/Glaister 2005).

It was not until 2009, after the long absence of the PAB screening mechanism, that a pre-screening exercise for new arrivals began in four camps. The process is being undertaken as a pilot exercise in Tham Hin, Ban Dong yang, NuPo and Site 1 camps and is intended to determine genuine asylum seekers. The pre-screening process is monitored by UNHCR using a standard interview form and the asylum decision is made by the RTG (TBBC 2009a, b). The results of the 2009 RTG pre-screening exercise are still forthcoming (TBBC 2010a, b) at the time of writing.

10.1.1.4 UNHCR

The Office of the UNHCR was established on 1 January 1951 by General Assembly resolution 319/IV. Its main responsibilities are to provide international protection and to search for durable solutions to the problem of refugees and other persons of concern by assisting governments involved to facilitate voluntary repatriation, local settlement or resettlement. UNHCR operates on an annual budget cycle. The budgets of most organisations in the UN system are prepared on a biennial basis, and UNHCR should be no exception. Biennial budgets facilitate long-term planning, contribute to financial stability and produce a better match between multiyear work programmes and the budgeting process. Biennial budgeting would afford the UNHCR planning and budgeting process the required flexibility to respond to emergency situations (Kuyama et al. 2004).

UNHCR's Executive Committee is made up of host countries whose funding support the Committee cannot operate without. They also provide UNHCR with permission to operate on their territory. On the other hand, UNHCR's role is often to challenge states either for causing refugee movements or for failing to provide adequate protection and assistance to refugees and asylum seekers (UNHCR 2000).

UNHCR was created to uphold and oversee implementation of the 1951 Refugee Convention. It was designated to work with Thai authorities to reach policy agreements and to overcome technical obstacles to the implementation of this policy. Since 1979, UNHCR has been responsible for Khao-I-Dang and other *holding centres* for Cambodian refugees in Thailand, but it had avoided seeking a role in the border camps. At one point in late 1979, UNHCR offered to be the lead UN agency on the border, but the terms it set, including the removal of all soldiers and weapons from the camps and the relocation of the camps away from the border, were considered to be unrealistic at the time. Moreover, at least some 93 international donors felt that UNHCR was not equipped to handle such a large and complex emergency. In January 1982, the newly designated United Nations Border Relief Operation (UNBRO) took over the coordination of the relief operation along the Thai–Cambodian border, but it had no explicit protection mandate and no mandate to seek durable solutions for the population in its care. Thailand's decision not to become a signatory to the 1951 Convention, together with the distant relationship between the two actors, may limit the UNHCR's role in any bargaining process with the RTG.

10.1.2 Power Relations: Interest and Influence

Each of these actors has different spheres of influence and also different interests, particularly the donors and the RTG. The RTG controls policy and regulations on displaced persons, while donors have the funds to support and determine working direction for projects with displaced persons. The intermediary bodies here are the NGOs who provide services to displaced persons. NGOs must comply with the policies and regulations of the RTG in working with displaced persons and at the same time request funding support from donors. Thus, NGOs walk a difficult line, balancing dual pressures from two dominant actors. At the same time, it seems that donors have limited capacity to pursue local integration as a dominant strategy with the RTG as Thailand is not a signatory to the 1951 Refugee Convention.

In reality in protracted refugee situations all actors are interdependent in seeking solutions and here they have each contributed to the state of the current situation in the shelters, and are all implicated in causing the protracted nature of the refugee situation. Government policy forces refugees to rely on external support. Despite this, it should be noted that donor funding for displaced persons did not support the model of development in the initial stages. Stakeholders may have thought that the situation would not last long enough to necessitate this. However, waiting over 17 years to begin to review aid, whether the catalyst be funding problems, economic crisis, or the lack of progress, was of little help. NGOs as service providers have traditionally been more familiar with aid in the form of relief, as it pertains to emergency responses. Combined, these factors resulted in the continuation of relief services for over 10 years and contributed to the protracted nature of this refugee situation. This has had effects on human capability in the shelters and demonstrates how such situations are affected by policy and operational approaches of stakeholders.

As has been noted at the second International Conference on Assistance to Refugees in Africa (ICARA II), held in Geneva in July 1984, the international community must recognise not only the needs of refugees but of their hosts, whose economic and social infrastructure must cope with the added burden of large numbers of refugees (Gorman 1986). In the case of Thailand, it has been an asylum seeker-receiving country for decades, fuelling what might be termed *asylum fatigue*. The RTG may view that allowing displaced persons to work outside the shelter is risky for a number of reasons. Protecting displaced persons is a major concern when these people are under the protection of UNHCR which distinguishes them from other migrant workers and has the potential to create a pull factor for new asylum seekers as well as competition with the local labour force. Providing work opportunities poses another risk in terms of the political sensitivities in the relationship with Myanmar. Security concerns related with local integration poses a major concern as well; the RTG may perceive that the local integration refers to displaced persons living in Thailand permanently, as nationalised Thais.

Nevertheless, these displaced persons are in shelters on Thai soil and the RTG has no choice but to be part of the coordinated response to finding durable solutions. All actors, donors, NGOs and the RTG, would do well to attempt to better understand the influencing factors on each other and to accept their interdependence as they move forward from here.

10.2 Stakeholder Cooperation and Communication: Management Modalities

Given the numerous and varied agencies involved in funding and delivering humanitarian assistance to the displaced people along the Thai–Myanmar border, a coordinated approach is vital for effective aid programmes. However, despite identifying this as a priority, donors and NGOs consistently reported a lack of effective communication practices or opportunities within and across stakeholder groups, but particularly in engaging the RTG. Appropriate mechanisms are lacking to manage the complex junction at which policy, funding direction and service delivery meet.

RTG policies and regulations govern all activities along the Thai side of the border. Implemented on Thai soil, all assistance programmes must comply with national and provincial regulations. To manage this, NGOs must apply annually to the RTG for permission to enter the border camps. NGOs submit all plans to the RTG for approval and report at regular intervals throughout the year.

NGOs interact with both national and provincial authorities but generally report an easier relationship with the latter, based on day-to-day contact and opportunities to develop relationships and form agreements. The CCSDPT is the representative body of NGOs working in the border camps and reports a relatively strong relationship with the RTG, meeting with the MOI several times a year.

However, despite a relatively cooperative and compliant environment, NGOs often struggle to meet their mandate due to the restrictive nature of RTG policy and the limited space to advocate for change. Communication is largely one way and prescriptive and as one respondent from a NGO articulated, policy change can only be achieved through coordinated advocacy on the part of donors, international agencies and civil society groups.

NGO operations are sometimes similarly restricted by donor policy direction. Donors fund NGOs through grants processes, with some allowing NGOs to allocate resources to programmes based on their determination of need. Other donors, though, restrict NGO activities by enacting their capacity to influence projects and interventions through guidelines on the specific use of funds. So while donors as funders and NGOs as implementers are in their essence assistance partners, this is the donor mechanism for managing the nature of humanitarian aid in the camps.

There are also complexities in developing donor policies within the context of RTG policies. Donor policy must also comply with RTG regulations and this often undermines the coordinated management of humanitarian assistance along the Thai–Myanmar border. Many donors find the operating environment restrictive, with limited opportunity to engage the RTG in any discussion of policy. Donors expressed frustration at the structural complexity of RTG management of the displaced people situation, needing to engage with the NSC, MOI, MOFA as well as provincial authorities.

While there are many factors contributing to this disconnect, including a lack of coordination amongst the donors themselves, it is clear that the operating environment in the border camps is somewhat inadequate. A gap in communications among stakeholders is recognised across the board. While there have been some attempts to stimulate dialogue and cooperation between the major stakeholders, more responsive management mechanisms are required for all actors to be as effective as possible in providing assistance to the displaced people in this protracted situation.

10.2.1 Funding Shortage and Coping Strategies

Donor aid policy has been gradually shifting towards LRRD since 2007, bringing both opportunities and challenges for humanitarian action. Despite this shift, the inability of donors to make long-term commitments of financial support means LRRD remains a challenge. Three trends impact on the availability of funds to NGOs to deliver services in the camps: food prices, currency exchange rates and the level of donor contributions. The number of residents in the camps has largely remained consistent in recent years.

Rising food prices and a drop in the value of major currencies in recent times mean that implementing agencies have less funding in real terms at their disposal to support camp populations with basic needs and other relief services. In order to cope, NGOs must be creative in service delivery, such as by adjusting the food basket from being culturally balanced to nutritionally balanced, thus replacing a portion of rice rations with an Asian mix. Another cost-saving initiative has seen standardised shelter equipment rations replaced with a system of awarding materials on the basis of individual assessment of household need. Bamboo is also being grown within some camps for internal use.

The absence of multiyear funding options for donors is a structural flaw of the funding system that supports the border camps. This makes it extraordinarily difficult for NGOs to plan with any certainty, even in the short and medium term. At least one NGO is seeking private funding to cover gaps left by the shift of donor focus away from basic needs to development projects. Others are attempting to view the situation more holistically, identifying opportunities to provide assistance to refugee populations by incorporating them into broader migrant health or education programmes supported by the RTG and other international funds.

The basic questions related to alignment of the 5-year strategy plan and the scale and scope of donor funding, including the operation of INGOs are: is the funding sufficient enough for the transition from the emergency to developmental phase; how can it be assured that this plan and identified strategies are comprehensive enough to lead towards supporting either one or all of the three durable solutions and what are the measures of success for this strategic plan?

10.3 The Impact of Stakeholder Policy and Durable Solutions for Displaced Persons

The movement from the emergency phase to development phase has been discontinuous since the beginning. Donors and INGOs need to better coordinate with and obtain real agreement from the RTG in order to develop more effective mechanisms and results. The provision of humanitarian aid to displaced persons inside the shelter along Thai–Myanmar border has lead to dependency after almost three decades of engagement. It is foreseeable that the promotion of self-reliance in this protracted situation may prove even more difficult than the initial emergency phase.

Since the outset, the RTG has considered the protracted situation along its Myanmar border to be an issue of national security, rather than any refugee or humanitarian crisis. The RTG has refrained from becoming a signatory to the 1951 Refugee Convention and has thus approached the situation with a policy of containment of irregular migration. In November 2005, the RTG terminated the UNHCR screening programme of new arrivals and since that time there has been no mechanism for identifying who new arrivals are, or what they are fleeing from. As a consequence, displaced persons inhabit the camps on a *temporary* basis, even though many have been there for 25 years. This has numerous implications for the pursuit of durable solutions for displaced persons, with restrictions on movement, employment and other opportunities for livelihood development and interaction with the local community outside the camps.

10.3.1 Resettlement

Since 2005, the resettlement programme has seen 67,000 refugees leave the displaced persons camps and settle in a third country. There is a general consensus among stakeholders that the resettlement programme has been successful for those who are eligible and wish to relocate. However, its viability as a durable solution has been undermined by the present lack of a PAB pre-screening process. No new arrivals have been screened or registered since 2005. The unwillingness of the RTG to pursue this mechanism prohibits the determination of displaced persons as eligible for resettlement. The programme is thus entirely finite as a solution. At this stage, resettlement is the only solution in place which could reduce the size of the camp population; however, the number of residents has remained steady due to the continuing influx of new arrivals.

Donors and NGOs are largely very supportive of the resettlement programme as a durable solution but it has been emphasised that this is not a solution in isolation. In their view, resettlement can only work as part of a coordinated package of solutions. There is some concern over whether a resettlement programme is in itself a pull factor bringing new arrivals into the camps and one which stimulates a brain drain from Myanmar. However, many donors dismissed the pull factor argument, believing that an active screening process would negate any incentive for non-refugees to seek out a place in the camps.

10.3.2 Repatriation

Several donors believe repatriation to be the desire of many displaced persons themselves, and surveys found this to be conditionally true, with 58.56 % of camp residents indicating that they would wish to return if guaranteed safety in Myanmar. Results of focus group discussions confirmed that displaced persons who wished to return to their hometown did so only with a guarantee of their safety and security. However, for those who have no personal connections such as relatives remaining inside Myanmar, or have no bound obligation to return, for instance children born inside shelters with no concept of life in Myanmar, resettlement or staying in Thailand are the only options. These responses reflected the need for the cultivation of a peace process for displaced persons who want to return home.

Repatriation as a durable solution has not been actively discussed. While many stakeholders agree that voluntary repatriation is an ideal durable solution, it is one which remains unfeasible until the situation inside Myanmar improves dramatically and safe and dignified return can be guaranteed. The RTG's current policy of no interference with the Myanmar Government also means there is no forum for discussion of repatriation as an option. Despite the *temporary* nature of the border camps, the RTG accepts that not all displaced persons will be able to return to Myanmar. Its policy, however, is one that sees their ongoing presence in Thailand as an issue for Thai national security.

10.3.3 Local Integration

The term *local integration* itself was found to be one which triggers alarm bells for stakeholders, with a variety of different interpretations among different actors. The concept of local integration is loaded with many potential ramifications for nationality, income generation and the socio-economic fabric of local communities. But there is no clear definition of what it entails precisely. Does local integration refer to the Thai nationalisation of displaced people, after which they would enjoy the same entitlements as natural-born Thais? Would it allow them freedom of movement and access to work, health and education in the communities surrounding the camps? Or would it involve the provision of income generating opportunities within the camps themselves? Consequently, as a durable solution it is regarded with scepticism and uncertainty by many stakeholders, not least the RTG. The long-term implications and political ramifications of this are not yet known.

Many donors and NGOs argue that the process of integration is already well underway, with education, health and agricultural projects in place. Pilot projects have already started in most camps, targeting vocational training, livelihood opportunities and health care integration, though these are not yet formalised. In Mae La camp, for example, agricultural projects introducing small-scale intensive farming, including fish ponds, help supplement the diets of the participating refugee families (Eick n.d.).

Most donors and NGOs rejected the idea that self-reliance activities constitute a pull factor into the camps, arguing that a reinstituted PAB process would negate this by screening out those not considered refugees. There is strong sentiment that any policy of integration would require the displaced persons community to be self-sustaining; they cannot be seen as a burden to local communities. New language around the notion of local integration must be developed to encourage the RTG and other actors to engage further with the concept, without inducing fear among Thai communities of being burdened or overrun with an influx of displaced people monopolising jobs and services. Ideas of *service integration*, *self-reliance* or *co-existence* are perhaps less confrontational to the local communities and the RTG.

Regardless of how integration is defined, at present, displaced persons are extremely limited in their opportunities for self-reliance. It will require a major shift in RTG policy before local integration of any kind can be considered a realistic or viable durable solution.

References

CCSDPT/UNHCR, 2007: *A Comprehensive Plan Addressing the Needs of Displaced Persons on the Thailand/Myanmar (Burma) Border in 2007/2008* (Bangkok: CCSDPT/UNHCR).

CCSDPT/UNHCR, 2009: *Five-year Strategic Plan working draft: Aid to Uprooted People Programme (AUP) Thailand 2009/2010* (Bangkok: UNHCR/CCSDPT).

Eick, M., (n.d.): *Thailand - World Refugee Day 20 June 2010: Refugees in Thailand: Another 25 years in limbo?* at: http://ec.europa.eu/echo/aid/stories/asia30_en.htm.

Gorman, R.F., 1986: "Beyond ICARA II: Implementing Refugee-Related Development Assistance", in *International Migration Review*, 20,2: 283–298.

IRC/Jesuit Refugee Service, 2005: *Nowhere to Turn: A Report on Conditions of Burmese Asylum Seekers in Thailand*; at: http://www.jrs.net/news_detail?TN=NEWS-20100603111409.

Lang, H., 2002: *Fear and Sanctuary: Burmese Refugees in Thailand* (Ithaca: Cornell Southeast Asia Program).

Lee, Chen Chen; Glaister, I., 2005: *Burmese asylum seekers in Thailand: still nowhere to turn*; at: http://www.fmreview.org/FMRpdfs/FMR30/33-34.pdf.

Macrae, J., 2002: The Changing Role of Official Donors in Humanitarian Action: a review of Trends and Issues. *HPG BriefingPaper*; at: http://www.odi.org.uk/resources/downdload/279.pdf.

Macrae, J. et al., 2002: Uncertain Power: the Changing Role of Official Donors in Humanitarian Action. *HPG Report 12 December*; at: http://www.odi.org.uk/resources/download/279.pdf.

TBBC, 2009a: *Programme Report, January–June 2009* (Bangkok: TBBC).

TBBC, 2009b: *Programme Report, July–December 2009* (Bangkok: TBBC).

TBBC, 2010a: *Programme Report, January–June 2010* (Bangkok: TBBC).

TBBC, 2010b: *Programme Report, July–December 2010* (Bangkok: TBBC).

UNHCR, 2000: *The State of the World's Refugees 2000: Fifty years of humanitarian action*; at: http://www.unhcr.org/4a4c754a9.html.

UNHCR, 2005a: *Handbook for Self-reliance: Book 1—Why self-reliance?* at: http://www.unhcr.org/44bf3e252.html.

UNHCR, 2005b: *Refugee Status Determination Identifying who is a refugee: self study module 2* (Geneva: UNHCR); at: http://www.unhcr.org/43144dc52.html.

Chapter 11
The Impacts of Existing Intervention Mechanisms, Including Gender-Related Aspects

Dares Chusri, Tarina Rubin, Ma. Esmeralda Silva, Jason D. Theede, Sunanta Wongchalee and Patcharin Chansawang

Abstract The current levels of support within the settlements are assessed from the perspective of the displaced persons. In general, despite differences in approach from different actors, and the RTG's stated policy of confinement and restriction of movement and access to services that might encourage local integration, the displaced persons themselves feel they have been well supported in terms of basic food, shelter, education and healthcare. However, problems resulting from long confinement are starting to impact, in terms of loss of self-confidence and self-reliance. There are also signs that funding is slowing down, partly related to the economic crisis in Europe and North America. Women, in particular, have experienced some disadvantage as a result of the way agencies and the RTG have supported traditional, male-dominated administration of the camps. There is consensus amongst all actors that change is needed now.

Keywords Refugee opinions · Settlement services · Humanitarian aid · Donor cooperation · Thai refugee policy

Existing intervention mechanisms, whether of donor, RTG or other actors, have already impacted on the displaced persons. This chapter will discuss the positive and negative impacts that have arisen from these interventions.

D. Chusri (✉) · T. Rubin · Ma. E. Silva · J. D. Theede · S. Wongchalee · P. Chansawang
Asian Research Center for Migration, Institute of Asian Studies, Chulalongkorn University, 3rd floor, Prachadhipok Rambhai-Barni Building, Bangkok 10330, Thailand
e-mail: dares_c@hotmail.com

T. Rubin
e-mail: tarina.Rubin@gmail.com

P. Vungsiriphisal et al. (eds.), *Humanitarian Assistance for Displaced Persons from Myanmar*, SpringerBriefs in Environment, Security, Development and Peace 17,
DOI: 10.1007/978-3-319-02795-1_11,

11.1 Existing RTG and NGOs Intervention Mechanisms

Although the RTG places strict restrictions on the number of operating NGOs and staff working inside shelters, there are some beneficial impacts of such a policy. This rigid rule allows for positive contributions to the development of displaced persons-led camp management of services and community-based management in collaboration with the Thai authorities who are limited in number. This strategy increases self-reliance and can reduce dependency on external management. For example, TBBC has been working in partnership with the Karen Refugee Committee (KRC) and Karenni Refugee Committee (KnRC) since 2004, supporting camp administration costs including stipends for camp committee members and staff involved in the delivery, storage and distribution of TBBC supplies, with capacity-building effect (TBBC 2010a, b).

Another positive outcome of RTG policy is cooperation in the judicial reform process inside temporary shelters between Ministry of Justice (MOJ) and IRC to provide legal aid to vulnerable groups, especially women. Displaced persons can access formal Thai justice through Legal Aid Centre (LACs) located inside the shelters.

Although such RTG regulations produce some positive results, other policies and regulations still in force have negative impacts on the quality of life of displaced persons and, subsequently, the image of Thailand in the eyes of the international community. Restricting access to work and movement forces displaced persons to rely on external support and causes the international community to overlook the reality that Thailand has been hosting these displaced persons for almost three decades. Some current policies are outdated and inappropriate at present in a region where socio-economic and environmental conditions have changed dramatically. In practice however, the RTG allows some flexibility in enforcing existing policy, permitting some NGOs to work on pilot projects related to livelihoods, for example. If the potential to roll out these pilot projects is realised through policy change, the benefits to the displaced persons will be substantial. It would also reflect the RTG's commitment to responsiveness and timeliness of its policies.

It is widely acknowledged that state bureaucracy is usually slow to instigate change and the same can be said of the Provincial Admission Board (PAB) process for displaced persons status determination. In operation since 2009, the results of pilot studies have not yet been disclosed. If the RTG could expedite this process it would help address or prevent many issues in this protracted displaced persons' situation. It could also strengthen the capacity of state officers to work effectively.

Gender programming has introduced various activities into the shelters. Those NGOs interviewed have gender policies in place, integrated into all aspects of their work in management and service areas. During field visits, it was noted that every shelter had women working side by side with men at the management level. The male camp residents interviewed admired and respected these working women. Women know where to go to ask for help if they have any problems. There are women's organisations such as the Karen Women Organisation (KWO) and

Karenni Women's Organisation (KnWO) which have a significant role in providing support and protection to women and children. It should be noted that while many organisations try to promote and protect women in various ways, it seems that men do not participate in these kinds of programmes. Training programmes that aim to empower women and provide protection will only be more effective if men have the opportunity to participate also, promoting understanding and avoiding resentment at female-targeted programmes only. Men are also in need of strengthened capacity in this area and both sexes should work together. Focus group discussions suggested that men felt neglected in this regard, as one man complained:

> Currently, women have been more developed than men (Male interviewee, 28-year old).
>
> Currently men have to be aware that women have more rights. If women would like to do something such as watching a CD (movie) after meal, they can do so. If men say something and make women angry, they say that they will report to LAC. So men do not dare to complain about anything to women, while women dare to say they want (Male displaced persons, 26 year).

11.2 Coordination Mechanisms Among Donors, RTG and INGOs

The communications gap in the current operating environment between the RTG and donors is an ongoing source of frustration for many donors. The nature of individual donor countries' bilateral relations with the RTG is enormously varied, from suggestions that the RTG has devolved itself of all responsibility in the running of the camps and no relationship exists to even speak of, to sentiments of close cooperation and belief that the RTG is a *neglected donor* receiving insufficient credit for its support for the border camps. While cooperation between NGOs and RTG officials at the provincial level is generally satisfactory, the majority of donors described a lack of open dialogue with the national government characterised by limited opportunities to meet, and even then, ad-hoc meetings with low-level representation from the RTG. Attempts to host workshops have proved fruitless, and the sheer number of RTG agencies involved in this protracted situation further confounds donor attempts to engage the Thai authorities.

However, within the donor group there has been a realisation in recent years that their ineffectiveness in multilateral advocacy to the RTG is related to a lack of coordination amongst themselves. This could be attributed in some part to the high turnover of donor staff, often posted to Thailand for a fixed period of 2–3 years. This revolving door environment has created discontinuity and hindered donors' ability to build and maintain personal relationships with the RTG.

Many donors also identified better collaboration as a necessary precursor to approaching the RTG for policy change. A recent donor-led effort to facilitate dialogue between donors, implementing agencies and the RTG has still not provided results in terms of cooperation with the RTG but has proved successful in providing a forum for improved donor collaboration.

The relationship between the government and donors is of course governed by the terms of RTG policy and regulations on displaced persons, as mentioned previously. Within this, however, the quality of the relationship still depends on the means and modalities of communication employed. If donors act aggressively or offensively to change RTG policy, it may be with negative consequence in which the RTG could feel coerced into accepting donor proposals which make no concessions, especially on the policy of displaced persons encampment. The RTG reaction is often expressed silently and can be perceived as a decision to ignore attempts at communication, to the frustration of both parties.

By contrast, the RTG relationship with NGOs is more based on compromise and coordination. If donors can better consult and listen to what the RTG puts forward, this will have a positive impact in practice, perhaps enabling more pilot projects on vocational training or movement towards some kind of policy shift. Some donors demonstrate good humanitarian donorship and are collaborative rather than aggressive, as are the NGOs, through regular communication, and a concerted effort to develop a friendly understanding of the cultural limitations of the RTG. This will help to increase trust and improve working relationships.

11.3 Linking Relief, Rehabilitation and Development: Challenges and Opportunities

At present, NGOs are engaged in capacity-building interventions such as candle-making and subsistence agriculture, as well as training displaced persons in camp management, or as field and office personnel. This makes use of the abundance of time at displaced persons' disposal given they do not work outside the camps, and at the same time develops their skills and should be an opportunity for self-reliance arise. One respondent discussed the need to continuously practice and hone the knowledge and skills that displaced persons possessed before entering the camp, otherwise once a person becomes designated a displaced person, they become *invisible* and the skills that they had before will disappear.

The provision of basic services such as food, shelter, health and education is funded by donors and provided directly to displaced persons. A respondent noted that the level and quality of these services is better than those in other protracted displaced persons situations. This could be attributed to the fact that providers of these services need to adhere to the strict global standards of their funders. It also shows that the service systems in these camps run parallel to that provided by the RTG to local communities. Some NGOs and donor countries are currently working on mechanisms that would allow the provision of these services to the displaced persons to be channelled through the Thai system. An example is in healthcare, where local Thai health services would be provided to the displaced persons in the camps, or as a potential alternative, where local communities could access camp health facilities. Respondents from donor countries expressed their openness to exploring and supporting alternative avenues for policy and programmatic collaborations with the RTG, such as formulating and supporting mechanisms to enable students to study in Thai schools and universities and for displaced persons to be incorporated into the local health system.

But an obstacle to scaling up and rolling out small-scale interventions is the fact that the camps are closed. An example of this is the agricultural project that one NGO is implementing in some of the camps. At present, the project is at the subsistence level because it is constrained by economies of scale, such as land area available for planting. This is also dependent on the amenability of the camp officials to making resources available to the project. The current levels of production are not enough to impact on the food requirements of the families in the camp. Should restrictions on the camps be eased, there is an opportunity for the project to expand and produce more, contributing substantially to the food needs in the camp, creating opportunities to sell the produce in the local markets, or both.

In terms of policy and programmatic collaborations, the reluctance of the RTG to engage in dialogue with donor countries is another stumbling block. Respondents revealed that they have had limited opportunities for meaningful discussion with the RTG on how these collaborations could be achieved, particularly on how donor countries could assist the RTG. A corollary issue to this is burden shifting and burden sharing between the RTG and donor countries. Financial support for the camps over the past two decades has been drawn from donors and NGOs with minimal financial input from the RTG.

An interesting point raised by one respondent focused on whose shoulders the burden should lie because up until now it has rested with the citizens of donor countries. Given the shifts in funding philosophies and shrinking funding levels, this respondent highlighted the need to consider how the RTG could take on some of the burden from donor countries. This respondent's position showed the extent of donor frustration at this protracted refugee situation. Donors may lose interest because of a lack of solutions. Although the RTG has restricted its displaced persons policy, it does not mean that Thailand is free of responsibility. In fact, donors and the host country have both common and differentiated responsibilities and play an important role in humanitarian support. Cooperation is needed to support *responsibility-sharing*. The only way that the RTG could assist is to create an environment in which displaced persons can be self-reliant, thus reducing external aid and increasing self-esteem and dignity of displaced persons.

11.4 Needs, Perceptions, Hopes and Expectations of Displaced Persons

This section reveals the results of the baseline survey conducted at Tham Hin, Ban Mai Nai Soi and Mae La temporary shelters in Ratchaburi, Mae Hog Sorn and Tak provinces, respectively. The survey questions explored the needs, perceptions,

Table 11.1 Aid dependency by sex and age

	Totally dependent	Partially, for food, shelter and jobs	Very little, only food and shelter	Other	No answer	Total
Sex						
Male	135 (30.41)	40 (9.01)	13 (2.93)	9 (2.03)	1 (0.23)	198 (44.59)
Female	183 (41.22)	41 (9.23)	16 (3.60)	4 (0.90)	2 (0.45)	246 (55.41)
Age group (years)						
18–24	86 (19.37)	26 (5.86)	5 (1.13)	8 (1.80)	1 (0.23)	126 (28.38)
25–59	221 (49.77)	53 (11.94)	22 (4.95)	5 (1.13)	2 (0.45)	303 (68.24)
60 and above	11 (2.48)	2 (0.45)	2 (0.45)	0 (0.00)	0 (0.00)	15 (3.38)
Total	318 (71.62)	81 (18.24)	29 (6.53)	13 (2.93)	3 (0.68)	444 (100.0)

Source The authors

hopes and expectations of displaced persons as they pertained to the roles of donors, international organisations, NGOs and the RTG.

Out of 444 individuals interviewed, 55.4 % female and 44.6 % male, seven out of ten indicated that they were totally dependent on the aid of NGOs. Broken down by age, most of those who indicated they were totally dependent on NGO aid were aged between 24 and 59-years old who could be considered the economically productive age group (Table 11.1).

Seven out of ten respondents indicated that they would like opportunity to be more self-reliant. Respondents within the economically productive age group of 25–29 years old would like to be more self-reliant (Table 11.2).

The results of the survey are consistent with the responses of the participants in the FGDs:

Table 11.2 Self-reliance by sex and age

	Yes	No	Don't know	Other	Did not answer	Total
Sex						
Male	163 (36.71)	26 (5.86)	9 (2.03)	0 (0.00)	0 (0.00)	198 (44.59)
Female	180 (40.54)	44 (9.91)	20 (4.50)	1 (0.23)	1 (0.23)	246 (55.41)
Total	343 (77.25)	70 (15.77)	29 (6.53)	1 (0.23)	1 (0.23)	444 (100.00)
Age group (years)						
18–24	103 (23.20)	23 (5.18)	0 (0.00)	0 (0.00)	0 (0.00)	126 (28.38)
25–59	230 (51.80)	73 (16.44)	0 (0.00)	0 (0.00)	0 (0.00)	303 (68.24)
60 and above	10 (2.25)	5 (1.13)	0 (0.00)	0 (0.00)	0 (0.00)	15 (3.38)
Total	343 (77.25)	101 (22.75)	0 (0.00)	0 (0.00)	0 (0.00)	444 (100.00)

Source The authors

Compared with Myanmar, here is better. But if we think about the future it is not good because we have no future. Just live life day by day without knowing the future. Each day we just cook rice to eat and have nothing to do. I wish to have job to do because I need privacy and want to help myself. No need to be burden to anyone (Male displaced persons, 28 years).

Our life is like a dwarf tree. It does not grow. It is under a big tree, so it cannot grow. I have a dream. In the future, I want to be an eagle because it has completed both the wings and legs. What we want to do, we cannot do because we have no opportunity. Like a bird in a cage (Male displaced persons, 34 years).

When asked about what they thought about the motivations of the NGOs in their engagement, almost 44 % of respondents acknowledged that NGOs provide services to them as they are people in need, while around 32 % of respondents believed that NGOs act because they cannot help themselves. This reveals that most respondents are aware they have no opportunity to be self-reliant, and thus, NGOs must come to help them.

Although camp regulations do not allow all the displaced persons to work or even go outside the shelters, in reality the research team found that many displaced persons in all the studied shelters have had some working experience outside the shelter, whether daily, periodical, seasonal or even ongoing for months or years. This is evidence that even though there are regulations in place, in reality these regulations cannot prevent the displaced persons from endeavouring to meet the basic life needs for themselves. It also reflects that even though the regular basic support services provided by NGOs can meet minimum essential needs, they cannot meet their wider needs. The FGD revealed that displaced persons need cash for their children to attend school (e.g. for lunch, sweets, stationary) and for a variety of other general needs, particularly food and cloth (Table 11.3).

When asked about the timeline of NGO support, almost 55 % of respondents believe they will need NGO support forever. Another 21 % feel they will no longer need NGO support when the times come that they can support themselves. For those who need NGO support, they do not foresee any channels or opportunities to become self-reliant. Respondents in FGD complained that they feel they have no value if they do not work. They do not want just to sit and wait for NGOs arrive with free services (Table 11.4).

Table 11.3 Why NGOs provide services

Why are NGOs helping you?	Male	Female	Total
They want to help people in need	86 (19.37)	109 (24.55)	195 (43.92)
Because I cannot help myself	65 (14.64)	76 (17.12)	141 (31.76)
They benefit from their services	1 (0.23)	2 (0.45)	3 (0.68)
It is their business	11 (2.48)	11 (2.48)	22 (4.95)
Don't know	34 (7.66)	46 (10.36)	80 (18.02)
Other	1 (0.23)	0 (0.00)	1 (0.23)
Did not answer	0 (0.00)	2 (0.45)	2 (0.45)
Total	198 (44.59)	246 (55.41)	444 (100.00)

Source The authors

Table 11.4 Need for NGO services

When do you think you will no longer need NGO services?	Male	Female	Total
Did not answer	0 (0.00)	1 (0.23)	1 (0.23)
Never, we need the NGOs to take care of our health and other things	105 (23.65)	138 (31.08)	243 (54.73)
Only when we can access the local services	9 (2.03)	10 (2.25)	19 (4.28)
Whenever we can take care of ourselves	41 (9.23)	52 (11.71)	93 (20.95)
Anytime	5 (1.13)	1 (0.23)	6 (1.35)
Don't know	38 (8.56)	44 (9.91)	82 (18.47)
Total	198 (44.59)	246 (55.41)	444 (100.00)

Source The Authors

> People outside the camp may think that displaced persons are lazy, in fact, some people maybe but not everyone. They may view us like dogs, that we do not do anything, just take and eat only. Displaced persons do not want to be like that. We have no opportunity to help ourselves. We are here, we cannot go back. Displaced persons are allowed to be here. We have to follow the rules (Male displaced persons, 35 years).

When it comes to opportunities for self-reliance, one out of three respondents wants to work either inside or outside of the temporary shelter. Women in particular want to work inside shelter. Some of the reasons they have shared include:

> I want to work here because I can take care of my family and also do some housework (Female displaced persons, 30 years).
>
> Anywhere we can work, we want to work outside but we are afraid that our employer will not pay us. We do not know what to do, we have not much knowledge (Male displaced persons, 24 years).
>
> Will they allow us to go outside? We have no rights to go out, I am afraid to be arrested and sent back (Male displaced persons, 28 years).

Interestingly, 23 % of the respondents are not aware of any means to be self-reliant. This is quite disturbing because it would seem that there is absolute dependence on the part of the displaced persons on external support (Table 11.5).

Only 7 % of respondents would like to return to Myanmar, highlighting the need for better information on options for self-reliance. Another concerning point is 15 % and almost 9 % of displaced persons respondents chose to stay in Thailand or go to another place that guarantees their safety respectively. This means that they are afraid to go back to Myanmar due to fear of persecution. It serves as a reminder to people who work with them to think about who should facilitate safe conditions inside Myanmar, and how.

Even though respondents were unaware of the situation of *donor fatigue*, some guessed that this is the case. Only 34 % of respondents expected donors to never stop funding while displaced persons remain in the shelters. Another 30 % were aware that donors may stop supporting NGOs sometime, but believed this to be an issue for the long term when they have to help other countries. A further 12 % felt

Table 11.5 Opportunities for self-reliance

	Male	Female	Total
Authors below chapter and affiliation			
Abstract (about 100–200 words)	35 (7.88)	66 (14.86)	101 (22.75)
Keywords: 5–10	72 (16.22)	71 (15.99)	143 (32.21)
Authors below chapter and affiliation	33 (7.43)	39 (8.78)	72 (16.22)
Abstract (about 100–200 words)	35 (7.88)	32 (7.21)	67 (15.09)
Keywords: 5–10	3 (0.68)	4 (0.90)	7 (1.58)
Authors below chapter and affiliation	15 (3.38)	24 (5.41)	39 (8.78)
Abstract (about 100–200 words)	3 (0.68)	7 (1.58)	10 (2.25)
Keywords: 5–10	2 (0.45)	3 (0.68)	5 (1.13)
Authors below chapter and affiliation	198 (44.59)	246 (55.41)	444 (100.00)

Source The Authors

that donors may stop funding soon as they have been providing funding for a long time already. This indicates that almost 425 respondents are aware that funding will one day no longer be available. The potential termination of donor funding is relevant to their previous responses regarding the need to work for self-reliance. Corollary to this are the options open to the displaced persons once there is no funding support available. One out of three respondents indicated that they will work towards supporting themselves and being self-reliant (Tables 11.6 and 11.7).

A majority of the displaced persons rated the services of NGOs as good or fair, education in particular. In relation to NGO food services, 63 % of respondents perceived them to be good quality. A couple of women voiced concerns during FGDs about the accuracy of the amount of rice rationed. One woman measured using a plastic container and found that the amount of rice was less than before, estimated around 200 g. The other participants had no complaint about this. However, it is acknowledged that respondents are perhaps unlikely to tell interviewers the truth about their perceptions, and may have just said what they think interviewers wanted to hear or kept silent. Though these few voices raised such

Table 11.6 Ongoing donor support

Will the donors ever stop their support for the NGOs?	Male	Female	Total
Never, as long as we are here	73 (16.44)	76 (17.12)	149 (33.56)
A long time in the future when they want to support other countries	55 (12.39)	78 (17.57)	133 (29.95)
Soon, because they have helped us for too long	17 (3.83)	36 (8.11)	53 (11.94)
Don't know	51 (11.49)	51 (11.49)	102 (22.97)
Other	1 (0.23)	0 (0.00)	1 (0.23)
Did not answer	1 (0.23)	5 (1.13)	6 (1.35)
Total	198 (44.59)	246 (55.41)	444 (100.00)

Source The authors

Table 11.7 Likely response to termination of funding

What will you do if the donors stop sending funds for the NGOs?	Male	Female	Total
We want to work to support ourselves	85 (19.14)	92 (20.72)	177 (39.86)
We will ask them not to stop	40 (9.01)	55 (12.39)	95 (21.40)
Other organisations will come after them for helping us	11 (2.48)	15 (3.38)	26 (5.86)
Repatriate with guaranteed security	6 (1.35)	7 (1.58)	13 (2.93)
Don't answer	41 (9.23)	53 (11.94)	94 (21.17)
Other	15 (3.38)	22 (4.95)	37 (8.33)
Do not know	0 (0.00)	2 (0.45)	2 (0.45)
Total	198 (44.59)	246 (55.41)	444 (100.00)

Source The Authors

issues, they cannot be used to generalise or question the accuracy of rice contribution. The food distribution monitoring system is the appropriate mechanism to assess accountability here.

Education is the service that most displaced persons are satisfied with, with 82 % reporting education services to be good. This was attributed to the RTG allowing displaced persons the chance to study Thai language and extend the education level to Grade 10 (Table 11.8).

But there are some services provided which a significant proportion of respondents perceive to be insufficient. Of those who complained that the food was not sufficient, many cited the reason being due to sharing with their relatives. Many asylum seekers are waiting for status determination from PAB screening and those who are not awarded status have limited access to food services, hence the need to share with their relatives. While 65 % of respondents found vocational training to be good, those who disagreed with this said that the waiting periods and the small size of the pilot project leaves much to be desired. Respondents also expressed frustration at having little opportunity to use their newly acquired skills and expressed as *if we do not use it, we will forget it* mentality.

Despite the fact that it is difficult to find any evidence of income generation inside the shelter, almost half of the respondents think that the services are good. Results highlight that this area needs strategic reconsideration to assist in the development of self-reliance among displaced persons. Similarly, gender training requires further public relations and strategy revision to help increase community participation in quite a new issue for displaced persons (Table 11.9).

Again, activities to prevent violence against women and children faced similar issue; these are new activities for displaced persons and need further publicity and advocacy. At this stage 65 % perceived it to be a good service (Table 11.10).

In all, 71 % of respondents reported that the legal assistance service is good. This programme is also quite new but useful and of benefit to all displaced persons, particular women (Table 11.11).

Table 11.8 Perceptions about various services provided by NGOs to displaced persons in camps

	Male (n = 198)	Female (n = 246)	Total (n = 444)
Food Services			
• Good	123 (27.70)	156 (35.14)	279 (62.84)
• Fair	38 (8.56)	43 (9.68)	81 (18.24)
• Not enough	31 (6.98)	39 (8.78)	70 (15.77)
• Don't know/did not answer	6 (1.35)	8 (1.80)	14 (3.15)
Shelter Items			
• Good	108 (24.32)	122 (27.48)	230 (51.80)
• Fair	38 (8.56)	41 (9.23)	79 (17.79)
• Not enough	48 (10.81)	76 (17.12)	124 (27.93)
• Other	0 (0.00)	1 (0.23)	1 (0.23)
• Don't know/did not answer	4 (0.90)	6 (1.35)	10 (2.25)
Health services			
• Good	146 (32.88)	181 (40.77)	327 (73.65)
• Fair	29 (6.53)	32 (7.21)	61 (13.74)
•Not enough	17 (3.83)	25 (5.63)	42 (9.46)
• Don't know/did not answer	6 (1.35)	8 (1.80)	14 (3.15)
Sanitation			
• Good	138 (31.08)	171 (38.51)	309 (69.59)
• Fair	36 (8.11)	33 (7.43)	69 (15.54)
• Not enough	20 (4.50)	36 (8.11)	56 (12.61)
• Don't know/did not answer	4 (0.90)	6 (1.35)	10 (2.25)
Education			
• Good	160 (36.04)	202 (45.50)	362 (81.53)
• Fair	14 (3.15)	24 (5.41)	38 (8.56)
• Not enough	20 (4.50)	13 (2.93)	33 (7.43)
• Don't know/did not answer	4 (0.90)	7 (1.58)	11 (2.48)
Vocational training			
• Good	125 (28.15)	165 (37.16)	290 (65.32)
• Fair	21 (4.73)	24 (5.41)	45 (10.14)
• Not enough	29 (6.53)	25 (5.63)	54 (12.16)
• Don't know/did not answer	23 (5.18)	32 (7.21)	55 (12.39)
Income generating activities			
• Good	81 (18.24)	104 (23.42)	185 (41.67)
• Fair	24 (5.41)	40 (9.01)	64 (14.41)
• Not enough	52 (11.71)	53 (11.94)	105 (23.65)
• Don't know/did not answer	41 (9.23)	49 (11.04)	90 (20.27)
Gender Training			
• Good	117 (26.35)	138 (31.08)	255 (57.43)
• Fair	23 (5.18)	28 (6.31)	51 (11.49)
• Not enough	18 (4.05)	23 (5.18)	41 (9.23)
• Don't know/did not answer	40 (9.01)	57 (12.84)	97 (21.85)

Source The Authors

Table 11.9 Activities to prevent violence against women and children

Violence against women and children prevention activities	Male	Female	Total
Don't know/did not answer	30 (6.76)	38 (8.56)	68 (15.32)
Good	122 (27.48)	165 (37.16)	287 (64.64)
Fair	29 (6.53)	23 (5.18)	52 (11.71)
Not enough	17 (3.83)	20 (4.50)	37 (8.33)
Total	198 (44.59)	246 (55.41)	444 (100.00)

Source The Authors

Table 11.10 Legal assistance

Legal assistance	Male	Female	Total
Don't know/did no answer	24 (5.41)	34 (7.66)	58 (13.06)
Good	138 (31.08)	176 (39.64)	314 (70.72)
Fair	23 (5.18)	19 (4.28)	42 (9.46)
Not enough	13 (2.93)	16 (3.60)	29 (6.53)
Other	0 (0.00)	1 (0.23)	1 (0.23)
Total	198 (44.59)	246 (55.41)	444 (100.00)

Source The Authors

Table 11.11 Negotiation with Myanmar

Do you think that it is the responsibility of any organisations to negotiate with your original country to take you home with guaranteed security?	Male	Female	Total
No	63 (14.19)	94 (21.17)	157 (35.36)
Yes	126 (28.38)	134 (30.18)	260 (58.56)
Did not answer	9 (2.03)	18 (4.05)	27 (6.08)
Total	198 (44.59)	246 (55.41)	444 (100.00)

Source The Authors

Related to repatriation, only 59 % of respondents believed that it is the responsibility of certain organisations to negotiate with Myanmar for the guarantee of their safe return. Another 35 % thought there was no need for anyone to negotiate with Myanmar. FGDs revealed that respondents never believed in the Myanmar government and do not believe that negotiation will be successful, thus there is no point wasting time on this. This sheds light on responses to the question of where they would choose to go after the camp. Not surprisingly, this is why they do not want to return home. They do not trust the Myanmar government, based on bad experiences, fleeing persecution and human rights abuses. Respondents indicated that at least 58.56 % would return home following attainment of peace inside

Table 11.12 Responsible Organisations

Specific responsible organisations for negotiations with Myanmar	Male	Female	Total
UN agencies	57 (21.92)	53 (20.38)	110 (42.30)
ASEAN	8 (3.07)	10 (3.84)	18 (6.92)
Royal Thai Government	19 (7.30)	18 (6.92)	37 (14.23)
NGOs	9 (3.46)	10 (3.84)	19 (7.30)
More than 1 organisations	33 (12.69)	43 (16.53)	76 (29.23)
Total	126 (48.46)	134 (51.51)	260 (100.00)

Source The Authors

Myanmar. However, this process requires leadership from international agencies to identify appropriate channels or mechanisms and facilitate the peace process (Table 11.12).

Of those who agreed that it was the responsibility of particular organisations to negotiate with Myanmar for their safe repatriation, 42.3 % believed it to be the role of UN agencies, 29.23 % multilateral organisations, 14.23 % the RTG, 7.3 % NGOs and 6.92 % ASEAN.

References

TBBC, 2010a: *Programme Report, January–June 2010* (Bangkok: TBBC).
TBBC, 2010b: *Programme Report, July–December 2010* (Bangkok: TBBC).

Chapter 12
The Limitations and Constraints on Effective Intervention Mechanisms

Dares Chusri, Tarina Rubin, Ma. Esmeralda Silva, Jason D. Theede, Sunanta Wongchalee and Patcharin Chansawang

Abstract Generally, the displaced persons themselves are relatively contented with the way they have been treated in the settlements by all the various stakeholders. They have found relative safety and security, and have access to basic life requirements such as food and shelter and, increasingly, to education, health care and other services. However, the displaced persons are in limbo, and have been for a long time in some cases, and lack hope and motivation, leading to increasing social and community issues in the shelters. For the donors, the issue has become a strain on resources, and a peripheral issue in world affairs. For the UN agencies and NGOs, with no solutions in sight, this protracted situation has taxed resources and patience. For the RTG, also, there are more major issues to attend to. All parties have different perspectives, and communication between them is poor. The RTG's approach has been more flexible in practice than is its policy, but it has been unable to agree a solution with the other actors.

Keywords Donor fatigue · Funding shortages · Confinement · Aid reliance · Livelihoods · Labour · UNHCR · NGOs

This chapter will summarise the various limitations and constraints on effective intervention mechanisms for durable solutions. Results of the baseline survey have also been examined to reveal the perceptions and suggestions put forward by the displaced persons who participated from the three targeted temporary shelters.

D. Chusri (✉) · T. Rubin · Ma. E. Silva · J. D. Theede · S. Wongchalee · P. Chansawang
Asian Research Center for Migration, Institute of Asian Studies, Chulalongkorn University, 3rd floor, Prachadhipok Rambhai-Barni Building, Bangkok 10330, Thailand
e-mail: dares_c@hotmail.com

T. Rubin
e-mail: tarina.Rubin@gmail.com

P. Vungsiriphisal et al. (eds.), *Humanitarian Assistance for Displaced Persons from Myanmar*, SpringerBriefs in Environment, Security, Development and Peace 17,
DOI: 10.1007/978-3-319-02795-1_12,

12.1 RTG Policy

The current policy environment means that refugee issues are likely to remain low on the national agenda in Thailand. Instead, RTG policy will continue to be concerned with issues of national security, the impact of the refugee situation on Thai communities, avoiding conditions which create pull factors for new asylum seekers, as well as bilateral considerations, including maintaining relations with Myanmar. Moreover, refugee policy issues remain contingent upon the overall political environment in Thailand. As a consequence, the policy of encampment remains in place today.

All interviewed RTG officers were sympathetic and would like to see the situation of refugees improve, as one interviewee described:

> Displaced persons have social problems, mental problems, issues with alcohol use and quarrelling among teenagers, etc. No matter how well we take care of them, this is not real life. Children grow and graduate, then what will they do?

Many government officials have compassion for displaced persons and most of them understand the protracted refugee situation clearly but they are keenly aware of RTG policy in relation to the camps. This makes them reluctant to say or do anything outside regulation, particularly making any promise or personal commitment.

Some authorities viewed hosting displaced persons as a burden to Thailand, partly due to negative perceptions associated with the hosting. However, in reality, the trends in durable solutions to refugee situations have been moving noticeably away from local integration in terms of actualised solution strategies, since the policy response by host countries has often been one of restriction of movement. Within this environment there has been no significant progress towards the displaced persons' economic self-reliance or access to the labour market, and opportunities for higher education remain limited. This is contrary to the UNHCR suggestion that sustained advocacy in line with the 5-year strategic plan will help achieve a gradual opening of the temporary shelters and gain the Government's permission for refugees to work and move about more freely (UNHCR 2010).

It seems that RTG will not be easily persuaded to change a policy which has been in place since the influx of Indochinese refugees in the 1970s. Policy guidelines of RTG have not changed since that time (Lee/Glaister 2005), as reaffirmed by another Thai authority in an interview: *Thai Policy toward displaced persons never changes*. Consequently, until policies of encampment are altered in a significant way, there is little possibility that dependency on humanitarian aid can be reduced in the short term (TBBC 2010a, b). Restriction of movement directly affects the promotion of self-reliance among refugees. The programme report of TBBC (2005) revealed several constraints on agriculture inside the shelter which place restrictions on household food production such as physical limitations including location, population density, limited space and seasonal water supplies.

A further constraint to the promotion of refugee self-reliance is the RTG policy which states *All NGOs must submit an annual proposal to obtain permission to operate from the MOI.* Going through the processes of applying for approval each year hampers the ability of NGOs to promote self-reliance through long-term planning and alignment with funding support. Long and tedious administrative processes also cause delays in the implementation of projects and programmes. Navigating through the many and complex processes in place results in delays and causes ambiguity in the transparency and accountability of the system. It also raises doubts about standards of work such as the PAB process, which as mentioned previously, has implemented a pilot project to pre-screen new arrivals since 2009 but not yet released the results.

Government officials must comply with the National Security Policy A.D. 2007–2011 and the Management Strategy for the problem of the status and rights of individuals A.D. 2005–2011, neither of which mention working opportunities for displaced persons. Perhaps emerging evidence from the livelihood pilot project evaluation by NGOs and this research study by ARCM will be useful to stimulate new policy development and strategic planning by the RTG.

Although Thailand has not ratified the Refugee Convention, it has ratified a number of other core international human rights treaties in the UN system that can confer protection to displaced people. The first treaty, the Convention on the Elimination of All Forms of Discrimination against Women (CEDAW), was ratified in 1985 to guarantee that men and women are treated equally by the state. The Convention on the Rights of the Child (CRC) was then put in force in 1992 to protect all children in the state without discrimination. In 1996, the Thai state ratified the International Covenant on Civil and Political Rights (ICCPR), a significant treaty for the mechanisms of the UN system and one of the so-called International Bills of Human Rights. It describes every fundamental norm of human rights that all should respect and protect, especially civil and political rights. Another International Bill of Human Rights, ratified by Thailand in 1999, is the International Covenant on Economic, Social and Cultural Rights (ICESCR), focused on monitoring the implementation of economic, social and cultural rights. Only in 2003 did Thailand accept the Convention of the Elimination of All Forms of Racial Discrimination (CERD), which especially applies to ethnic minorities. All the treaties have a reporting system to which state parties are obliged to make periodic submissions.

In 2007 Thailand ratified the Convention against Torture (CAT). The Convention aims to prevent torture and other cruel, inhuman or degrading treatment or punishment. Signatories are legally bound by these international mechanisms to apply international laws domestically, ensuring that no such domestic laws contradict ratified international human rights laws. However, it is clear that Thailand has not yet realised the legal requirements of international standards it has ratified (Napaumporn 2008). Even though Thailand has not ratified the 1951 Refugee Convention, the aforementioned conventions cover the basic human rights, including the right to work of refugees for their self-reliance.

12.2 Characteristics of Funding Policy and Intervention Mechanisms

As discussed previously, there exists a disconnection between NGO and donor perspectives on the state of *emergency* in the camps. NGOs continue to believe the situation is an emergency, thus requiring that interventions provide for basic humanitarian needs. In contrast, some donors believe the emergency has ended, given the protracted nature of the situation. The EU's reallocation of funds from ECHO to AUP development-oriented projects is the prime example, but this shift is also apparent in the decision of some donors to support activities within Myanmar itself. The impact here is that these different approaches require different technical capacities and resources on the part of the NGOs. Under a humanitarian umbrella, the funding process is commonly expedited in order to address the emergency nature of the situation. But within a development framework, proposals may be subject to a competitive bidding process which takes time and often necessitates the allocation of counterpart funding from the NGO. An example of the impact of this is that even though the reallocation of funds to AUP aims to increase support for the developmental approach, the proposals of not all current implementing NGOs will be approved and may result in discontinuity of their projects, including those aimed at the promotion of self-reliance.

However, new influxes of refugees have arrived from time to time over the years as the conflict inside Myanmar continues, even as recently as the end of 2010. This would indicate that the emergency situation is ongoing and needs emergency funding and skilled management for the delivery of timely humanitarian aid. Funding shortages and the dynamic of emergency may create new tensions among stakeholders.

Another constraint is the year by year funding process, inconsistent with the nature of development work which demands continuous funding or funding security. Each donor provides funds in line with their interest, rather than coordinating to ensure comprehensive funding. This may leave gaps in the development process and issues such as food insecurity.

12.3 Self-Reliance and Livelihood Interventions

Although a community-based service delivery model is helpful in strengthening the capacity of refugees to be self-reliant, it requires regular monitoring to ensure accountability, especially in even ration distribution. Several interviewees raised the issue of the accuracy of rice distribution and the quality of some non-food items during group discussions and interviews:

> We doubt that we get the right amount of rice we should get. We went home and we measured it by our barrel, which has been used for years, and we found that the level of

rice has decreased. It means we did not get the full amount of rice. Did they start cutting our ration? We heard that if NGOs have no money, they will cut our rice (Female refugee)

Refugees live in difficult conditions and have nothing much to eat. We should get the full amount of rice distribution. Otherwise it is not enough for us (Female refugee)

Why do we get the pen without the ink? We cannot use it (Male refugee)

There are still ongoing challenges for achieving food security in the shelters. Even though NGOs try to promote agricultural projects through linking vocational training projects to community-based production for food safety-net programmes, all studied shelters are crowded and did not have enough space to do so. Moreover, the limited number of trainees that can participate in each training course cannot meet the needs of refugees. Agriculture training courses take many months or years to complete, thus waiting periods are long and refugees sometimes lose interest. Some refugees would like to raise chickens but have heard that this has been prohibited due to the Bird flu pandemic.

Some service activities still follow the old model of relief, rather than a development model. This may be related to the current transition period and the need for more time to design relevant and appropriate activities so to encourage refugee self-reliance.

NGO field workers walk to distribute Sarong to displaced persons. The question is why they do not promote displaced people to produce it by weaving it. Because it may be more expensive? (Thai authority).

12.4 Stakeholder Relationships, Communication and Collaboration: Consideration of Expectations

The roles of various stakeholders in this protracted situation are inextricably linked. Thus, there is an absolute need for improved communication and collaboration among stakeholders in order to collectively identify appropriate durable solutions for displaced persons. None of the suggested solutions can be effectively or sustainably implemented without the support of all stakeholder groups, especially the RTG. Opportunities for dialogue must be created to improve understanding among actors across the board, but achievement of this first demands better awareness and sensitivity towards the cultural context of the border situation and the organisational cultures of those involved.

It would appear that donor attempts to engage the RTG have been largely unsuccessful to date, causing some to attempt to seek unilaterally to change in the nature of assistance in the camps. Take, for example, the withdrawal and reallocation of relief funds to target specific development projects. Without effective communication, this policy transition has been perceived as impulsive, forceful and an abandonment of a commitment to supporting basic needs in the camps. Regardless of whether this is an accurate interpretation of the policy agenda, this sort of bold approach has led to miscommunication and the alienation of certain assistance partners.

This highlights a lack of cultural sensitivity, both towards the Thai context and organisationally, considering the breadth of actors involved in delivering assistance. Over pressure from foreign countries to direct policy down a certain path, or else, will not succeed in garnering the RTG's support.

Instead, as many stakeholders remarked in interview, working within the Thai context requires devoting time to building relationships that support ongoing communication flows, rather than limiting interactions to one-off official business meetings. It is important to identify common ground, to work together positively on areas of shared concern before moving forward to addressing more complex issues with a diversity of opinion.

Consensus exists that mutual understanding will be better facilitated via a forum with representation from all stakeholders, donors, NGOs, INGOs and the various agencies of the RTG. So at what point do donor, NGO and RTG policy goals converge? Donors whose assistance priorities greatly differed did agree that education and health are the areas in which common ground can be forged with the RTG. Engaging the Ministries of Education (MOE) and Public Health (MOPH) to work with the NSC and MOI could create opportunities to allow displaced children to travel safely to study in Thai schools or to better integrate health services with the local community to avoid parallel systems and the duplication of effort.

Despite current frustrations, the only way for any solutions to be truly durable is for stakeholders to communicate and cooperate. While it will not solve all differences of opinion, attention to cultural context and the application of a considered approach which does not raise the defences of any one party will greatly improve the collaborative environment among stakeholders. Finding areas of shared concern to address in the first instance is important for incremental change, which may pave the way for further cooperation.

12.5 Resettlement, Repatriation and Local Integration: The Remaining Challenges for Effective Intervention Mechanisms

12.5.1 Resettlement

Many challenges remain to ensure effective intervention mechanisms. One such challenge is the current lack of a PAB process. This has a direct effect on the availability of the resettlement option for refugees. There is no avenue for verifying whether the people coming into the camps are really refugees. Since there is no means for the authorities to identify people who could be resettled in third countries, the resettlement option is unfeasible at this point.

Without a PAB process, there is also no means of controlling the influx of people into the camps. At present, any person who crosses the border from Myanmar and joins the camp is considered a refugee and is, therefore, entitled to the goods and services provided within the camps. Despite the difficult conditions in the camps, it is still preferable to the conditions in their home country and forms a fairly significant pull factor. Without the ability to target goods and services to those in greatest need, the NGOs working directly in the camps are burdened with providing goods and services to everybody.

Another challenge for the resettlement option is its direction as opinion varies among actors about it should continue or end due to its potential as a pull factor.

12.5.2 Repatriation

Almost all of the respondents do not perceive repatriation to be a viable solution at this point in time. It will only become viable when the conditions in Myanmar improve considerably such that its citizens do not live in fear and with the threat of violence. Respondents from donor countries cite that the Myanmar problem is an ASEAN concern and suggest its neighbours should have a stronger hand in pushing Myanmar for reforms. But the current hands-off position of ASEAN means this will not happen in the near future.

12.5.3 Local Integration

The number of restrictions placed on the shelters effectively makes them closed camps. This is congruent with Thai national security concerns that are at the forefront of RTG refugee policy agenda and in line with its latent policy to limit or stop the mainstreaming of refugees into local Thai communities. But all respondents cite these constraints as a major stumbling block in encouraging service integration where refugees can access basic services such as health and education through the Thai system as well as access some opportunities to earn a living. An easing, not lifting, of some of the restrictions would go a long way in the scaling up of NGO interventions as well as provide opportunities for collaborations between donor countries and the RTG at the policy and strategic level. An avenue that could be explored is the formulation of a comprehensive migration policy. This policy would include a PAB process that would effectively screen refugees entering the Thai border, as well as a framework for service integration and restrictions on the movements of the refugees that are screened in into the Thai workplace.

References

Lee, Chen Chen; Glaister, I., 2005: *Burmese Asylum Seekers in Thailand: Still Nowhere to Turn*; at: http://www.fmreview.org/FMRpdfs/FMR30/33-34.pdf.

Napaumporn, B., 2008: *Monitoring the Implementation of Human Rights with International Mechanisms in Thailand: Human Rights Situations in Lessons Learned on Human Rights and Statelessness*; at: http://gotoknow.org/blog/bongkot-humanrights-and-statelessness-eng/259676.

TBBC, 2005: *Programme Report, July–December 2005 including emergency funding appeal for 2006* (Bangkok: TBBC).

TBBC, 2010a: *Programme Report, January–June 2010* (Bangkok: TBBC).

TBBC, 2010b: *Programme Report, July–December 2010* (Bangkok: TBBC).

UNHCR, 2010: *2010 UNHCR country operations profile—Thailand Working Environment*; at: http://www.unhcr.org/cgi-bin/texis/vtx/page?page=49e489646.

Chapter 13
Conclusions and Recommandations

Dares Chusri, Tarina Rubin, Ma. Esmeralda Silva, Jason D. Theede, Sunanta Wongchalee and Patcharin Chansawang

Abstract The root cause of this issue remains unresolved; the conflict within Myanmar. At the same time, there are signs of change in Myanmar, with the release of Aung San SuuKyi and the increasing engagement of ASEAN and the wider international community. Donors and funders are urged to maintain their support for now, and to increase pressure through trade and other links to make Myanmar a safe place for repatriation. The agencies are encouraged to continue moving from emergency response to developmental programmes, including within Myanmar. Collaboration on solutions, such as CCSDPT/UNHCR's 5-year plan, is encouraged as long as all options are considered, not just local integration. The RTG must continue to be flexible, and to see strategies to encourage self-reliance of the displaced persons as preparation for eventual repatriation of the majority once Myanmar is free of conflict.

Keywords Ethnic conflict · Myanmar · ASEAN · 5-Year plan · Self-reliance · Repatriation

This part has provided a range of perspectives on the roles of donors, international organisations, non-governmental organisations and UN agencies in providing humanitarian assistance to the displaced persons in shelters along the Thailand–Myanmar border. It has examined the rationale behind international intervention, funding policies and organisational mandates; implementation strategies and the dynamics of cooperation among stakeholders; as well as the operating environment and impacts for effective intervention. Findings from both secondary data

D. Chusri (✉) · T. Rubin · Ma. E. Silva · J. D. Theede · S. Wongchalee · P. Chansawang
Asian Research Center for Migration, Institute of Asian Studies, Chulalongkorn University, 3rd floor, Prachadhipok Rambhai-Barni Building, Bangkok 10330, Thailand
e-mail: dares_c@hotmail.com

T. Rubin
e-mail: tarina.Rubin@gmail.com

P. Vungsiriphisal et al. (eds.), *Humanitarian Assistance for Displaced Persons from Myanmar*, SpringerBriefs in Environment, Security, Development and Peace 17,
DOI: 10.1007/978-3-319-02795-1_13,

analysis and quantitative and qualitative field study were consolidated and summarised. Based on this, practical and realistic recommendations are provided for policy options to reach durable solution for displaced persons in temporary shelters along Thai–Myanmar border.

13.1 Conclusions

13.1.1 Root Causes

Internal conflict in Myanmar between ethnic minority groups and the Myanmar government has been ongoing with no sign of peaceful, mutual agreement since 1984. The result of continuing human rights violations due to this conflict has been massive flows of ethnic minority groups leaving their homelands and fleeing persecution from the Myanmar government and seeking asylum in Thailand. These people have not only lost their land, becoming displaced, but also become stateless persons upon seeking asylum in Thailand. Temporary shelters along Thai–Myanmar border were designated their temporary home, but in reality encampment of more than 25 years is too long to be temporary. The prolonged confinement of displaced persons from Myanmar in temporary shelters and the restrictions imposed on them have not only affected their socio-psychological well-being but have also increased their dependence on external assistance. For those who have long left their homes, the chance for a safe and dignified return home is elusive; their hometowns remain only in bitter and aggrieved memories. Those who were born in the shelters have no past and future, only current life in the shelter. All displaced persons inside the temporary shelters have lost the opportunity for self-determination.

13.1.2 Funding Policy: Constraints and Impacts

Donor aid policy has been gradually shifting towards *linking relief and development* (LRRD) since 2007. The EC has started scaling down EU contributions to the Burmese displaced persons camps in Thailand. While the lack of financial commitment from donors to support multiyear funding and the realignment from emergency aid to a developmental model yield many challenges, the opportunity for self-reliance among displaced persons is entirely unsupported by the RTG policy. Whether aid flows will trend upwards or downwards in the next year cannot be predicted, as most donor countries stated that their assistance contributions rely on approval from their cabinet or congress. Moreover, some donor countries are still slowly recovering from recent economic crisis and have not committed to any increase in support. Donor fatigue is not only caused by these factors, but also mainly due to the lack of progress and a perception of little outcome for the money injected into the shelters. As the process is annual, this makes development planning very difficult as NGOs cannot predict what funds it will have at its disposal. As such, engagement in areas that require multiyear commitments, such as development and rehabilitation for returning displaced persons populations, are very difficult (Loescher and Milner 2006; UNHCR 2007). Funding shortages may also affect food security.

13.1.3 RTG Policy: Constraints and Impacts

Together with long influxes of Indochinese displaced persons, Thailand has had much experience in dealing with displaced people. The RTG policy mandate has not change since the beginning, premised upon temporary asylum and repatriation for displaced persons, preventing new influxes and restrictions on movement. Despite this, in practice the RTG seems somewhat more flexible and acts according to each situation. Policy change may only eventuate through the alignment of multiple factors, including those that relate not only to displaced persons. For example, in some instances, change develops from other internal Acts which confer protection to everyone in Thailand, such as rights of the child on birth certificate and education. According to RTG policy, the local integration strategy is not possible, but these most recent developments mean that refugees who born in the camps are eligible for birth certificates from the Thai government.

Despite the RTG providing support to displaced persons in term of encouraging the initiatives of development programmers on health, education and vocational training, as proposed by NGOs, much remains to be done. First, RTG policies remain opaque and access to information on clearly directed policies for long-term solutions for displaced persons is difficult. This, of course, rekindles other stakeholders' suspicion of the government's commitment. Sometimes, though not always, this lack of transparency stems from traditional Thai bureaucratic attitudes of secrecy and in sharing information or concerns about *burden shifting*. Second, there is still a gap in the donor–host government relationship that may affect cooperation for durable solutions.

Although Thailand has not ratified the 1951 Refugee Convention, the nation has already ratified many core international human rights treaties in the UN system: CEDAW, CRC, ICCPR, ICESCR, CERD and CAT. As a signatory, Thailand is *legally bound* as the state party to apply those international laws domestically. It is obvious that Thailand has not yet fulfilled the legal requirements of those ratified international standards, though there have been some changes.

13.1.4 Role of International Organisations

Within CCSDPT practice, administrative development is already in place in camp and project management by displaced persons. NGOs continue to be involved in the shelters under the same mandate that has not changed since the start; their core philosophy is humanitarian action and aid for people in need or those most vulnerable. Some of them expressed the view that the displaced persons situation is still a *protracted emergency* because of the potential for large numbers of displaced persons to continue to cross the border is quite likely as long as the instability inside Myanmar persists. This is in contrast with other organisations who perceived the emergency situation to be over, as so much time has passed and even though there are still some new asylum seekers arriving shelters. However, considering the number is not massive, this can be seen more as a *protracted displaced people situation*, rather than an emergency. However, most NGO programme activities have also gradually changed to a development model. NGO operations are constrained by RTG policy and funding requirements from donors. UNHCR also has to cooperate with RTG and work under RTG policy.

13.1.4.1 Pilot Projects

Donors are supporting the CCSDPT and the UNHCR in their efforts to implement a 5-year strategic plan to find durable solutions to expand the displaced persons' self-reliance. Pilot projects have already started in most camps in fields such as vocational training, livelihood opportunities and health care integration (Eick n.d.). Most of the pilot projects are small scale and subsistence level implementation within the shelters only. At the time of writing, these pilot projects are still going on, and the results of the programme evaluation should provide lessons learned for further expansion.

13.1.4.2 Five-Year Strategic Plan

UNHCR and CCSDPT have developed a 5-year strategic plan to provide strategic direction to durable solutions for displaced persons. It is selective durable solution that tends to focus on local integration rather than a comprehensive solution. The obvious constraint is the ambitious expectation to think that the camps would be closed immediately. This needs to be a phased process with systems first in place.

Surprisingly, little discussion and attention has been paid to repatriation for displaced persons at both national and international level, with a corresponding lack of investment in strengthening the process of initiative planning. Some say that it is not the time to think about repatriation as conflict and the human rights violation situation are ongoing inside Myanmar. However, if following 25 years of protracted refugee situation is not the time to talk about, when is? The occasion of spontaneous peace or democratic is very rare without the international cooperation. Although repatriation is not an option at the moment, it is an obligation and collective international responsibility to pressure the Myanmar regime to create a good, safe environment that people can return to in Myanmar. The ongoing phenomenon of the influx of displaced persons from Myanmar has formed a protracted displaced persons situation which will remain forever if the root cause of the problem is ignored by all stakeholders. How long do we have to wait for the decline of protracted internal conflict situation inside Myanmar? Is it time for repatriation to feature on the international agenda?

13.1.4.3 Stakeholder Relationship: Communication Gaps and Different Cultural Background of Organisation

Relationship between donors and the RTG vary from donor to donor, depending on their approach, frequency of communication, manner, cultural sensitivity and equality. A lack of effective communication between donor groups themselves, between donors and RTG and donor and NGOs prohibits information sharing and coordination process. Even though there is donor meeting forum, not every donor participates in the meeting. There is no official forum meeting between donor and RTG. Between RTG and CCSDPT, most of NGOs working at the field level will participate in annual meeting with the MOI once a year only, while they deal with local authorities on a day-to-day basis and to drive more personnel relationships.

There is lack of a neutral communication forum: donors and RTG have no direct contact with each other and there are no other forums to engage between them. There is an expectation from some donors to see the RTG's international cooperation and funding committed to the displaced persons but there is none in place. RTG avoids engagement by declining invitations or sending low level representation to high level meetings. While TBBC hosts retreats with UNHCR/CCSPDT and RTG, donors are not invited. Some thus view that those existing forums are not neutral as they are led by organisations with their own agenda, and this is why some people choose not to participate.

13.2 Recommendations

Stakeholders in this displaced people situation should respond to a range of areas:

13.2.1 Donors

13.2.1.1 A Response that Covers All Categories of LRRD Interventions

In keeping with principles of good humanitarian donorship, donors should together ensure that adequate funding is available to respond to the full spectrum of LRRD needs in the shelters and in planning. Commitment to multiyear funding support that aligns with development plans is required. The funding patterns of donors should reflect their humanitarian action responsibilities. If this condition proves difficult to achieve due to the conflicting foreign policy interests of each government, a coordinating body should be appointed to adopt a neutral role, independent from any influential organisation, to coordinate among the donor group to produce a multiyear funding plan. Within this plan, each donor can fill a specific funding gap. A Partnership Program Agreement such as this should support a Multiyear Grants Scheme for LRRD projects of up to 3–5 years duration at least. This will require a commitment from donors to providing sufficient, ongoing funding to support the period of transition from relief to development programming, designed to develop the self-reliance of displaced persons. The donor group should identify categories of intervention in development with concordant principles, relevant to the CCSDPST strategy and with clear objectives to guide intervention. Donors should also reach agreement on each responsibility to ensure a response to all LRRD interventions proposed by CCSDPT.

13.2.1.2 A Holistic and Comprehensive Approach

Donors should approach displacement holistically, in both the original and host countries and in both the emergency and development phases. Donors should recognise displaced persons and internally displaced persons (IDPs) as part of the same dynamic of forced migration, while providing for different responses, vulnerabilities and needs.

13.2.2 RTG

> When you wear a robe, you become the symbol of the Dharma, just as when you put on a police officer's uniform, you become a symbol of the law, or you sit behind a teacher's desk you become the symbol of authority. This can be a danger, but it also gives you the opportunity to think about how to work together with people to create a code of ethics in a community (ThichNhatHanh 2010).

The RTG should disclose clear policy direction with regard to the self-reliance or development of displaced persons and provide suggestions or recommendations on the feasibility of project operation. The RTG should consider the current protracted refugee situation and explore ways to adopt international law, through all ratified treaties, for displaced persons' development. The PAB system should be reactivated as a priority to work more effectively in screening and determining displaced persons status so that new asylum seekers can access protection and basic needs and services, including resettlement options in a timely manner. The result of pre-screening pilot projects in four temporary shelters should be disclosed soon to demonstrate public accountability in a project conducted since 2009.

The RTG is encouraged to be more responsive to attempts by the donor and NGO community to collaborate on issues pertaining to displaced persons in the temporary shelters. Providing further clarity on the roles of different RTG agencies and individuals is an important first step to better engagement and improving understanding and cooperation among the stakeholder community. Moreover, human rights concepts and principles should be promoted to the relevant authorities to apply in practice. An action plan for displaced persons development also should be developed. This is in the spirit of the Thailand National Security Policy and the ratification by the RTG of various associated declarations and conventions on human rights. Therefore, policy formulation of a new Management Strategy for the Problem of the Status and Rights of Individuals should identify strategies and measures for development of displaced persons in terms of self-reliance at least. As the host government, the RTG together with partners such as CCSDPT, UNHCR and UNDP, must be open to participation based on the evidence and scientific research which proposes viable alternatives and identifies the need for common/mutual agreement and sincere participation in strategic planning to develop the self-reliance of displaced persons. This participative process is significant to all partners in that they will have a constructive working forum and an opportunity to together translate policy into implementation and sustainable practice.

The RTG also should lobby ASEAN countries to establish a peace dialogue with Myanmar in order to facilitate sustainable durable solutions in the future.

13.2.3 UNHCR/CCSDPT

These bodies are prime movers to facilitate coordination, consultation and collaboration with donors and high level of RTG representatives to obtain mutual agreement on development strategies for displaced persons, particularly the development of economic self-sufficiency. A concrete, realistic and comprehensive plan is needed which addresses short-term, medium term and long-term planning.

Regular meetings should be scheduled between key executive stakeholders, donors, NSC, MOI, MOFA and other relevant government agencies, at the policy level to promote communication and a positive, collaborative working environment.

13.2.3.1 Comprehensive Plan

CCSDPT/UNHCR and donors need to undertake a strategic reassessment of the appropriate mechanisms for dealing with the long-term interests of the RTG in the displaced persons' issue, including the extent and feasibility of economic self-reliance in line with funding support in place. This will also require the engagement of civil society in advocacy with the RTG, with appropriate Thai and state culture representatives in discussions to support policy changes aimed at finding durable solutions. CCSDPT/UNHCR, donor and RTG should together determine the meeting agenda and provide close coordination and a transparent process, using the principles of partnership, and through a working group which comprises representatives of UNHCR/CCSDPT/UNDP and RTG. However, the extent to which these actors will work together in partnership remains a challenging question.

The strategic plan needs to balance and address all three options for durable solutions. Repatriation requires international cooperation to negotiate and advocate for peace building inside Myanmar. It requires a prime mover such as UNHCR to facilitate this process. Resettlement also should be addressed in terms of the agreement on policy direction needed from all partners; whether to sustain or end the programme if it is seen to create pull factors or brain-drain. If resettlement continues to be a viable and desired option, ongoing advocacy with third countries is needed.

Clarification and prioritisation are also required to determine the nature and extent of self-reliance and interventions. What changes are needed? What does the strategic plan seek to change—the overall situation, conditions, attitudes or behaviours? Who will instigate change—service providers, communities or individuals?

An *action plan* is also needed which will guide transformation of the strategic into practice. This will require mutual acceptance of the plan among actors and clear definition of key terminology, e.g. *local integration*. The action plan must include activities, assumptions, indicators, time frames, responsibilities and a budget. It must identify short, medium and long-term plans for advocacy at the international level to realise the three durable solutions; resettlement, self-reliance and repatriation.

13.2.3.2 Policy Formulation

Given that the timeframe of the actual *Thailand National Security Policy* and *Management Strategy for the Problem of the Status and Rights of Individuals* will end this year, these policies must be revised. CCSDPT, UNHCR and/or UNDP persons should more active in establishing a consultative forum with the office of the National Security Council and propose research results on the feasibility of displaced persons self-reliance to the RTG.

13.2.3.3 Pilot Projects

Programme evaluations are needed to assess outcomes and impacts on livelihoods, including the relevance, effectiveness, efficiency and sustainability of projects. Results will be used as a guide for further project design, planning and expansion.

13.2.4 UNHCR

The peace building process inside Myanmar requires the diplomatic efforts of the international community. The challenge is how to ensure the sensitivity of national and international human rights bodies and their continued active participation in finding solutions to the protracted displaced persons situation. Negotiation and dialogue to bring durable peace to Myanmar must be facilitated. The issue of the repatriation of displaced persons to Myanmar should be addressed in the international agenda to solicit international support and collaboration in conflict resolution and easing human rights violations inside Myanmar. UNHCR should be the lead agency involved in the peace negotiation process, as it is its experience and mandate to provide both international protection and solutions for displaced persons. This process needs strong leadership to engage and facilitate national, regional and international advocacy efforts, i.e. from the National Human Rights Commission (NHRC), ASEAN, UNHCR exe-com and the United Nations General Assembly.

13.2.5 All Actors

The results of this study suggest that trust and cooperative relationships between key actors is critical. Working with various partners demands sensitivity and a commitment to honouring the cultural integrity of those we work with. All stakeholders must be ethical in their approach to working with their partners and the displaced persons.

Displaced persons development processes are complex. Designing activities and making sound policy and funding decisions require constant engagement and need true cooperation from donors, RTG and NGOs. There is still a long way to go in making these diverse partnerships more effective and improving coordination mechanisms. A mutually acceptable resolution of the displaced persons issue must be a common goal of all partners. Donors and NGOs need to better coordinate with and solicit sincere cooperation from the RTG in order to achieve more effective intervention mechanisms and results.

There is a need for a forum of donors which meets at least annually with relevant RTG agencies. More channels for regular communication among the tripartite of RTG, donors and NGOs are needed, with sensitivity and respect for cultural orientation prioritised and interactions based on trust and optimistic views of each other. This demands increasing communication flows, improving mutual trust and establishing mechanisms for regular meetings, not just annual, to strengthen cooperation and communication between stakeholders.

A more positive working atmosphere will be better facilitated by adjusting the language of displacement and durable solutions to use positive, productive phrases rather than those with negative connotations: *responsibility sharing* rather than *burden shifting* or *burden sharing; partnership* and the application of partnership principles in working together; a mutually accepted definition of *local integration* which will inform its nature and extent; *displaced persons self-reliance* to replace *local integration* where it is the objective of development interventions. In some cases, *integration* can be used without reference to local integration, as in *integration with the existing service*.

References

Eick, M., (n.d.): *Thailand—World Refugee Day 20 June 2010: Refugees in Thailand: Another 25 years in limbo?* at: http://ec.europa.eu/echo/aid/stories/asia30_en.htm.

Loescher, G; Milner, J, 2006: *Protracted Refugee Situation in Thailand: Towards Solutions.* Presentation to the Foreign Correspondents' Club of Thailand.

Loescher, G; Milner, J, 2007: *Protracted Refugee Situations: Causes, Consequences, and Trends.* Paper presented at the RSC 25th Anniversary Conference.

ThichNhatHanh, 2010: *A Safe Place. Workplace practice: A code of Ethics, Keeping the Peace.* Bangkok: DMG Books.

UNHCR, 2007: *Handbook for Emergencies: The Emergency Preparedness and Response Section.* Geneva: UNHCR. at: http://www.reliefweb.int/rw/lib.nsf/db900sid/AMMF-75TFLQ/$file/unhcr-feb2007pdf?openelement.

Appendix A
Context of Study Areas

Ban Mai NaiSoi, Mae Hong Son Province

The shelter was first set up in 1989 in Karenni state and has been moved many times. It moved across the border into Thailand in 1993 but was forced back into Myanmar in 1995. After the Karenni had agreed to ceasefire with the Burmese Army, the residents moved to the current area. In 2002, the Thai authority consolidated the Karenni shelters in Mae Hong Son by closing Ban NaiSoi, formerly Site 3, which was located 5 km down the hill from Site 1. The shelter was given the name Ban Mai NaiSoi or Site 1,[1] consists of Ban Tractor and Ban Kwai.

The shelter is situated 3 km from the border, 26 km from Mae Hong Son, divided into two zones: Ban Pang Kwai and Ban Pang Tractor (Table A.1).

The majority of Ban Mai NaiSoi population is 94 % Kayah/Karenni ethnic, which comprise of various sub-groups with different dialects. Non-Karenni groups are Karen 3 %, Shan 3 %, Burman 1 %, Kachin 1 % and Mon 1 %. The religious beliefs of the population are Christian 48 %, Buddhist 42 % and Animist 10 % (MOI).

There are 13 primary schools, four elementary schools and two high schools. There is also a special school called "accelerating school" for those who recently arrived and have had no educational background in their home state. The schools

Table A.1 Population

Camp	UNHCR/MOI registered population February 2011[a]	TBBC verified caseload February 2011[b]		
		Female	Male	Total
Ban Mai NaiSoi	12,117	6,925	7,480	14,405

Source TBBC, February 2011

[a] UNHCR figure includes registered, pending PAB and some students but excludes new arrivals

[b] The TBBC verified caseload includes all persons verified as living in the camps and eligible for ration, registered or not registered with UNHCR (including outside students). Rations are provided only to those personally attending distributions, actual feeding figures are typically 4 % lower than the caseload. It excludes all permanently out of camp

[1] There are four camps in Mae Hong Son: Ban Mai NaiSoi (Site 1), Ban Mae Surin (Site 2), Ban Mae La Oon and Ban Mae Ra Ma Luang.

P. Vungsiriphisal et al. (eds.), *Humanitarian Assistance for Displaced Persons from Myanmar*, SpringerBriefs in Environment, Security, Development and Peace 17,
DOI: 10.1007/978-3-319-02795-1, © The Author(s) 2014

are open from 8.30 am to 3.15 pm every day. The language used in instruction is Karenni in primary school and Burmese in elementary and high school. Though Karenni is considered to be a sub-group of Karen, its language is a little similar to Karen. There are many ethnic groups in the camp such as Paku, Kayah, Pa-O, etc.

Mae La camp, Tak Province

The shelter was first established in 1984 near the border for approximately 1,000 asylum seekers from Karen state after the Burmese Army launched its attack and successfully broke through the Karen front lines and maintained in the area. Soon the shelter was moved from the border to the current area (Zone C). After the fall of the Manerplaw (headquarters of Karen ethnic insurgents), the Burmese Army and Democratic Karen Buddhist Army (DKBA, a faction of the Karen armed groups which split off and aligned itself with the Burmese Army in 1994) launched several attacks to smaller shelters closer to the border. The RTG decided to consolidate those small shelters and transferred the people to Mae La, making it the biggest shelter of nine settlements.

Mae La shelter was under attack by DKBA in 1997 and a mortar shell landed on section A of the shelter in March, 1998 and had caused security concern and tension to the shelter from the threats the attack.

Mae La shelter is located in Ban Mae Oak Hoo, Mae La sub-district, Tha Song Yang district. The area is mostly clay and has a stream called Huay Oak Hoo, which passes through most parts of the camp. Huay Oak Hoo is also the main water source for the people in the camp. The shelter runs along national road number 105, between Mae Sot and Mae Sarieng (in Mae Hong Son Province). The shelter backs up to a mountain ridge which runs along the border with Myanmar. It is 8 km from the border and 60 km from Mae Sot District. The shelter area is approximately 1,150 Rais or 1.8 km^2, divided into three zones (A–C) (Table A.2).

The people living in the shelter can be divided into three groups as: persons who have been accepted by the Provincial Admission Board (PAB) as "people who flee from fighting in Myanmar" and have registered with UNHCR; persons who were rejected by PAB, awaiting to be repatriated but pending as the conflict situation in Myanmar still continues and persons awaiting submission to the PAB.

The population of 49.5 % female and 50.5 % is divided into four age groups: 14 % of children under 5 years, 35 % of 5–17 years, 47 % of 18–59 years and 4 % of elderly over 59 years. The major ethnic is Karen 97 %, Burman 2 % and 1 % of

Table A.2 Populations

Camp	UNHCR/MOI registered population February 2011	TBBC verified caseload February 2011		
		Female	Male	Total
Mae La	29,945	22,608	23,090	45,698

Source TBBC, February 2011

other ethnics. The population religious beliefs in Mae La are Buddhist 38 %, Christian 47 %, Muslim 13 % and Animists 2 %. There are 24 Christian churches (15 Baptist, 1 Anglican, 6 Seventh Day Adventist and 1 Roman Catholic), 4 Buddhist monasteries and 5 Muslim mosques in the shelter.

The shelter has a total of 26 schools, including 5 high schools, 5 middle schools and 16 primary schools. There is one school teaching Thai run by an MOI Volunteer officer, as part of the RTG policy.

Tham Hin Shelter, Ratchaburi Province

Suan Phung District has arranged two preliminary reception centres, one is Huay Sot at Moo 3, Suan Phung sub-district, another is Huay Khokmoo at Ban Boewi, Moo 4, Tanaosri sub-district, to shelter the influx of Karen people fleeing from fighting between the Burmese army and the ethnic Karen fighters along Thai–Myanmar border in March 1997.

In May, 1997, Surasi Task Force established Tham Hin Temporary Shelter to accommodate people relocated from both Huay Sot and Huay Khokmoo. Later on the task force started to relocate people from other shelters into Tham Hin. Later in 2001, a new zone (Zone 4) was expanded to receive the remainder of political asylum seekers from the closure of UNHCR Maneeloy shelter in the same province. The closed location to the border has led to security tension though there have never been real attacks. In March 2005, about 400 UNHCR Persons of Concern (POC) residing in urban areas, were transferred to Tham Hin as part of the RTG's policy.

Tham Hin shelter is located at Ban Tham Hin, Moo 5, Suan Phung sub-district, Suan Phung District, Ratchaburi Province, with 44 rais or 70,400 m^2 of land. The landscape is mountainous and the area is surrounded by mountains. It is called Hupkratorn, which is 10 km away from the border, 270 km from Bangkok. There is a stream called Nong-Khun flowing across the area (Table A.3).

The population consists of 51 % female and 49 % male and can be broken down into age groups: 15 % of children under 5 years, 36 % of 5–17 years, 44 % of 18–59 years and 5 % of elderly over 59 years. The major ethnic is Karen as of 98 % and 2 % of other ethnics.

Table A.3 Population

Camp	UNHCR/MOI registered population 28 February 2011	TBBC verified caseload 28 February 2011		
		Female	Male	Total
ThamHin	4,293	3,886	3,696	7,582

Source TBBC, February 2011

Appendix B
List of Key Informants

Position/Organisation	Period of interview (m/y)
Royal Thai Government	
• Ministry of Education	
- Deputy Secretary General, Office of Basic Education Commission	10/10–11/10
- Officer, Office of Non-formal and Informal Education, Office of the Permanent Secretary	11/10
• Ministry of Foreign Affairs	
- Director, Social Division, International Organisation Department	11/10
- Director, East Asian Department	12/10
• Ministry of Human Security and Social Development	
- Child Protection Unit	9/10
• Ministry of Interior	
- Director, Foreign Affairs Division, Office of Permanent Secretary for Interior	6/10
- Chief, Policy Planning Section, Operation Centre for Displaced	10/10
- Person (OCDP)	8/10
- Officers, Policy Planning Section, OCDP	8/10
- Officers, NGO Coordination Section, OCDP	8/10, 12/11
- Officer, Department of Provincial Administration	10/11
- District officer, Maung district, Mae Hong Son (MHS) Province	8/10
- District officer, Suan Phung District, Ratchaburi Province	7/10
- District officer, Tha Song Yang District, Tak Province	9/10–1/11
- Provincial officer, Tak Province	8/10
- Senior Deputy District Officer, Maung District, MHS Province	10/10
- Senior Deputy District Officer, Suan Phung District, Ratchaburi	8/10
- Senior Deputy District Officer, Tha Song Yang District,	9/10–11/10
- Territorial Voluntary Defence Corps, Tha Song Yang District	8/10
- Territorial Voluntary Defence Corps, MHS	7/10
- Territorial Security Defence Corps, Suan Phung	7/10
- Head, Local Administration Office, Suan Phung	8/10
- Local Administration Officer, NaiSoi Sub-District	9/10
- Head, Local Administration Office, Tha Song Yang Sub-District	12/10

(continued)

P. Vungsiriphisal et al. (eds.), *Humanitarian Assistance for Displaced Persons from Myanmar*, SpringerBriefs in Environment, Security, Development and Peace 17,
DOI: 10.1007/978-3-319-02795-1,

(continued)

Position/Organisation	Period of interview (m/y)
• Ministry of Justice	
- Officer, Rights and Freedom Protection Division	
• Ministry of Public Health	
- Director, Strategy and Policy Planning Bureau	11/10
- Deputy Director, Mae Sot Hospital	9/0
- Health Staffs, Suan Phung Health Station	7/10
• Ministry of Defence	
- Border Affairs	12/10
• National Secretary Council (NSC)	
- Secretary General, Office of NSC	11/10
- Director, Internal Security Affairs Division	9/10
- Officers, Internal Security Affairs Division	9/10–10/10
- Officer, Intelligent Unit	11/10–12/10
- Humanitarian Organisations	
- Field Staff, COERR, Mae La	9/10
- Field Staff, IRC, MHS	8/10
- Field Staff, World Education, Mae Sod	9/10
- Field Staff, ZOA	9/2010
- Deputy Director, TBBC	10/10
Displaced Persons	
- Camp Committees, Tham Hin	7/10
- Karen Women Organisation, Tham Hin	7/10
- Head Teacher, Tham Hin	7/10
- Camp Committees, Ban Mai NaiSoi	8/10
- Karen Womens Organisation, Ban Mai NaiSoi	8/10
- Camp Committees, Mae La	9/10
- Karen Women Organisation, Mae La	9/10
- Youth Organisation, Mae La	9/10
UN and International Organisation	
- IOM, Regional Programme Coordinator for Resettlement and Voluntary Return	6/10
- UNHCR, Senior Programme Officer	10/10
- UNDP	10/10
Private Sector	
- Committee, Tak Chamber of Commerce	9/10

Appendix C
Displaced Person Status Determination Procedure

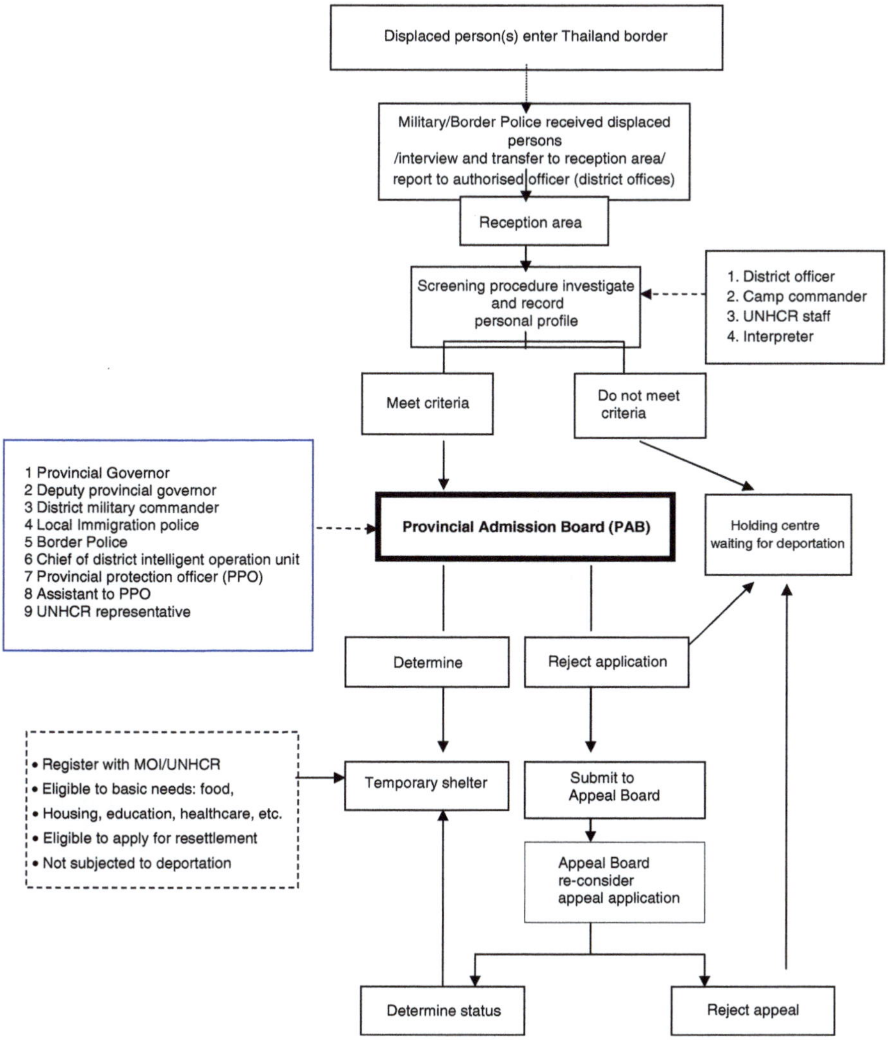

P. Vungsiriphisal et al. (eds.), *Humanitarian Assistance for Displaced Persons from Myanmar*, SpringerBriefs in Environment, Security, Development and Peace 17,
DOI: 10.1007/978-3-319-02795-1, © The Author(s) 2014

Appendix D
Detailed Descriptions of Study Areas

Tham Hin, Suan Phung District, Ratchaburi Province

Tham Hin is the southernmost camp in Thailand, also the camp with the most cramped living conditions. Tham Hin is situated about 10 km from the border with Myanmar. It is 53 km (1 h) from Ratchaburi Province, 295 km (4.5 h) from Sanklaburi District, Kanchanaburi Province and 270 km from Bangkok (3 h). The camp covers an area of 44 rai[2] or 70,400 m^2. Tham Hin was formed in May 1997 following offensives by the Burmese military in Tenasserim Division, which caused extensive displacement of civilians across the Thailand–Burma border. Three temporary sites were established for the displaced persons: Huay Sot and Bor Wii in Suan Phung District, Ratchaburi Province and Phu Muang in Dan Makham Tia District, Kanchanaburi Province. Agreement was reached in April 1997 to move the three sites to the current camp location, and this was completed 2 months later with an initial population of 7,202. In December 2001, with the closure of the UNHCR camp for political displaced persons at Maneeloy, a new zone (Zone 4) was created for the remaining residents. In March 2005, about 400 Bangkok-based POC who were registered with the UNHCR were transferred to Tham Hin as part of the RTG's policy of ensuring all asylum seekers from Burma were based in camps, rather than urban areas.

The camp has never been attacked, though Burmese Army troop movements in the area have sometimes led to increased security awareness [Tham Hin: Thailand Burma Border Consortium (TBBC), n.d.]. There are 2,251 households in the camp. The camp population totalled 7,531 persons as of November 2010 (Burmese border displaced person, 2010), 51 % male and 49 % female. Residents are divided into five age groups: 21–65 years (41 %), 6–18 years (35 %), 5 and under (16 %), 18–21 years (6 %) and over 65 years (2 %).

The majority of the camp are Karen ethnicity (95 %) and divided into two religions: Christian (90 %) and Buddhist (9 %). Karen is the native language (94 %); however for those over the age of 18, several other languages are spoken:

[2] Rai is a unit of area, equal to 1,600 m^2 (40×40 m), used for measuring land area in Thailand. Retrieved from http://www.siam-legal.com/realestate/thailand-convert-rai-square-meters.php.

DOI: 10.1007/978-3-319-02795-1,

Burmese (63 %), Thai (30 %) and other (2 %). The majority of the people living in the camp (aged 18 years and over) have a primary level education (41 %), while some completed secondary school (35 %) and others were never educated (22 %).

The majority of the employed camp population are involved in fishing, farming or other agricultural activities. Involvement in the education sector is the next most common, either as professional teachers or trainers involved in adult education within the camp. There are also a number of skilled labourers, including tailors, interpreters, mechanics and other professional services. A large number of camp residents also have experience in the health sector, either as medics or nurses, or as trainers or water and sanitation workers. The remainder of the employed population work as daily-hired labourers, performing various, mainly manual tasks.

The vast majority of the population has likely had exposure to television and radio but limited experience with modern public transportation or other modern conveniences. Most are aware of television, radio and the Internet; however, their actual use of such equipment may be limited. The most common technology used is radio, with many of the displaced persons listening to Burmese radio (UNHCR, n.d. cited in International Rescue Committee, n.d.).

Mae La Camp, Tak Province

Mae La camp is located in Ban Mae Oak Hoo, Mae La sub-district, Tha Song Yang district. The area is mostly clay and a stream called ‘Huay Oak Hoo’ passes through most parts of the camp. Huay Oak Hoo is also the main water source for the people in the camp. There are three zones, A–C, inside the camp. It is situated 8 km from the border and is about 57 km or 1 h from Mae Sot District. The camp covers an area of about 1,150 rai (Burmese border displaced person, 2010) or 1,840,000 m^2.

The camp was originally established in 1984 following the fall of the Karen National Union (KNU) base at Mae La, a Thai village on the border with a population of 1,100. Shortly afterward, due to security concerns, the camp was moved to the site where Zone C currently lies. After the fall of Manerplaw in January 1995, a number of camps were attacked in cross-border raids and the Thai authorities began to consolidate camps to improve security. Mae La was designated as the main consolidation camp in the area.

In April 1995, Mae La increased in size from 6,969 to 13,195 due to the closure of five camps to the north—Mae Ta Waw, Mae Salit, Mae Plu So, KlerKho and Kamaw Lay Kho—and the move of Huay Heng later that year. Over the following year, the camp doubled in size again to 26,629 as those lost in the move returned to the camp. In March 1997, some displaced persons were relocated here following the closure of Huai Bone camp (aka Don Pa Kiang) and again in February 1998 when Shoklo camp was closed. The camp was attacked in 1997 by DKBA troops with support from Burmese Army units. There have been no incursions since then, but a mortar shell landed in Section A5 in March 1998. Every dry season, the area becomes tense with concerns relating to camp security—threats of armed attack and/or attempts to burn the camp.

Mae La is considered as a centre of studies for displaced persons, thus the current population includes several thousand students who come to study (some from other camps but mostly from Myanmar). They are registered only as temporary inhabitants.

The Karen State situated opposite Mae La camp is very rural with no large settlements or infrastructure. The Karen National Liberation Army (KNLA) maintains its 7th Brigade Headquarters nearby, and there are several Burmese Army and Democratic Karen Buddhist Army outposts in the area (the DKBA is a faction of the KNLA which split off and aligned itself with the Burma Army in 1994) (Mae La: TBBC, n.d.).

As of November 2010, the camp population had reached 46,673 (Burmese border displaced person, 2010). They are divided into three groups: Persons who have been accepted by the PAB as people who are fleeing from fighting in Myanmar and have been registered with UNHCR. Their number totals 32,906; persons who have been rejected by PAB and should to repatriate to Myanmar as they did not flee from fighting. However, as the conflict in Myanmar has continued, they have not been able to return. This group accounts for 9,034 people and persons awaiting submission to the Board—137 people.

The largest age group is 18–59 year olds (47 %), followed by 5–17 year olds (35 %) and those less than 5 years (14 %). The majority are Karen (97 %) (Mae La: TBBC, n.d.).

Ban Mai NaiSoi Shelter, Mae Hong Son Province

Ban Mai NaiSoi shelter, also known as Camp 1, is situated 3 km from the border and 26 km (45 min) from Mae Hong Son (Ban Mai NaiSoi: TBBC, n.d.). The first camp here was set up in 1989 and has been moved many times. At one stage in August 1993, the camp was moved across the border into Myanmar but was forced back in July 1995. It was moved to its present location in March 1996. The camp consists of two zones divided by 1.5 km of protected forest; Ban Pang Kwai and Ban Pang Tractor.

In 2002, the Thai authorities made a decision to consolidate the Karenni camps in Mae Hong Son by closing Ban NaiSoi, formerly Camp 3, located 5 km down the hill from Camp 1. Consequently, all 4,421 displaced persons were forced to relocate by February 2003 to Camp 1 with logistical and technical support provided by the International Rescue Committee (IRC). The majority of displaced persons settled in the area of Ban Tractor. As of November 2010, there are 15,121 displaced persons living in the shelter (Burmese border displaced person, 2010).

The majority of the camp population is Karenni (94 %). There are many Karenni ethnic sub-groups in the camp such as Paku, Kayah and Pa-O. The largest age group are those 18–59 years (47 %), followed by 5–17 year olds (33 %) (Ban Mai NaiSoi: TBBC, n.d.). Both Christians and Buddhists live together in the shelter.

Appendix E
Details of Interviewees

Detailed Descriptions of the INGOs and UN Agencies Interviewees

Table E.1:

Table E.1 Interviewees: donors

Interviewees	Donors
Minister—Counsellor	Australian Embassy
The Project Team Leader and Programme Officer (Development)	Canadian Embassy
Head of Political Section/ DFID Political Officer	DFID, UK Embassy
Attache (Cooperation) Good Governance and Civil Society	European Union
1st Secretary, Political	Norwegian Embassy
Deputy Head of Mission Counsellor (Political) and Senior Programme Officer	Royal Danish Embassy
Political and Economic Affairs	Royal Netherland Embassy
Regional Humanitarian Aid Coordinator South-East Asia	Swiss Embassy
Deputy Displaced Persons Coordinator for SEA and Assistant Displaced Persons Coordinator for SEA	USA Embassy
Total 12 People	Total eight Donor Government one International Donor

Source The Authors

P. Vungsiriphisal et al. (eds.), *Humanitarian Assistance for Displaced Persons from Myanmar*, SpringerBriefs in Environment, Security, Development and Peace 17,
DOI: 10.1007/978-3-319-02795-1,

Table E.2 Interviewees: RTG

Interviewees	RTG organisations
1 High level	Foreign Affairs Division Office of the Permanent Secretary for Interior, MOI
2 Deputy Director Officers, 2 Senior Deputy District Chiefs (Senior Deputy Director Officer)	3 District Governors of 3 Targeted Temporary Shelters, Department of Provincial Administration, MOI
1 High level, 1 Officer	Operations Center for Displaced Persons (OCDP), MOI
2 High level, 4 Officers	National Security Council, Office of the Prime Minister
Total 12 People	Total 2 Ministries

Source The Authors

Table E.3 Interviewees: INGOs

Interviewees		INGOs, UN agencies
Bangkok	Studied shelters	
1 Executive	–	ARC
1 Executive, 1 Staff	2 Staff, 3 Field workers	COEER
1 Executive, 1 Staff	1 Staff	IRC
1 Executive	1 Field worker	JRS
2 Executives	–	TBBC
1 Executives	–	CCSDPT
2 Executive, 1 Staff	3 Field workers	ZOA
1 Senior Officer	–	IOM
2 Programme Specialists	–	UNDP
1 Senior Officer	–	UNHCR
1 Officer	–	WHO
Total 16 People	Total 10 People	Total 11 Organisations

Source The Authors

Focus Group Discussions and In-Depth Interviews with Displaced Persons (Tables E.2, E.3)

A total of 16 FGDs were conducted with 80 displaced persons: 40 female and 40 male in three selected temporary shelters from July to September 2010 (Table E.4).

IDIs were conducted with 18 displaced persons: nine female and nine male in the three targeted temporary shelters (Table E.5).

Table E.4 Focus group discussions with displaced persons

Date (2010)	Number of group interview			Number of interviewees			Temporary shelter
	F	M	Total	F	M	Total	
12–14 Jul	2	3	5	10	14	24	Tham Hin, Ratchaburi
9–10 Aug	2	2	4	10	10	15	Ban Mai NaiSoi, Mae Hong Son
1–3 Sep	4	3	7	20	16	36	Mae La, Tak
Total	8	8	16	40	40	80	3 Shelters

Source The Authors

Table E.5 In-depth interviews with displaced persons

Date (2010)	Number of interviewees		Temporary shelter
	F	M	
12–14 Jul	3	3	Tham Hin, Ratchaburi
9–10 Aug	3	3	Bann Mai NaiSoi, Mae Hong Sorn
1–3 Sep	3	3	Mae La, Tak
Total	9	9	3 Targeted Temporary Shelters

Source The Authors

Appendix F
Displaced Person Respondent Characteristics

Four hundred forty four displaced persons respondents in three targeted temporary shelters were recruited in this study. 55.4 % (246 respondents) were female and 44.6 % (198 respondents) were male (Fig. F.1).

Mae La shelter hosts half of all respondents, with a further 25 % living in both Tham Hin and Ban Mai NaiSoi (Fig. F.2).

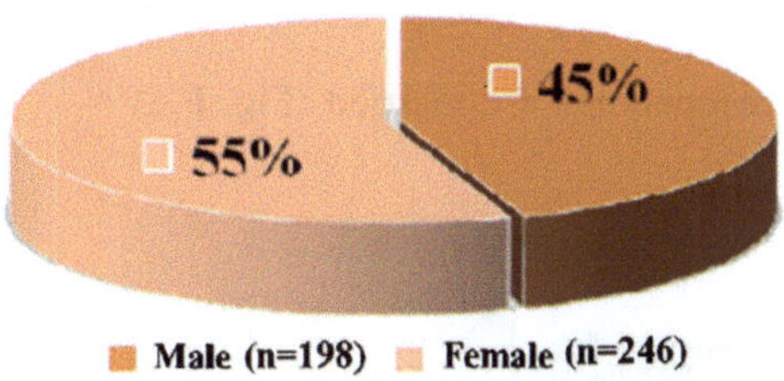

Fig. F.1 Respondents characteristics. *Source* The Authors

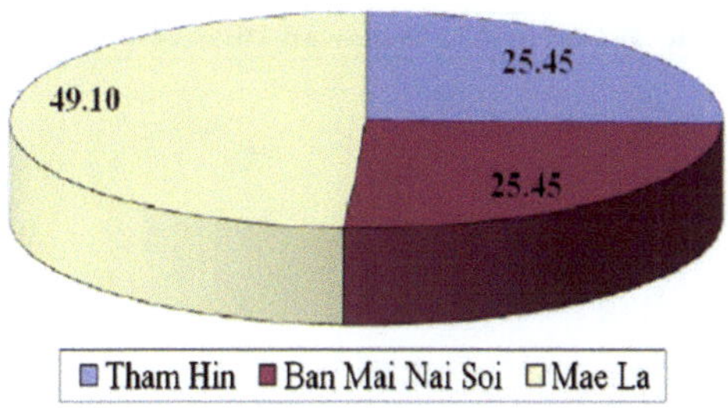

Fig. F.2 Resident of temporary shelter. *Source* The Authors

P. Vungsiriphisal et al. (eds.), *Humanitarian Assistance for Displaced Persons from Myanmar*, SpringerBriefs in Environment, Security, Development and Peace 17,
DOI: 10.1007/978-3-319-02795-1, © The Author(s) 2014

The majority of respondents are aged 25–59 years (68 %) (Fig. F.3).

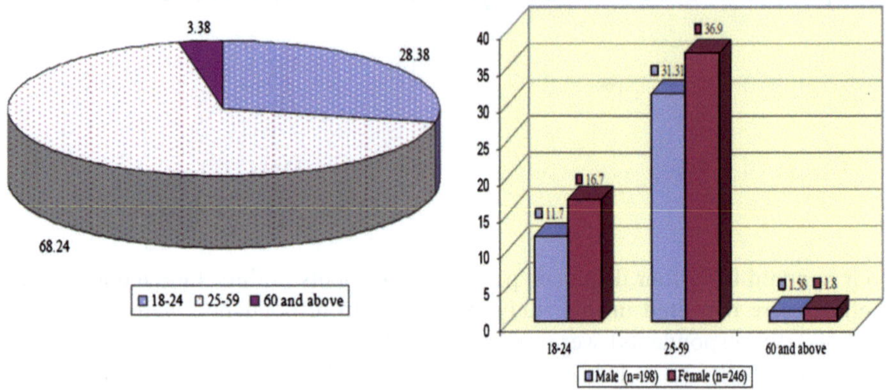

Fig. F.3 Age group by years. *Source* The Authors

Almost 69 % of respondents are married (Fig. F.4).

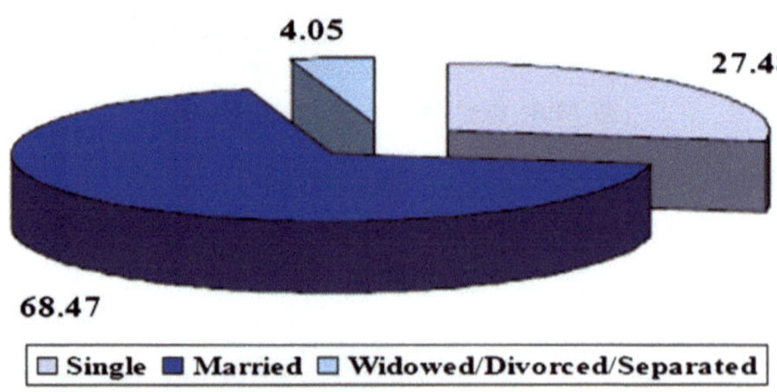

Fig. F.4 Marital status. *Source* The Authors

Almost 57 % of respondents are registered as displaced persons, while 33 % are non-registered and the rest PAB (Fig. F.5).

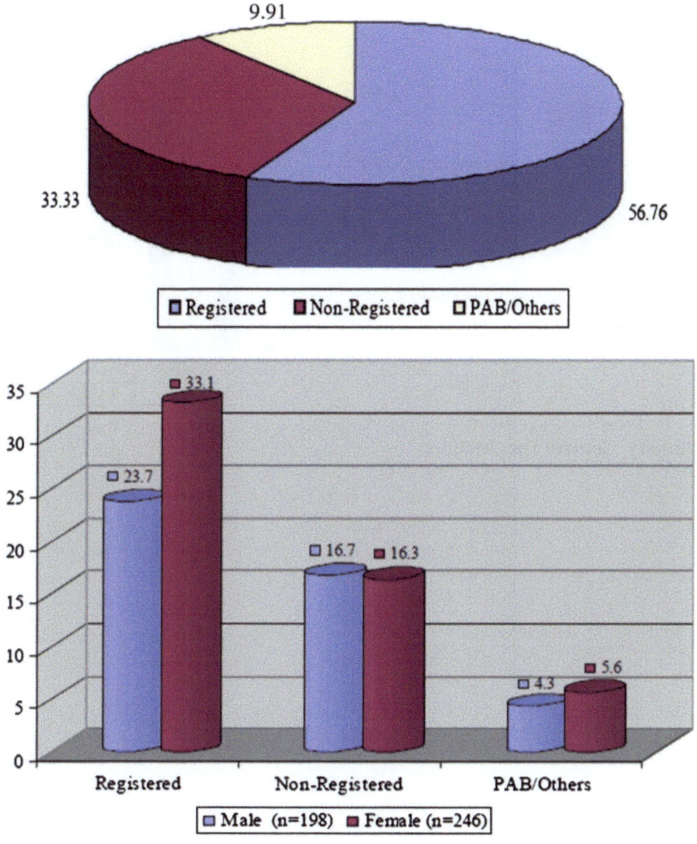

Fig. F.5 Status of respondents. *Source* The Authors

Karen/S'gaw is the largest ethnic group (48 %) among respondents (Fig. F.6). The largest group (41 %) has lived in the shelters between 11 and 20 years (Fig. F.7).

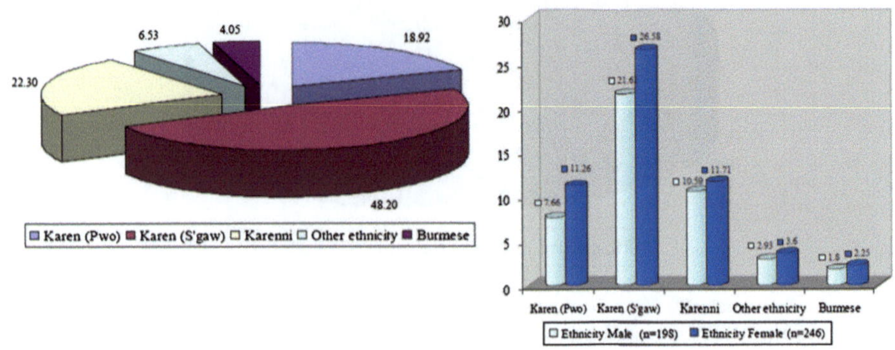

Fig. F.6 Ethnicity. *Source* The Authors

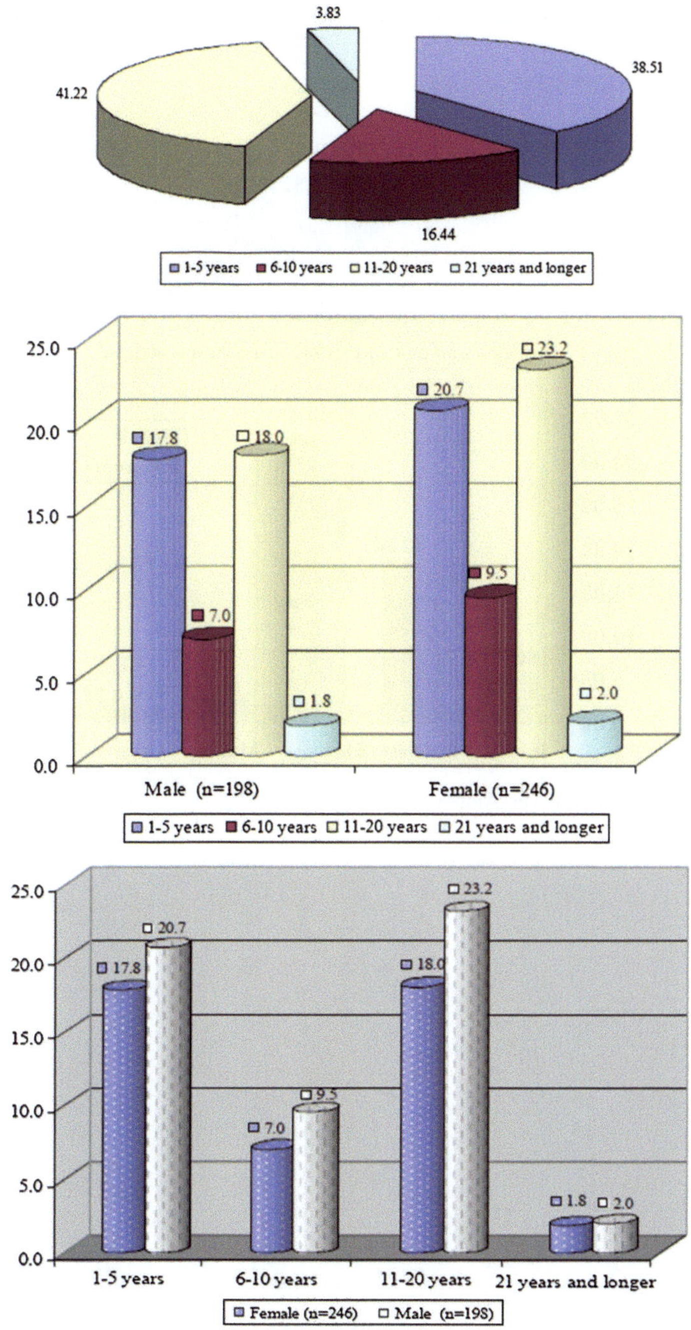

Fig. F.7 Length of stay in the Inside shelter. *Source* The Authors

56 % of respondents are Christian and 31 % are Buddhist (Fig. F.8).

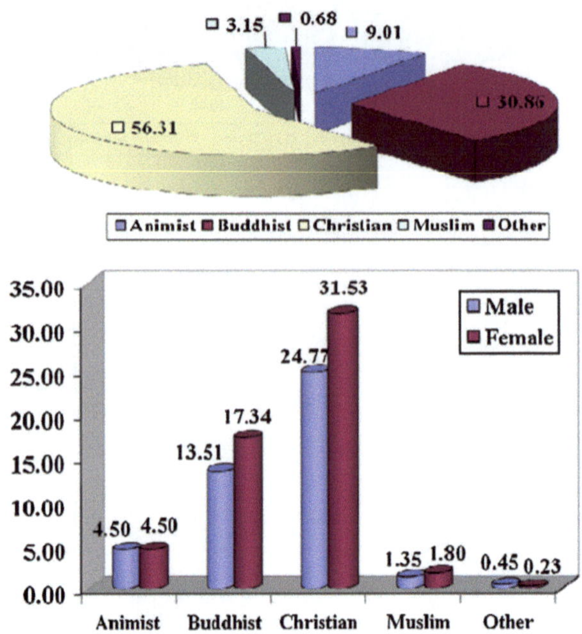

Fig. F.8 Religion. *Source* The Authors

75 % of respondents were literate and of these, 68 % had graduated from Myanmar rather than within the temporary shelter (Fig. F.9).

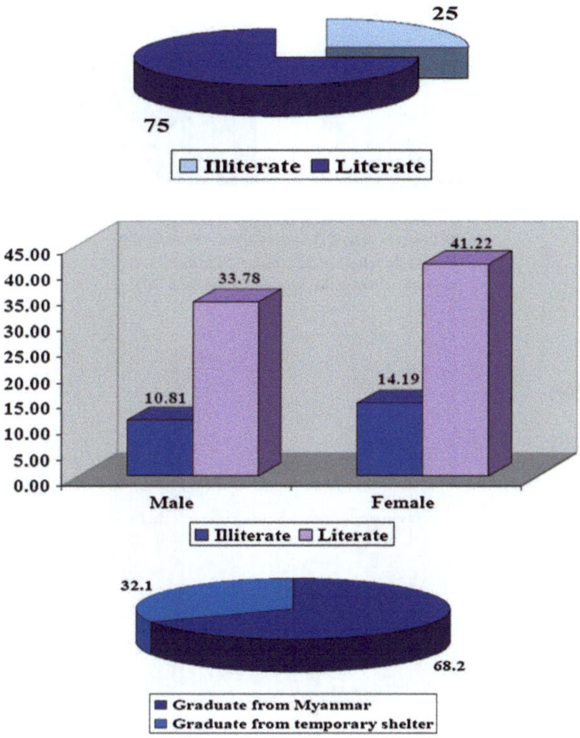

Fig. F.9 Education. *Source* The Authors

Of the literate respondents who had graduated from Myanmar, 50.7 % reached middle school level (Fig. F.10).

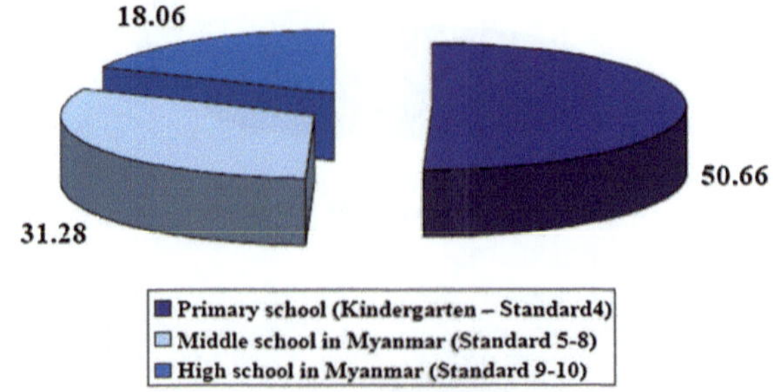

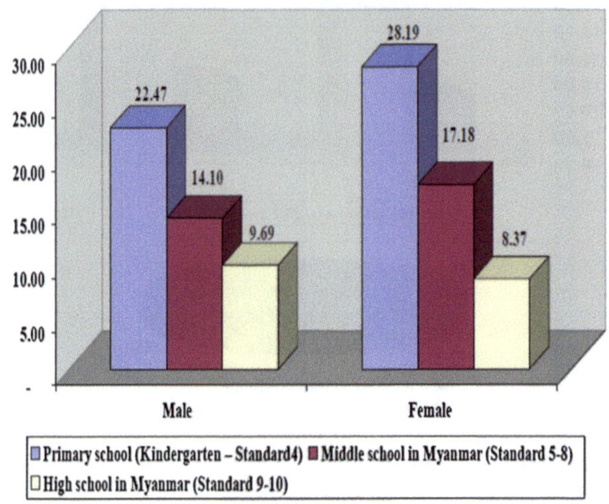

Fig. F.10 Respondents who had graduated from Myanmar. *Source* The Authors

Around half (51.4 %) of the respondents reported the current number of people in their household to be 5–8 persons, while 38.4 % share with 1–4 persons (Figs. F.11, F.12).

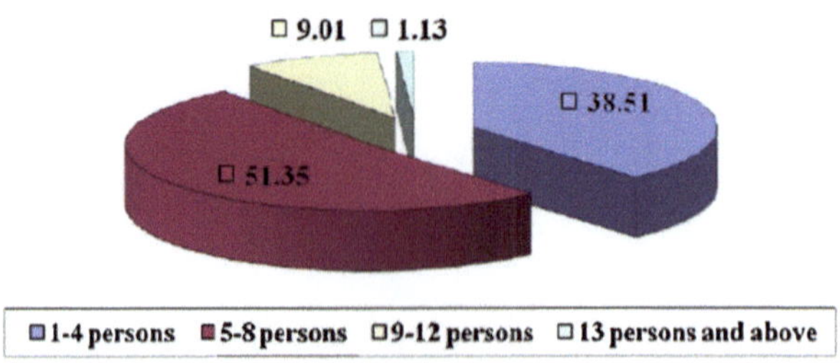

Fig. F.11 Household members. *Source* The Authors

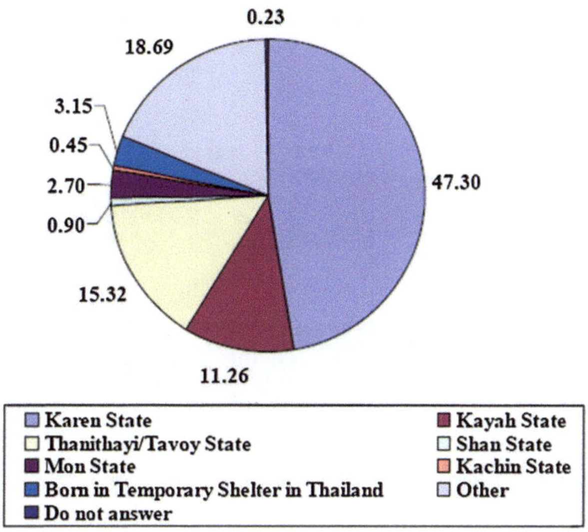

Fig. F.12 Birthplace. *Source* The Authors

52 % of respondents are employed and 48.1 % earn between 501 and 1,500 baht per month (Fig. F.13).

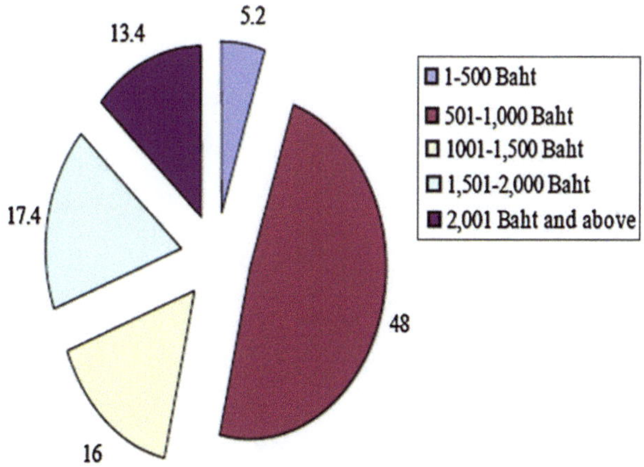

Fig. F.13 Income per month. *Source* The Authors

37.4 % of Thai–Karen language was used during interview (Fig. F.14).

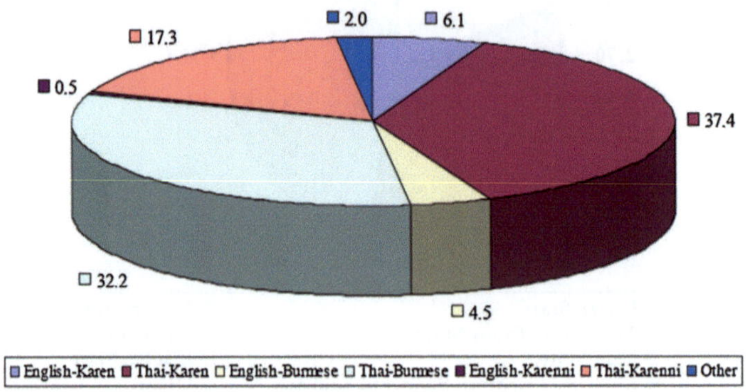

Fig. F.14 Language used in interviews. *Source* The Authors

Appendix G
Key Informant Questions

1. What are the current and future policy directions of your organisation? What are the dynamics, needs and constraints of funding to grantees/ displaced people?
    1. Please tell us about the working philosophy or objectives of your organisation. When did your organisation begin supporting Burmese refugees?
    2. Do you feel it is still an emergency situation to support the Burmese refugee after more than 20 years? Why or why not?
    3. What was your policy mandate at the beginning of the Burmese emergency? Since the beginning of your work has there been any policy mandate shift? If yes, when did this happen? What has changed and why? What are the factors that have changed? What are the strengths, limitations and impacts of those changes?
    4. Do you think the current policy has worked so far? Why and Why not? What are the different impacts of the current policy in terms of gender?
    5. What type of funding aid do you fund, *bilateral or multilateral aid,* and since when? If funding is *bilateral aid*, are the most of the funds earmarked assistance?
    6. How much do you fund in each year? What of the trends in funding, is it static or is there change, for what reason?
    7. Who are your grantees? How do you decide who should get your support? Please explain the structure and linkage with those NGOs (such as UN agencies or CCSDPT). When did this relationship begin?
    8. What is your perception of the meaning *refugee aid and development approach*?
    9. What is the concept of "*self-reliance of refugees*"? How will this concept lead to durable solutions?
    10. What strategies do you employ to encourage your grantees and government authorities, to make commitments to linking relief, rehabilitation and development (LRRD)? What factors limit the progress of LRRD?
    11. Is there an oversight system to verify the accountability of your grantees? If yes, how?
    12. Do you have any plans which specify certain timeframes or criteria for phasing out support for these displaced people? Why and why not?

P. Vungsiriphisal et al. (eds.), *Humanitarian Assistance for Displaced Persons from Myanmar*, SpringerBriefs in Environment, Security, Development and Peace 17, DOI: 10.1007/978-3-319-02795-1,

2. What strategy does your organisation apply to cooperate with the Royal Thai Government (RTG)?

   1. How and how often do you cooperate /work with the RTG?
   2. Is the relationship with the RTG easy? Please Explain.
   3. How does your organisation manage and/or cope with RTG requests? On which issues does your organisation and RTG easily find agreement? On which issues do you disagree?
   4. What RTG policy constraints does your organisation face in term of developing an intervention programme for durable solutions for displaced people? Are there any positive ones?
   5. Since the beginning of your work, what RTG policy/regulations have been shifted or changed? What are the factors? What are the impacts of those changes?
   6. What contribution was provided by your organisation to the RTG policy/regulation shift?
   7. What kinds of lessons learned are useful for working effectively with the RTG?
   8. What challenges have you identified in implementing with the RTG?
   9. Do you think the stakeholders involved will cooperate more deeply to obtain better results in the future? Are there conflicting interests or perspectives?

Appendix H
Questionnaire for Sustainable Solutions to the Displaced People Situation along the Thai–Myanmar Border

Questionnaire for "Sustainable Solutions to the Displaced People Situation along the Thai-Myanmar Border" (แบบสอบถามโครงการทางออกที่ยั่งยืนของผู้หนีภัยการสู้รบชายแดนไทย-พม่า) (ထိုင်း မြန်မာ နယ်စပ်တလျှောက်ရှိ ယာယီကယ်ဆယ်ရေးစခန်းများတွင် ရွှေပြောင်းနေထိုင်လာသူများ၏ ရေရှည်အတွက်ဖြစ်နိုင်သောဖြေရှင်းမှုများအား သုတေသနပြုလုပ်ရန်အတွက် စာတမ်းကောက်ယူခြင်း)

No. เลขที่ အင်တာဗျူးနံပါတ်စဉ် ___________

Date of interview วันที่ နေ့စွဲ______________ (dd/mm/yyyy) (วัน/เดือน/ปี) (ရက်/လ/ခုနှစ်)

Name of interviewer ผู้สัมภาษณ์ အင်တာဗျူးသူအမည် ________________________

Name of translator ล่าม ဘာသာပြန်သူအမည် ____________________________

Name of the temporary shelter ศูนย์พักพิง စာတမ်းကောက်သည့်ယာယီစခန်းအမည်

☐ 1. Tham Hin ถ้ำหิน သမ်း(မ်)ဟင်

☐ 2. Ban Mai Nai Soi บ้านใหม่ในสอย ဘန်မယ်နန်ဆွိုင်

☐ 3. Mae La แม่หละ မဲလ

Interview starting time เริ่มสัมภาษณ์เวลา အင်တာဗျူးစတင်သည့်အချိန်______________________

Interview ending time เสร็จสิ้นเวลา

အင်တာဗျူးပြီးဆုံးသည့်အချိန် ________________________

Language used during the interview ภาษาที่ใช้ အင်တာဗျူးတွင်သုံးသည့်ဘာသာစကား:

☐ 1. English-Karen อังกฤษ-กะเหรี่ยง ☐ 2. Thai-Karen ไทย-กะเหรี่ยง

☐ 3. English-Burmese อังกฤษ-พม่า ☐ 4. Thai-Burmese ไทย-พม่า

☐ 5. English-Karenni อังกฤษ-คะเรนนี ☐ 6. Thai-Karenni ไทย-คะเรนนี

☐ 7. Other (specify) อื่นๆ (โปรดระบุ) အခြားဘာသာစကား ....

Notes

P. Vungsiriphisal et al. (eds.), *Humanitarian Assistance for Displaced Persons from Myanmar*, SpringerBriefs in Environment, Security, Development and Peace 17, DOI: 10.1007/978-3-319-02795-1, © The Author(s) 2014

Demographic Information ข้อมูลส่วนบุคคล ဒေသန္တရအချက်အလက်များ

1. Status of respondent สถานะของผู้ตอบแบบสอบถาม အင်တာဗျူးခံရသူ၏ လက်ရှိအနေအထား

   ☐ 1. Registered ลงทะเบียน စာရင်းသွင်းပြီး

   ☐ 2. Non-Registered ไม่ลงทะเบียน စာရင်းမသွင်းရသေး

   ☐ 3. PAB/Others พีเอบีหรืออื่น စာရင်းသွင်းရန်စိစစ်ဆေးမှုပြုလုပ်နေသောအဆင့်

2. Sex เพศ လိင် ☐ 1. Male ชาย အမျိုးသား ☐ 2. Female หญิง အမျိုးသမီး

3. Age อายุ အသက်____________ (years ปี နှစ်)

4. Birth place สถานที่เกิด မွေးဖွားရာဒေသ

☐ 1. Karen State รัฐกะหรี่ยง ကရင်	☐ 6. Kachin State รัฐคะฉิ่น ကချင်
☐ 2. Kayah State รัฐคะยา ကယား	☐ 7. Born in Temporary Shelter in Thailand ศูนย์พักพิงในประเทศไทย ထိုင်းယာယီစခန်း
☐ 3. Thanithayi/Tavoy State รัฐทะวาย တနင်္သာရီ	☐ 8. Other (specify) อื่นๆ (โปรดระบุ) (အခြားဒေသ) ____________
☐ 4. Shan State รัฐฉาน ရှမ်း	
☐ 5. Mon State รัฐมอญ မွန်	

5. Marital status สถานภาพสมรส အိမ်ထောင်အခြေအနေ

   ☐ 1. Single โสด အပျိုလူပျို ☐ 2. Married สมรส အိမ်ထောင်ရှိ

   ☐ 3. Widowed หม้าย မုဆိုးဖိုမုဆိုးမ

   ☐ 4. Divorced/Separated หย่า/แยกกันอยู่ အိမ်ထောင်ကွဲ

   ☐ 5. Other (specify) อื่นๆ (โปรดระบุ) အခြား(တိကျစွာပြောပါ)____________

6. Highest level of education จบการศึกษาสูงสุด အမြင့်ဆုံးပညာရေး

☐ 1. Never attended school ไม่ได้เรียน ကျောင်းမနေဘူးပါ	
☐ 2. Primary school in Myanmar (Kindergarten – Standard 4) ประถมศึกษาในประเทศพม่า (อนุบาล – สแตนดาร์ด 4) မူလတန်း (သူငယ်တန်းမှ၄တန်းအထိ) ☐ 3. Middle school in Myanmar (Standard 5-8) มัธยมศึกษาตอนต้นในประเทศพม่า (สแตนดาร์ด 5-8) အလယ်တန်း (၅ တန်းမှ ၈ တန်းအထိ) ☐ 4. High school in Myanmar (Standard 9-10) มัธยมศึกษาตอนปลาย (แสตนดาร์ด 9 -10) အထက်တန်း (၉ တန်းမှ ၁၀ တန်းအထိ) ☐ 5. Primary school in the temporary shelter (Kindergarten – Standard 6) ประถมศึกษาในศูนย์พักพิงฯ (อนุบาล - แสตนดาร์ด 6) မူလတန်း (သူငယ်တန်းမှ၆တန်းအထိ)	☐ 6. Secondary school in the temporary shelter (Standard 7-10) มัธยมศึกษา (แสตนดาร์ด 7-10) အလယ်တန်း (၇တန်းမှ၁၀တန်းအထိ) ☐ 7. Post-10 Course ชั้นพิเศษหลังจากแสตนดาร์ด 10 (၁၀တန်းအလွန်) ☐ 8. College/University วิทยาลัย/มหาวิทยาลัย (ကောလိပ်၊တက္ကသိုလ်) ☐ 9. Non-formal education การศึกษานอกระบบ (ကျောင်းပြင်ပပညာရေး) ☐ 10. Vocational training หลักสูตรฝึกอาชีพ (အသက်မွေးဝမ်းကျောင်းသင်တန်း) ☐ 11. Other (specify) อื่นๆ (โปรดระบุ) အခြား (တိကျစွာပြောပါ) ____________

7. Ethnicity กลุ่มชาติพันธุ์ လူမျိုး

☐ 1. Karen (Pwo) กะเหรี่ยงโปว์ ပိုးကရင်	☐ 2. Karen (S'gaw) กะเหรี่ยงสะกอ စကောကရင်	☐ 3. Karenni คะเรนนี ကယား
☐ 4. Kachin คะฉิ่น ကချင်	☐ 5. Mon มอญ မွန်	☐ 6. Pa-O ปะโอ ပအို့

Survey Questionnaires by Asian Research Center for Migration (ARCM), Institute of Asian Studies, Chulalongkorn University

☐ 7. Burmese พม่า မြန်မာ	☐ 8. Arakan อะระกัน ရခိုင်	☐ 9. Shan ไทใหญ่ ရှမ်း
☐ 10. Rohingya โรฮิงยา ရိုဟင်ဂျာ	☐ 11. Other (specify) อื่นๆ(โปรดระบุ) အခြား______ ☐ 12. Unknown ไม่ทราบ (မသိပါ)	

8. Religion ศาสนา ဘာသာ

☐ 1. Animist นับถือผี အန်နီးမစ်	☐ 2. Buddhist พุทธศาสนา ဗုဒ္ဓဘာသာ	☐ 3. Christian คริสตศาสนา ခရစ်ယာန်
☐ 4. Muslim อิสลาม မူစလင်	☐ 5. No Religion ไม่มีศาสนา ဘာသာမရှိ	☐ 6. Other (specify) อื่นๆ (โปรดระบุ) အခြား (တိကျစွာပြောပါ)_________

9. Current or last occupation อาชีพปัจจุบันหรือล่าสุด လက်ရှိ (သို့မဟုတ်) နောက်ဆုံးလုပ်ခဲ့ဘူးသောအလုပ်

☐ 1. Employed (specify occupation) รับจ้าง (ระบุ) အလုပ်အကိုင်________________________________

☐ 2. Self-employed (specify occupation) ทำงานส่วนตัว (ระบุ) ကိုယ်ပိုင်အလုပ် _____________________

☐ 3. Unemployed ไม่ได้ทำงาน အလုပ်မရှိ

☐ 4. Student นักเรียน ကျောင်းသား

10. Length of stay in the Temporary Shelter ระยะเวลาที่อยู่ในศูนย์พักพิง နေထိုင်သည့်ကာလ

________________years ปี (နှစ်)

11. Number of current family members in household จำนวนสมาชิกในครอบครัวปัจจุบัน

အိမ်ထောင်စုအတွင်း မိသားစုဝင် အရေအတွက် ______________คน

12. If you had your preference in the future, where would you like to go after you finish your stay in the Temporary Shelter? ယာယီစခန်းတွင်နေထိုင်ပြီး၍ အခြားနေရာသွားရမည်ဆိုလျှင် မည်သည့်နေရာကိုသွားရန်ဆန္ဒရှိပါသလဲ

ในอนาคตถ้าเลือกได้ ท่านคิดว่าอยากไปอยู่ที่ใด

☐ 1. Stay in Thailand อยู่ในประเทศไทย ထိုင်းမှာနေမယ်

☐ 2. Resettlement country ไปประเทศที่สาม ပြန်လည်နေရာချထားပေးတဲ့ နိုင်ငံတွေမှာနေမယ်

☐ 3. Hometown in Burma กลับบ้านเกิดในประเทศพม่า မြန်မာပြည်ကအိမ်ကိုပြန်မယ်

☐ 4. Other safe area in Burma ไปอยู่พื้นที่ปลอดภัยในประเทศพม่า မြန်မာပြည်လုံခြုံတဲ့တနေရာမှာနေမယ်

<u>Policy Survey Questions คำถามด้านนโยบาย</u>

13. What is your primary reason for remaining in the Temporary Shelter? (อะไรเป็นเหตุผลหลักที่ทำให้ท่านเลือกอยู่ในศูนย์พักพิง)

1.☐ Safety (ความปลอดภัย) 2.☐ Family unity (การอยู่ร่วมกับครอบครัว)

3.☐ Children's education (การศึกษาของเด็ก) 4.☐ Food rations (ได้ส่วนแบ่งอาหาร)

5.☐ Having no choice (ไม่มีทางเลือกอื่น) 6.☐ Other, specify (อื่นๆ ระบุ............................)

14. Do you feel physically safe staying in the Temporary Shelter? (ท่านรู้สึกปลอดภัยในการอยู่ในศูนย์พักพิงหรือไม่)

1.☐ Safe (ปลอดภัย) 2.☐ Fair (ธรรมดา)

3.☐ Unsafe (ไม่ปลอดภัย) 4.☐ Other, specify (อื่นๆ ระบุ..............)

15. How would you characterize your relationship with the Thai authorities in the Temporary Shelter? (ความสัมพันธ์ของท่านกับเจ้าหน้าที่ของไทยเป็นอย่างไร)

1.☐ Very good (ดีมาก) 2.☐ Good (ดี) 3.☐ Fair (ธรรมดา)
4.☐ Poor (ไม่ค่อยดี) 5.☐ Very poor (ไม่ดีมาก)

16. If you face difficulties while staying in the Temporary Shelter, whom do you turn to for help? List from first 3 priority (1=most) (ถ้าท่านมีปัญหาในศูนย์พักพิง ท่านไปขอความช่วยเหลือจากใคร เรียงตามลำดับ 3 ลำดับ (1=มากที่สุด))

1.☐ Temporary Shelter committee (กรรมการศูนย์ฯ) 2.☐ Religious leader (ผู้นำศาสนา) 3.☐ Community leader ผู้นำชุมชน
4.☐ NGO staff (เจ้าหน้าที่องค์กรพัฒนาเอกชน) 5.☐ Thai authorities (เจ้าหน้าที่ของไทย)
6.☐ Other, specify (อื่นๆ ระบุ...................)

17. When you have needed assistance from the Thai authorities, how have you approached them? (ถ้าท่านต้องการความช่วยเหลือจากเจ้าหน้าที่ของไทย ท่านติดต่อเจ้าหน้าที่อย่างไร)

1.☐ Contacted directly (ติดต่อโดยตรง)
2.☐ Through Temporary Shelter committee (ติดต่อผ่านกรรมการศูนย์ฯ)
3.☐ Through NGO staff (ติดต่อผ่าน จนท.องค์กรพัฒนาเอกชน)
4.☐ Through other community member (ติดต่อผ่านคนในชุมชน)
5.☐ Did not attempt to approach them (ไม่ติดต่อ)

18. What do you think towards policies/regulation on well-being in the Temporary Shelter? (ท่านคิดว่านโยบาย/ระเบียบของรัฐบาลไทย เกี่ยวกับความเป็นอยู่ที่ดีภายในศูนย์พักพิงเป็นอย่างไร)

1.☐ Very good (ดีมาก) 2.☐ Good (ดี) 3.☐ Fair (ธรรมดา) 4.☐ Poor (ไม่ดี) 5.☐ Very poor (ไม่ดีมาก)

19. What do you think towards the following policies/regulation in the Temporary Shelter? (ท่านคิดว่านโยบาย/ระเบียบของรัฐบาลไทยในด้านต่างๆ ต่อไปนี้ ในศูนย์พักพิงเป็นอย่างไร)

Policies/Regulation นโยบาย/ระเบียบ	1.Good ดี	2.Fair ธรรมดา	3.Poor ไม่ดี	5.No idea ไม่มีความเห็น
19.1 Healthcare สาธารณสุข				
19.2 Education การศึกษา				
19.3 Security control of the Temporary Shelter การควบคุมความมั่นคงปลอดภัยของศูนย์ฯ				

20. What do you think towards the following policies/regulation? (ท่านมีความเห็นต่อนโยบาย/ระเบียบของรัฐบาลไทยในด้านต่างๆ ต่อไปนี้ อย่างไร)

Policies/Regulation นโยบาย/ระเบียบ	1.Totally agree เห็นด้วยอย่างมาก	2.Agree เห็นด้วย	3.Disagree ไม่เห็นด้วย	4.Totally disagree ไม่เห็นด้วยอย่างมาก	5.No idea/ Don't know ไม่มีความเห็น/ไม่รู้
20.1 Resettlement in third countries การไปตั้งถิ่นฐานในประเทศที่สาม					
20.2 Security control of the Temporary Shelter การควบคุมความมั่นคงปลอดภัยของศูนย์ฯ					
20.3 Allow working opportunity inside the temporary shelter only การอนุญาตให้ทำงานได้เฉพาะในศูนย์พักพิง					
20.4 Integration Temporary Shelter resident to local community การผสมกลมกลืนคนในศูนย์พักพิงกับชุมชนท้องถิ่น					

21. What do you think towards the RTG restriction of movement for Temporary Shelter resident? (ท่านคิดว่านโยบาย/ระเบียบของรัฐบาลไทยเกี่ยวกับการห้ามออกไปนอกศูนย์พักพิง เป็นอย่างไร)

1.☐ Totally agree (เห็นด้วยอย่างมาก)
2.☐ Agree (เห็นด้วย)
3.☐ Disagree (ไม่เห็นด้วย)
4.☐ Totally disagree (ไม่เห็นด้วยอย่างมาก)
5.☐ No policy/regulation (ไม่มีนโยบาย/ระเบียบ)

22. Which policy do you want to be changed as first priority ? (ท่านต้องการให้มีการเปลี่ยนแปลงนโยบาย/ระเบียบด้านใด เป็นลำดับแรก)

1.☐ Restricted movement (การออกไปนอกศูนย์พักพิง)
2.☐ Education (ด้านการศึกษา)
3.☐ Employment (โอกาสในการทำงาน)
4.☐ Resettlement (การไปตั้งถิ่นฐานในประเทศที่สาม)
5.☐ Integration to Thai community (การผสมกลมกลืนคนในศูนย์พักพิงกับชุมชนท้องถิ่น)

23. What has been the most significant policy/regulation change during your stay in the Temporary Shelter? (ระยะเวลาที่อยู่ในศูนย์พักพิง ท่านเห็นความเปลี่ยนแปลงนโยบาย/ระเบียบของรัฐบาลไทยด้านใดมากที่สุด)

1.☐ Educational opportunities (ด้านการศึกษา)
2.☐ Vocational trainings (การฝึกอาชีพ)
3.☐ Security protections (การคุ้มครองความปลอดภัย)
4.☐ Employment opportunities (การจ้างงาน)
5.☐ Other, specify (อื่นๆ ระบุ ....)

III. Roles of donors, international organizations, non-government organizations and UN agencies in providing humanitarian assistance to the Displaced People บทบาทของแหล่งทุน องค์กรพัฒนาเอกชนในประเทศและระหว่างประเทศ และหน่วยงานของสหประชาชาติในการให้ความช่วยเหลือด้านมนุษยธรรมแก่ผู้ลี้ภัย

24. Currently, how much do you depend on the aid of the NGOs? **(ปัจจุบันนี้ท่านต้องพึ่งพาความช่วยเหลือจาก เอ็นจีโอมากน้อยเท่าไร)**

1.☐ Totally dependent **(พึ่งพิงทุกเรื่อง)**

2.☐ Partially, food, shelter and jobs **(บางส่วน เช่นอาหาร ที่พักอาศัยและงาน)**

3.☐ Very little, only food and shelter **(พึ่งพิงเล็กน้อย เพียงแต่อาหารและที่พักอาศัยเท่านั้น)**

4 ☐ Don't know/ No idea **(ไม่รู้ ไม่มีความเห็น)**

25. Would you like to get opportunity to become more self-reliant? **(ท่านอยากมีโอกาสช่วยเหลือ(พึ่งพิง)ตนเองหรือไม่)**

1☐ Yes **ใช่อยากมี** (answer Q. 26 **ให้ตอบคำถามข้อ 26**)

2☐ No **ไม่อยากมี** (skip to Q.27 **ข้ามไปตอบข้อ 27**)

3☐ Don't know **ไม่รู้ ไม่มีความเห็น** (skip to Q.27 **ข้ามไปตอบข้อ 27**)

26. In which way would you like to become more self-reliant? **(ท่านคิดว่าอยากจะช่วยเหลือหรือพึ่งพิงตนเองโดยวิธีใด)**

1☐ I want to work inside or outside the Temporary Shelter **(ต้องการทำงานภายในหรือภายนอกค่าย)**

2☐ I want to study more and/or learn a new job **(ต้องการเรียนต่อหรือได้รับการฝึกอบรมเกี่ยวกับงาน)**

3☐ I would like to get Thai documents to stay here **(อยากได้รับเอกสารเพื่ออยู่ในประเทศไทย)**

4☐ I just want to go back to my country **(อยากกลับบ้าน)**

5☐ I would go anywhere else in a safe country **(ไปประเทศไหนก็ได้ที่ปลอดภัย)**

27. What do you think about the following NGOs services ? (please ✓ in the box that you choose) **ท่านคิดว่าบริการขององค์กรพัฒนาเอกชนด้านต่างๆต่อไปนี้เป็นอย่างไรบ้าง (ใส่✓ ลงในช่องที่เป็นความเห็นของท่าน)**

NGOs services	**1.Good ดี**	**2.Fair ปานกลาง**	**3.Not enough ไม่เพียงพอ**	**4.Don't know ไม่มีความเห็น**
27.1 Food อาหาร				
27.2 Shelter items ที่อยู่อาศัย				
27.3 Health (clinic) บริการด้านสุขภาพ				
27.4 Sanitation ด้านสุขาภิบาล				
27.5 Education ด้านการศึกษา				
27.6 Vocational training การอบรมด้านอาชีพ				
27.7 Income generation การส่งเสริมอาชีพ(สร้างรายได้)				
27.8 Gender training activities กิจกรรมฝึกอบรมด้านเพศสภาพ				
27.9 Violence against women and children prevention activities กิจกรรมด้านการป้องกันความรุนแรงต่อเด็กและสตรี				
27.10 Legal assistance การให้ความช่วยเหลือด้านกฎหมาย				

Survey Questionnaires by Asian Research Center for Migration (ARCM), Institute of Asian Studies, Chulalongkorn University

28. When do you think you won't need anymore those services (as above question)? เมื่อใดที่ท่านคิดว่าไม่ต้องการบริการต่างๆ เหล่านั้น (ในข้อข้างบน) อีกต่อไป

1☐ Never, we need the NGOs to take care of our health and others (everything)(เรายังต้องการให้องค์กรพัฒนาเอกชนช่วยดูแลสุขภาพของเราและเรื่องอื่นๆ(ทุกเรื่อง)ต่อไป)

2☐ Only when we can access the local services (เมื่อใดก็ตามที่เราสามารถเข้าถึงบริการ ท้องถิ่นได้)

3☐ whenever we can take care of ourselves (เมื่อใดก็ตามที่เราสามารถดูแลตัวเองได้)

4☐ Any time (เมื่อใดก็ได้)

5☐ Don't Know (ไม่รู้ไม่มีความเห็น)

29. Do you know why these organizations are helping you? (ทำไมองค์กรพัฒนาเอกชนเหล่านี้จึงมาช่วยเหลือท่าน)

1☐ They want to help people in need (พวกเขาต้องการช่วยคนที่มีความจำเป็นจะต้องได้รับการช่วยเหลือ)

2☐ Because I can not help myself. (เขาต้องช่วยฉันเพราะฉันช่วยเหลือตัวเองไม่ได้)

3☐ They benefit from their services (เขาได้ประโยชน์จากการช่วย)

4☐ It is their business (เป็นงานของเขา)

5☐ Don't Know (ไม่รู้ไม่มีความเห็น)

30. Do you think the donors will ever stop their support to the NGOs? (ท่านเคยคิดไหมว่าแหล่งทุนอาจจะยุติการสนับสนุนองค์กรพัฒนาเอกชน)

1☐ Never, as long as we are here (ไม่เคยคิดเพราะตราบใดที่เรายังอยู่ที่นี่เขาต้องสนับสนุน)

2☐ Long time in the future when they want to support other country (เป็นไปได้เมื่อเขาต้องการสนับสนุนประเทศอื่น แต่คงอีกนานในอนาคต)

3☐ Soon, because they have helped us for too long (คงเร็วๆ นี้เพราะเขาช่วยมานานแล้ว)

4☐ Don't know (ไม่รู้ไม่มีความเห็น)

31. What will you do if the donors stop sending funds for the NGOs? (หากแหล่งทุนยุติการสนับสนุนความช่วยเหลือกับองค์กรพัฒนาเอกชนท่านคิดว่าท่านจะทำอะไร)

1☐ We want to work to support ourselves (เราต้องการทำงานเพื่อสนับสนุน/ช่วยเหลือตัวเอง)

2☐ We will ask them not to stop (เราจะขอให้เขาช่วยเหลือเราต่อไป อย่ายุติการช่วยเหลือ)

3☐ Other organizations will come after them for helping us (คงมีแหล่งทุนอื่นๆที่จะเข้ามาช่วยเราต่อไป)

4☐ Repatriation with guarantee security (กลับไปบ้านเกิดแต่ต้องรับรองความปลอดภัย)

5☐ Don't know (ไม่รู้ไม่มีความเห็น)

6.☐ other specify (อื่นๆ ระบุ...)

32. Do you think that it should have any organizations to negotiate with your original country to take you home with security? (ท่านคิดว่าควรมีหน่วยงานไปเจราจากับประเทศต้นทางของท่าน เพื่อให้ท่านกลับบ้านอย่างปลอดภัยหรือไม่)

1☐No. (skip to answer 34) ไม่ควรมี (ข้ามไปตอบคำถามข้อที่ 34)

2☐ Yes. (please answer next question) ใช่ควรมี (กรุณาตอบคำถามข้อถัดไป)

33. Please specify (can choose more than 1) กรุณาระบุว่าควรเป็นใครบ้าง(เลือกได้มากกว่า1)

1☐ UN agencies (หน่วยงานของยูเอ็น) (specify ระบุ.................................. ....)

2☐ ASEAN (อาเซี่ยน)

3☐ Royal Thai Government (รัฐบาลไทย)

4☐ NGOs (specify)……………………………(องค์กรพัฒนาเอกชน ระบุ……………………………)

5☐ Other (specify)……………………………(อื่นๆ ระบุ ……………………………)

IV: Resettlement Questions

34. Are you aware of the Resettlement Program? (ท่านทราบเกี่ยวกับโครงการการตั้งถิ่นฐานหรือไม่?)

1☐ Yes ทราบ (If yes, from which source(s) ถ้าทราบ จากแหล่งข้อมูลใด) 2☐ No ไม่ทราบ (If no, skip to Question 39)

1.1☐ Temporary Shelter commanders/Thai officials (ผู้ประสานงานในศูนย์พักพิง / เจ้าหน้าที่)

1.2☐ Friends/Relatives (เพื่อน / ญาติ)

1.3☐ NGOs (องค์กรเอกชน)

1.4☐ Informants who are knowledgeable about resettlement) (คนในแคมป์ที่รู้ข้อมูล)

1.5☐ Others__________ (อื่นๆ……………………)

35. Have you ever applied to the Program? (ท่านเคยสมัครโครงการการตั้งถิ่นฐานหรือไม่?)

1☐ Yes (ใช่) 2☐ No ไม่

If Yes, when did you apply? ถ้าเคย ท่านสมัครเมื่อไหร่

1 ☐ Less than 1 month (น้อยกว่า 1 เดือน)

2 ☐ 1-3 months (1-3 เดือน)

3 ☐ 4-6 months (4-6 เดือน)

4 ☐ More than 6 months (มากกว่า 6 เดือน)

If No, why?__________________________ (Multiple answer is permitted) (ถ้าท่านไม่ได้สมัครเข้าร่วมโครงการเพราะเหตุใด ตอบได้มากกว่า 1 ข้อ)

1☐ Separation from family (ไม่อยากจากครอบครัว)

2☐ Afraid of resettlement adjustment (กลัวเรื่องการปรับตัวในการตั้งถิ่นฐาน)

3☐ No confidence in the Program (ไม่เชื่อมั่นในโครงการ)

4☐ Prefer waiting for a return to Myanmar (ต้องการเดินทางกลับพม่า)

5☐ Prefer staying in Temporary Shelter (พอใจที่จะอยู่ในศูนย์พักพิง)

6☐ Prefer staying in Thailand but outside the Temporary Shelter (อยากอยู่เมืองไทย แต่ไม่ใช่ในศูนย์พักพิง)

7☐ Others…………………………. (อื่นๆ……………………………………)

For those who used to apply for resettlement, please answer 36 and 37. (สำหรับผู้ที่เคยสมัครเข้าโครงการการตั้งถิ่นฐาน กรุณาตอบข้อ 36 - 38)

36. Did you feel you received adequate information to make an informed decision about resettlement? (ท่านคิดว่าท่านได้รับข้อมูลเพียงพอในการตัดสินใจที่จะไปตั้งถิ่นฐานหรือไม่)

1☐ Yes (ใช่) 2☐ No (ไม่ใช่) 3☐ Don't know (ไม่ทราบ)

37. In case you have been accepted, have you ever withdrawn/declined to be resettled? (ในกรณีที่ท่านได้รับการตอบรับเข้าโครงการแล้ว ท่านเคยขอถอนตัว / ปฏิเสธที่จะไปตั้งถิ่นฐานหรือไม่)

1☐ Yes 2☐ No

38. What finally made you choose to apply for resettlement? (อะไรเป็นเหตุผลสำคัญที่ทำให้ท่านเลือกที่จะสมัครเข้าโครงการการตั้งถิ่นฐาน)

1☐ Hope for a better future in another country (มีความหวังที่จะมีอนาคตที่ดีกว่าในประเทศอื่น)

2☐ Frustration about life in the Temporary Shelter (ไม่พอใจชีวิตในศูนย์พักพิง)

3☐ Acceptance of inability to return to Myanmar (ไม่เห็นหนทางที่จะได้กลับไปพม่า)

4☐ No other better options (ไม่มีทางเลือกอื่นใดที่ดีไปกว่านี้)

5☐ Other, specify……………..(อื่นๆ..............................)

39. Are you informed how frequently has the resettlement program been Temporary Shelteraigned in the Temporary Shelter? (ในศูนย์พักพิงมีการประกาศโครงการการรับไปตั้งถิ่นฐานบ่อยมากน้อยแค่ไหน)

1.☐	2.☐	3.☐	4.☐
Every day (ทุกวัน)	Every week (ทุกอาทิตย์)	Every month (ทุกเดือน)	Others............(อื่นๆ)

40. Do you think that resettlement is the best option, at this time, for those living in the Temporary Shelter? ท่านคิดว่าการไปตั้งถิ่นฐานเป็นทางเลือกที่ดีที่สุดหรือไม่ในขณะนี้สำหรับผู้ที่อาศัยอยู่ในศูนย์พักพิง

1.☐	2.☐	3.☐
Yes (ใช่)	No (ไม่ใช่)	Don't know (ไม่ทราบ)

41. If you were to choose the resettlement country, which country would you choose? หากท่านสามารถเลือกประเทศที่จะไปตั้งถิ่นฐานได้ ท่านจะเลือกประเทศไหน

1.☐ United States (สหรัฐอเมริกา)

2.☐ Japan (ญี่ปุ่น)

3.☐ Canada (คานาดา)

4.☐ Australia (ออสเตรเลีย)

5.☐ Norway (นอร์เวย์)

6.☐ Other (please specify……………..) (อื่นๆ ระบุ..................................)

42. Why did you choose to be settled to the mentioned country? (Select one the most significant factor) เหตุใดท่านจึงเลือกที่จะไปตั้งถิ่นฐานในประเทศนั้น (เลือกเพียงคำตอบเดียว)

1.☐ Many people from your community/ethnic group? (มีคนจากชุมชนเดี่ยวกัน / กลุ่มชาติพันธุ์เดียวกันอาศัยอยู่)

2.☐ Education opportunity (มีโอกาสได้ศึกษาเล่าเรียน)

3.☐ Generous welfare (มีสวัสดิการพร้อมทุกด้าน)

4.☐ Job opportunities (มีโอกาสได้ทำงาน)

5.☐ Have friends and family member in the country (มีเพื่อนและสมาชิกในครอบครัวอยู่ที่ประเทศนั้นแล้ว)

6.☐ Good climate and weather (ภูมิอากาศดี)

7.☐ Others (อื่นๆ)

43. From what you have heard, how do those who have been resettled generally feel about their choice? (จากข้อมูลที่ท่านได้รับทราบมา ผู้ที่ได้เดินทางไปตั้งถิ่นฐานแล้วโดยทั่วไปรู้สึกอย่างไรกับการเลือกตัดสินใจในการไปตั้งถิ่นฐาน)

1.☐	2.☐	3.☐	4.☐	5.☐
Very good	Good	Average	Poor	Very poor
(รู้สึกดีมาก)	(รู้สึกดี)	(รู้สึกพอใช้ได้)	(รู้สึกไม่ดี)	(รู้สึกไม่ดีมาก)

44. Do you think that the resettlement program has had a positive or negative impact on the Temporary Shelter? (ท่านคิดว่าโครงการรับไปตั้งถิ่นฐานมีผลกระทบในแง่บวกหรือแง่ลบต่อศูนย์พักพิง)

1.☐	2.☐	3.☐
Positive (แง่บวก)	Negative (แง่ลบ)	Don't know (ไม่ทราบ)

If negative please proceed to 44.1

If positive please proceed to 44.2

44.1 Please put 1 – 5 on the following negative impacts from most to least

(1-most impact to 5-least impact) โปรดเรียงลำดับผลกระทบในแง่ลบจากมากไปหาน้อย จำนวน 5 เรื่อง

1.☐ Reduction in quality for Temporary Shelter services (บริการต่างๆ ที่มีอยู่ในศูนย์พักพิงต้องลดคุณภาพลง)

2.☐ Less effective Temporary Shelter administration (การบริหารงานในศูนย์พักพิงจะมีประสิทธิภาพลดลง)

3.☐ Loss of ethnic solidarity (สูญเสียความเป็นปึกแผ่นของชาติพันธุ์)

4.☐ Negative emotional environment in the Temporary Shelter (ผลกระทบทางจิตใจและอารมณ์ในด้านลบต่อผู้ที่อยู่ในศูนย์พักพิง)

5.☐ Brain drain / Loss of skilled workers (สมองไหล / การสูญเสียแรงงานที่มีทักษะ)

6.☐ Separation of family members (สมาชิกในครอบครัวต้องแยกกันอยู่)

44.2 Please put 1-5 on the following positive impacts from most to least

(1-most impact to 5-least impact) โปรดเรียงลำดับผลกระทบในแง่บวกจากมากไปหาน้อย จำนวน 5 เรื่อง

1.☐ Reduced crowding (ลดความแออัดในศูนย์พักพิง)

2.☐ Remittances from resettled persons (มีรายได้จากเงินส่งกลับของผู้ที่ไปตั้งถิ่นฐาน)

3.☐ Better education or health programs (มีโอกาสได้ศึกษาเล่าเรียน หรือ ได้เข้าร่วมโครงการด้านสุขภาพ)

4.☐ More livelihood opportunities in the Temporary Shelter (มีโอกาสการดำรงชีวิตที่ดีมากกว่าการมีชีวิตในศูนย์พักพิง)

5.☐ Positive emotional environment in the Temporary Shelter (ส่งผลต่อจิตใจและอารมณ์ในแง่บวกต่อผู้ที่อยู่ในศูนย์พักพิง)

<u>Resettlement Questions for those already Accepted for Resettlement</u>

45. Did you find the application process difficult? (ท่านพบว่าขั้นตอนการรับสมัครยากหรือไม่)

1.☐ Yes (ใช่) 2.☐ No (ไม่) 3.☐ No opinion (ไม่มีความเห็น)

46. How long have you been waiting for resettlement beginning with the start of the application process until today? (ท่านต้องรอคอยนานเพียงใดในการสมัครเข้าโครงการการตั้งถิ่นฐานนับจากวันเริ่มต้นสมัครจนถึงปัจจุบัน)

1.☐ Less than 1 month (น้อยกว่า 1 เดือน) 2.☐ 1-3 months / เดือน 3.☐ 4-6 months / เดือน

4.☐ More than 6 months / เดือน

47. Do you feel adequately prepared vocationally for life in your resettlement country? (ท่านคิดว่าได้รับการเตรียมความพร้อมมากพอในการฝึกอาชีพเพื่อการดำรงชีวิตในประเทศที่ท่านไปตั้งถิ่นฐานหรือไม่)

1.☐ Yes (ใช่) 2.☐ No (ไม่) 3.☐ Don't know (ไม่ทราบ)

48. Do you feel confident in your ability to communicate in language in your resettlement country? (ท่านรู้สึกมั่นใจในความสามารถในการใช้ภาษาในประเทศที่ไปตั้งถิ่นฐานหรือไม่)

1.☐ Yes (ใช่) 2.☐ No (ไม่) 3.☐ Unsure (ไม่แน่นอน)

49. Do you plan on sending remittances to relatives in the Temporary Shelters or in Myanmar? (ท่านวางแผนที่จะส่งเงินกลับไปให้ญาติที่อยู่ในศูนย์พักพิงหรือในพม่าหรือไม่

1.☐ Yes (ใช่) 2.☐ No (ไม่) 3.☐ Unsure (ไม่แน่นอน)

50. What is your major concern about life in your resettlement country? (ข้อใดเป็นสิ่งที่ท่านกังวลมากที่สุดในการใช้ชีวิตในประเทศที่ไปตั้งถิ่นฐาน)

1.☐ Colder climate (อากาศที่หนาวเย็น)

2.☐ Difficulty to adjust to the new culture / disconnection from community/culture (ความยากลำบากในการปรับตัวให้เข้ากับวัฒนธรรมใหม่ / การที่ต้องถูกตัดขาดจากชุมชน / วัฒนธรรมของตนเอง)

3.☐ Inability to communicate (ไม่สามารถสื่อสารภาษาได้)

4.☐ Lack of ability to find employment (ขาดความสามารถในการหางานทำ)

5.☐ Safety (ความปลอดภัย)

6.☐ Homesick (คิดถึงบ้าน)

51. What type of job would you like to do in your resettlement country? (งานประเภทใดที่ท่านต้องการทำในประเทศที่รับไปตั้งถิ่นฐาน)

1.☐ Agricultural (งานด้านเกษตร)

2.☐ Manufacturing (งานอุตสาหกรรม)

3.☐ Public/social service (งานด้านบริการสาธารณะ / สังคม)

4.☐ Office work (งานสำนักงาน)

5.☐ Services (Retail/restaurant) (งานบริการ ค้าปลีก / ร้านอาหาร)

6.☐ Domestic work (Housekeeping) (ทำงานบ้าน)

Bibliography

"Thai Government Says Myanmar Refugees Can Stay Despite Hostage Crisis", in: *Agence France-Presse*, 25 January 2000.

Antiporta, J. B., 2000: *ODA Trend Updates: Some Perspective on Donors and NGO Experiences*; at: http://www.mode.org/oda/pdf/ODA%20Trends.pdf.

Austin, J. et al, 2008: "Reproductive Health: A Right for Refugees and Internally Displaced Persons". *Reproductive Health Matters*, 16,31: 10–21. http://www.raiseinitiative.org/library/pdf/rhm31.pdf.

Baek, B. S.; Subramanium, G., 2008: *Myanmarese Refugees in Thailand: the Need for Effective Protection*; at: http://scholarship.law.cornell.edu/cgi/viewcontent.cgi?article=1000&context=dsp_papers.

Baker, S.; Holumyong, C.; Thinlai, K., 2010: *Research Gap Concerning the Heal of Migrants from Cambodia, Lao PDR and Myanmar in Thailand* (NakonPathom, Nonthaburi: Mahidol University and WHO).

"Review of Policy on Burmese Exiles Urged: Our Hospitality Long Abused", in: *Bangkok Post*, 27 January 2000.

Banki, S.; Lang, H., 2007: *Planning for the Future: The Impact of Resettlement on the Remaining Camp Population;* at: http://www.tbbc.org/resources/resources.htm#idisplacedpersons.

Bebbington, A., 2005: "Donor–NGO Relations and Representations of Livelihood in Non-governmental Aid Chains". *World Development*, 33,6: 937–950.

Berg, J. E., 2009: *To Go or Not to Go; Factors Influencing Young, Educated Karen Refugees Considering Resettlement*. Master of Multicultural and International Education Thesis, Oslo University, Faculty of Education and International Study.

Betts, A., 2009: *Development Assistance and Refugees: Towards a North-South Grand Bargain?* Oxford: University of Oxford, Refugee Studies Centre, Department of International Development Oxford; at: http://repository.forcedmigration.org/show_metadata.jsp?pid=fmo:4961.

Betts, A., 2008: *International Cooperation in the Global Refugee Regime*. Oxford: University of Oxford, Department of Politics and International Relation; at: http://www.globaleconomicgovernance.org/wpcontent/uploads/Betts%20WP%20International%20Cooperation%20in%20the%.

Betts, A., 2006: "Comprehensive Plans of Action: Insights from CIREFCA and the Indochinese CPA". *New Issues in Refugee Research, Working Paper No. 120* (Geneva: UNHCR).

Bowles, E., 1997: *Assistance, Protection and Policy in Refugee Camps on the Thailand–Burma Border: An Overview*. Oxford: Oxford University, Refugee Studies Centre; at: http://repository.forcedmigration.org/show_metadata.jsp?pid=fmo:1760.

Brees, I., 2008: "Refugee Business: Strategies of Work on the Thai–Burma Border". *Journal of Refugee Studies*, 21,3: 380–397

Calabia, D., 2007: "Burmese Refugees: End the Exploitation of Burmese in Thailand". *Refugee International Bulletin* 1–2.

CCSDPT (n.d.). *About Us;* at: http://www.ccsdisplaced personst.org/aboutus.htm.

P. Vungsiriphisal et al. (eds.), *Humanitarian Assistance for Displaced Persons from Myanmar*, SpringerBriefs in Environment, Security, Development and Peace 17, DOI: 10.1007/978-3-319-02795-1,

CCSDPT 2007: *CCSDPT Planning for the Future: The Impact of Resettlement on the Remaining Camp Population* (Bangkok: CCSDPT).

CIDA 2010: *Canada Renews Support for Burmese Refugees and Displaced People 2010*; at: http://www.acdi-cida.gc.ca/acdi-cida/ACDI-CIDA.nsf/eng/FRA-3694947-KE7.

Demusz, K., 1998: "From Relief to Development: Negotiating the Continuum on the Thai-Burmese". *Journal of Refugee Studies*, 11,3: 231–244.

ECHO (n.d.). http://en.wikipedia.org/wiki/ECHO_(European_Commission

European Commission 2007: *Regional Programming for Asia: Strategy Document 2007–2013*; at: http://www.eeas.europa.eu/asia/rsp/07_13_en.pdf.

European Commission (n.d.): *European Commission Assistance Regarding Uprooted People*; at: http://ec.europa.eu/europeaid/where/asia/regional-cooperation/refugees-uprooted-people/refugees-and-uprooted-people_en.htm.

European Commission 2009: *Annual Reports on Humanitarian Aid 2009*. Brussels: European Commission; at: http://ec.europa.eu/echo/media/publications/annual_reports_en.htm.

European Commission (n.d.): *Humanitarian Aid & Civil Protection: ECHO's Finances; at:* http://ec.europa.eu/echo/funding/finances_en.htm.

European Commission (n.d.): *Linking Relief, Rehabilitation and Development—An Assessment*; at: http://europa.eu/legislation_summaries/humanitarian_aid/r10002_en.htm.

European Union (n.d.): *The History of the EU Formation*; at: http://www.minbuza.nl/en/KeyTopics/EuropeanUnion/The_History_of_the_EU.

"Executive Committee of the High Commissioner's Programme", in: *Regional update: Asia and the Pacific, 30 September 2010: Update on UNHCR's operations in Asia and the Pacific2010*; at: http://www.reliefweb.int/rw/RWFiles2010.nsf/FilesByRWDocUnidFilename/SNAA-89W8DE-full_report.pdf/$File/full_report.pdf.

Gorman, R.F., 1986: Beyond ICARA II: Implementing Refugee-Related Development Assistance. *International Migration Review*, 20,2: 283–298.

Hammerstad, A., 2005: *Making or Breaking the Conflict Cycle: The Relationship between Underdevelopment, Conflict and Forced Migration. Developing DFID's Policy Approach to Refugees and Internally Displaced Persons* (Oxford: Refugee Studies Centre).

IOM 2008: *Situation Report on International Migration in East and South-East Asia* (Bangkok: IOM).

IRC (n.d.). *OPE Thailand: Tham Him Camp; Camp Profile*; at: http://www.churchworldservice.org/PDFs/refugees/Burmesefs.pdf

IRC 2005: *Assessment of the Labour Market and Labour Activities in the Ban Kwai/Ban Tractor Refugee Camp and the Surrounding Environs* (Bangkok: IRC).

IRC/Jesuit Refugee Service 2005: *Nowhere to Turn: A Report on Conditions of Burmese Asylum Seekers in Thailand*; at: http://www.jrs.net/news_detail?TN=NEWS-20100603111409.

Jacobsen, K., 2002: "Can Refugees Benefit the State? Refugee Resources and African State building". *Journal of Modern African Studies*, 4,40: 577–596.

Kate, M., 2005: The Provision of Protection to Asylum-Seekers in Destination Countries. *Working Paper No 114* (Geneva: UNHCR).

Keely, C. B., 2005: *The State of the International Forced Migration Regime: Developing DFID's Policy Approach to Refugees and Internally Displaced Persons* (Oxford: Refugee Studies Centre).

Khin, Y., 2002: Assessing Adolescent Reproductive Health in the Karenni Refugee Community, Mae Hong Son, Thailand. *Master Thesis on Public Health.* Rollins School of Public Health (Atlanta: Emory University).

Lee, Chen Chen; Glaister, I., 2005: *Burmese Asylum Seekers in Thailand: Still Nowhere to Turn;* at: http://www.fmreview.org/FMRpdfs/FMR30/33-34.pdf.

Loescher, G. et al, 2007: "Protracted Refugee Situation and the Regional Dynamics of Peacebuilding". *Conflict, Security and Development*, 7,3: 491–501.

Long, C. (n.d): *Keys to Effective PVO/NGO Collaboration*; at: http://www.usaid.gov/our_work/cross-cutting_programmes/private_voluntary_cooperation/pvoconf_sum_pvocollaboration.pdf.

Macrae, J., 2002: The Changing Role of Official Donors in Humanitarian Action: a review of Trends and Issues. *HPG Briefing Paper;* at: http://www.odi.org.uk/resources/downdload/279.pdfa.

Minear, L., 1994: Development within conflict: The Challenge of Man-Made Disasters. *Background Paper for the Paris Colloquium 30 May–1 June 1994;* at: http://repository.orcedmigration.org/show_metadata.jsp?pid=fmo:1226.

Ministry of Public Health 2008: *Guideline for Disease Surveillance in Displaced Persons Camps, Thai-Myanmar Border Thailand, 2008* (Bangkok: Hang copy).

MOI 1954: *Document 1678/2497, issued on 8 April* (Bangkok: Ministry of Interior).

Napaumporn, B., 2008: *Monitoring the Implementation of Human Rights with International Mechanisms in Thailand: Human Rights Situations in Lessons Learned on Human Rights and Statelessness*; at: http://gotoknow.org/blog/bongkot-humanrights-and-statelessness-eng/259676.

National Security Council 2011: *Policy A.D, 2007–2011*. http://www.nsc.go.th/files/attach_doc/strategy_doc/PolicySecurity50.pdf.

Refugee Studies Programme 1997: *Assistance, Protection, and Policy in Refugee Camps on the Thailand-Burma Border: An Overview* (Oxford: Oxford University).

Rowley, E. A.; Burnham, G. M.; Drabe, R. M., 2006: "Protracted Refugee Situation: Parallel Health System and Planning for the Integration of Services". *Journal of Refugee Studies*, 19,2: 158–186. http://jrs.oxfordjournals.org/content/19/2/158.full.

Schultz, C. M., 1994: "Promoting Economic Self-Reliance: A Case Study of Afghan Refugee Women in Pakistan". *Journal of International Affairs*, 42,2; at: http://www.questia.com/googleScholar.qst?docId=5000189518.

Senate Committee on Foreign Affairs 2004: *Study on Ethnic Groups and Thai–Burma Border Security Issues* (Bangkok: Secretariat of the Senate).

Srithmrongswat, S.; Wisessang, R.; Rtjaroenkhajorn, S., 2009: *Financing Healthcare for Migrants: A Case Study from Thailand* (Bangkok: IOM/ WHO).

TBBC 2010: *Burmese Border Displaced Person*. http://www.tbbc.org/camps/2010-11-nov-map-tbbc-unhcr.pdf.

TBBC (n.d.): *Bamboo Planting Ceremony Near ThamHin*; at: http://www.tbbc.org/announcements/2010-09-24-news- bamboo-planting.htm

TBBC (n.d.): *Ban Mai Nai Soi ;* at: http://www.tbbc.org/camps/skb.htm#th.

TBBC (n.d.): *Camp Management. Authorities and Organisations*; at: http://www.tbbc.org/camps/management.htm.

TBBC (n.d.): *ThamHin: Thailand Burma Border Consortium*; at: http://www.tbbc.org/camps/skb.htm#th.

TBBC (n.d.): *Mae La: Thailand Burma Border Consortium*; at: http://www.tbbc.org/camps/skb.htm#th.

Thailand Development Research Institute 2006: *Thailand Economic Information Kit*. (Bangkok: TDRI).

UNDP 2010: *4R Approach: Repatriation, Reintegration, Rehabilitation, and Reconstruction*; at: http://www.undisplacedpersons.org/cpr/we_do/4r_approach.shtml.

UNHCR 1996: *Handbook on Voluntary Repatriation: International Protection* (Geneva: UNHCR); at: http://www.unhcr.org/publ/PUBL/3bfe68d32.pdf.

UNHCR 2000: *The State of the World's Refugees 2000: Fifty years of humanitarian action; at:* http://www.unhcr.org/4a4c754a9.html.

UNHCR 2007: *Enlargement of the Executive Committee of the Programme of the UNHCR*. General Assembly, United Nations *A/RES/61/136*; at: http://www.iom.int/jahia/webdav/shared/shared/mainsite/policy_and_research/un/61/A_RES_61_136_EN.pdf.

UNHCR 2010: *Executive Committee of the High Commissioner's Programme. Sixty-first Session, Geneva, 4–8 October 2010. Update on UNHCR's Operations in Asia and the Pacific—2010.* http://www.reliefweb.int/rw/rwb.nsf/db900sid/SNAA-89W8DE?OpenDocument/

UNHCR (n.d.): *Thailand. 2011 UNHCR Country Operations Profile—Thailand; Constraint; at:* http://www.unhcr.org/cgi- bin/texis/vtx/page?page=49e489646.

UNHCR (n.d.): *The Needs: 2011 UNHCR Country Operations Profile—Thailand: Working Environment; at:* http://www.unhcr.org/cgi-bin/texis/vtx/page?page=49e 489646.

UNICEF Thailand (n.d.): *Thailand Country Profile; at:* http://www.unicef.org/thailand/overview_2040.html.

United Nations 2007: Enlargement of the Executive Committee of the Programme of the United Nations High commissioner for Refugees, 61/136: Resolution adopted by the General Assembly. *Sixty-first Session Agenda Item 41, 81st Plenary Meeting, 19 December 2006; at:* http://www.iom.int/jahia/webdav/shared/shared/mainsite/policy_and_research/un/61/A_RES_61_136_EN.pdf.

US Department of State, Bureau of Population, Refugees and Migration (n.d.). *Funding*; at: http://www.state.gov/g/prm/c27111.htm.

US Department of State, Bureau of Population, Refugees and Migration (n.d.).What is the Bureau's role in the Department of State? at: http://www.state.gov/g/prm/c25756.htm.

Werker, E., 2007: "Refugee Camp Economies", *Journal of Refugee Studies*, 20,3: 461–480. http://jrs.oxfordjournals.org/content/20/3/461.short.

WHO/IOM, 2010: *Health of Migrants: The Way Forward: Report of a Global Consultation, Madrid, Spain, 3–5 March 2010* (Geneva: WHO).

Chulalongkorn University

Chulalongkorn University, Thailand's first institution of higher education, officially came into being in March 1917. The groundwork and preparation for it in terms of planning and development, however, took place more than a century ago. The worldwide economic, social and political changes in the late nineteenth century contributed to Siam's decision to adapt herself in order to avoid conflict with the Western powers ("Siam" became "Thailand" in the year 1939). Thus the royal policy of King Chulalongkorn (Rama V) was to strengthen and improve government so that the country could successfully resist the tide of colonialism. One of the major parts of the policy, which would later prove to be deep-rooted and highly effective, was to improve the Siamese educational system so as to produce capable personnel to work in both the public and private sectors. As a result, a school was founded in 1871 at the Royal Pages' Barracks within the Grand Palace compound.

The development of Chulalongkorn University continued. From 1934 to 1958, the university emphasised the improvement of undergraduate education, and more faculties were established. In 1961, the university set up the Graduate School to be responsible for graduate-level education. From 1962 till the present, the university has focused on graduate education and has set up research centres and institutes. The University, known familiarly as 'Chula', has grown constantly in the near-century since its founding.

P. Vungsiriphisal et al. (eds.), *Humanitarian Assistance for Displaced Persons from Myanmar*, SpringerBriefs in Environment, Security, Development and Peace 17, DOI: 10.1007/978-3-319-02795-1, © The Author(s) 2014

At present Chulalongkorn University is composed of 19 faculties, 23 colleges and 17 research institutes. Currently, there are over 38,000 students including 24,951 undergraduates, 13,391 postgraduates (10,881 on the Master's Degree and 2,150 on the Doctoral Degree programmes) and 2,800 faculty members. Its 87 international programmes have enjoyed a long and deserved high reputation for all-round academic attainment.

According to many Asian university rankings, Chulalongkorn University is Thailand's highest-ranked institution, with the highest scores in many subjects including Arts and Humanities, Social Sciences and Management, Natural Sciences, Engineering and Technology and Life Sciences and Medicine.

Chulalongkorn University's Strategy 2012–2016 has been undertaken to formulate guidelines for the university's development plan. The initiative focuses on different aspects of development and improvement with the objective of raising the university to a level of excellence that will qualify it as a "*World Class National University*" and as the "*Pillar of the Kingdom*".

The Institute of Asian Studies

INSTITUTE OF ASIAN STUDIES
CHULALONGKORN UNIVERSITY

The Institute of Asian Studies (IAS) is an interdisciplinary research, teaching and service organisation. IAS was established in 1967 as a unit within the Faculty of Political Science at Chulalongkorn University. After a considerable expansion of activities at IAS in 1979, an upgrade in the Institute's status was determined to be necessary. Consequently, on 10 May 1985, IAS was officially recognised as a separate institute at Chulalongkorn University, granting IAS a status equivalent to that of a faculty at the university.

Today, the strategic vision for IAS is to continue to serve the Thai community and the Asian region as a source of knowledge and expertise for a broad range of subject areas in the region including economic, social, political and security concerns. This has been accomplished through the diligence and cooperation of a team of highly qualified researchers who possess specialised knowledge about each country and subregion within Asia.

P. Vungsiriphisal et al. (eds.), *Humanitarian Assistance for Displaced Persons from Myanmar*, SpringerBriefs in Environment, Security, Development and Peace 17, DOI: 10.1007/978-3-319-02795-1, © The Author(s) 2014

Asian Research Center for Migration

The Asian Research Center for Migration, based at the IAS of Chulalongkorn University, is an internationally recognised centre of excellence in social science research. Located on the historic campus of Chulalongkorn University in the heart of Bangkok, ARCM is an important contributor to the research output of Thailand's oldest and most respected institution of higher learning, conducting critical policy-relevant research on international migration into, out of and within the South-East Asian Region.

History

ARCM was initially founded in 1987 as the Indochinese Refugee Information Center. The Center was established with the mission of conducting research on the flows of refugees from Cambodia, Laos, Vietnam and other South-East Asian countries seeking asylum in Thailand. After the Indochinese refugee crisis had abated in Thailand and the refugee camps were closed under the Comprehensive Plan of Action, the Center began to conduct research on new refugee situations that had begun to emerge in South-East Asia.

P. Vungsiriphisal et al. (eds.), *Humanitarian Assistance for Displaced Persons from Myanmar*, SpringerBriefs in Environment, Security, Development and Peace 17,
DOI: 10.1007/978-3-319-02795-1, © The Author(s) 2014

In recognition of this newly broadened research focus, the Center was reconstituted as the Asian Research Center for Migration in 1995. Since that time, the thematic areas of ARCM's research have expanded significantly and now include projects on all forms of international migration in South-East Asia with a particular emphasis on Thailand as a sending, receiving and transit country.

Research Activities

Through published research, statistical data, consultation and policy recommendations related to cross-border migration in the South-East Asia Region, the objective of ARCM's research activity is to support evidenced-based decision-making by governments, international agencies and private sector organisations on migration-related issues. These activities are conducted by a multidisciplinary team of committed researchers, including both Thai and international experts, with backgrounds in a diverse range of academic fields relevant to migration such as sociology, anthropology, political science, economics and law.

About the Editors

Premjai Vungsiriphisal (Thailand) is a senior researcher at the Asian Research Center for Migration (ARCM), IAS, Chulalongkorn University. She completed her MA in Public Health Culture Studies at Mahidol University. Her Ph.D. on Educational Policy Alternatives for Children of Migrant workers in Thailand within the ASEAN Context is being undertaken at the Faculty of Education, Chulalongkorn University. Her research covers various aspects of migrant issues. Her past research includes work on Migrant children in difficult circumstances in Thailand, Cross-border Migration and HIV Vulnerability on the Thai–Myanmar Border, Children Caught in Conflict: Case study of refugee children along the Thai–Myanmar Border, Assessing the situation of the worst forms of child labour in Samutsakorn, Cultural aspects of the Thailand–Cambodia relationship: Case Study in Surin Province, Contemporary art and cultural diversity in Thailand, Research and development of education modules for migrant children in the border area, Migration and Deception of Migrant Workers in Thailand and Sustainable Solutions to Displaced Persons along the Thai–Myanmar Border: Analysis of RTG Policy. During 2006–2008, she initiated and coordinated a series of Think-Tank Forums on Education for Migrant and Refugee Children, with participants from various Government offices and Non-Governmental Organizations (NGOs). She was granted a Mellow Fund Fellowship to be a visitor at the Refugee Studies Centre, Oxford University, UK during August–September 2007 and EU-Asia Link funding for a staff exchange with the Institute of Social Studies, The Hague, Netherlands, during August–October 2009. Recently, she was a Visiting Research Scholar at the Graduate School at the African and Asia Areas Study, Kyoto University, during August–October 2011.

Address: Ms. Premjai Vungsiriphisal, Asian Research Centre for Migration, IAS, Chulalongkorn University Phayathai road, Bangkok 10330, Thailand.

Email: premjai.v@gmail.com
Website: http://www.arcmthailand.com/

P. Vungsiriphisal et al. (eds.), *Humanitarian Assistance for Displaced Persons from Myanmar*, SpringerBriefs in Environment, Security, Development and Peace 17, DOI: 10.1007/978-3-319-02795-1, © The Author(s) 2014

Dares Chusri (Thailand) received a Ph.D. in Public Health from the College of Public Health Sciences, Chulalongkorn University, Bangkok. She has long experience in working for displaced persons (both migrants and refugees) in humanitarian work and development assistance programmes since 1980. She served with CARE International and the International Committee of the Red Cross (ICRC) for the Cambodian refugee camp at Site 8 and Khao-I-Dang, Aranyaprathet from late 1988 until the refugees were repatriated in 1993. While pursuing her studies, she has carried out a remarkable amount of consultancy, to conduct a large health project using qualitative evaluation techniques and tools and community-based approaches to work with marginalised and coastal community groups in southern Thailand with many organisations including IFRC, IOM and ECT—for whom she conducted research on HIV-AIDS awareness and responses among migrant workers and the Human Rights Center at UC-Berkeley, for whom she co-authored a publication in 2005. As a Country Director of USCRI Thailand, her efforts to advocate for refugees' right to work have reached the Thai Parliament and public. She is also affiliated to ARCM as a consultant conducting surveys and qualitative study related to Myanmar refugees in Thailand for UNDP and UNFPA. Currently, she is an independent researcher specialising in project evaluation, qualitative research, HIV/AIDS, TB, migrant workers and refugees, networking and policy advocacy.

Address: Dr. Dares Chusri, Asian Research Centre for Migration, IAS, Chulalongkorn University Phayathai road, Bangkok 10330, Thailand.

Email: dares_c@hotmail.com
Website: http://www.arcmthailand.com/

Supang Chantavanich (Thailand) is a professor emeritus at the Faculty of Political Science, Chulalongkorn University. She is also the Director of the Asian Research Center for Migration (ARCM) within the IAS at Chula. During 2010–2011, she cooperated with UNDP to lead the research project *"Sustainable Solutions to the Displaced Person Situation on the Thai–Myanmar Border"* with EU funding. The project covered six studies of situational and policy analyses of displaced persons along the western borders in Thailand. The studies are finally revised into *Springer Briefs in Environment, Security, Development and Peace* (*ESDP*), Volumes 15–18.

After she graduated in Sociology from the University of Grenoble, France, Supang Chantavanich focused her teaching and research areas on South-East Asian society and culture, sociological theories, qualitative research, migration and development, the overseas Chinese, education and healthcare of migrant people and labour migration and forced migration including refugee and human trafficking. Recently, she led a research team at ARCM which conducted a study of migrant fishermen from Myanmar and Cambodia in Thailand with the International Labour Organization. Another regional study on "Politics, Governance, Experience and Response to Flooding from the Locals' and Migrants' Perspective in ASEAN" is currently being conducted with researchers from eight ASEAN countries. The study addresses human security and conflicts among people affected by floods in the region.

Address: Prof. Supang Chantavanich, Asian Research Centre for Migration, IAS, Chulalongkorn University, Phayathai road, Bangkok 10330, Thailand.

Email: supang.c@chula.ac.th
Website: http://arcmthailand.com

About the Other Authors

Address: Graham Bennett, Independent Consultant, 137 Barclay Road, London E17 9JL, UK.
Email: grahambennett777@hotmail.co.uk.

Address: Waranya Jitpong, Asian Research Centre for Migration, IAS, Chulalongkorn University, Phayathai Road, Bangkok 10330, Thailand.
Email: wec135@hotmail.com.

Address: Chanarat Poomkacha, Asian Research Centre for Migration, IAS, Chulalongkorn University, Phayathai Road, Bangkok 10330, Thailand.
Email: cpoomkacha@abeam.com.

Address: Kamonwan Roengsumran, Asian Research Centre for Migration, IAS, Chulalongkorn University, Phayathai Road, Bangkok 10330, Thailand.
Email: kamonwan24@yahoo.com.

Address: Tarna Rubin
Email: tarina.rubin@gmail.com.

Address: Esmeralda Silva, Department of Health Policy and Administration, College of Public Health, University of the Philippines Manila, 625 Pedro Gil Street, Ermita, Manila, Philippines.

P. Vungsiriphisal et al. (eds.), *Humanitarian Assistance for Displaced Persons from Myanmar*, SpringerBriefs in Environment, Security, Development and Peace 17,
DOI: 10.1007/978-3-319-02795-1,

About this Book

This study of the RTG and donors' polices towards humanitarian assistance for refugees from Myanmar examines the protracted refugee situation at the Thai–Myanmar border which has persisted for more than 25 years. RTG policy has not been proactive and it remains ambivalent towards the situation. Displaced persons are kept in closed settlements, and this has limited their self-reliance. However, a resettlement programme has finally been implemented and a significant number of refugees have been accepted in resettlement countries. On the other hand, repatriation is not recommended as a possible durable solution at the moment unless Myanmar becomes a safe place for return.

With regard to donors, international organisations and NGOs, their funding and intervention policies vary. Donors prefer to switch humanitarian assistance to development aid. Most NGO programmes are increasingly focused on development.

This book provides realistic policy recommendations for a durable solution for refugees at the borders. Practitioners and policymakers from governments, international organisations and NGOs will benefit from the findings and recommendations proposed. The volume is also helpful for those who study forced migration and its denouement in the globalised age.

P. Vungsiriphisal et al. (eds.), *Humanitarian Assistance for Displaced Persons from Myanmar*, SpringerBriefs in Environment, Security, Development and Peace 17, DOI: 10.1007/978-3-319-02795-1, © The Author(s) 2014

MIX
Papier aus verantwortungsvollen Quellen
Paper from responsible sources
FSC® C105338

If you have any concerns about our products,
you can contact us on
ProductSafety@springernature.com

In case Publisher is established outside the EU,
the EU authorized representative is:
Springer Nature Customer Service Center GmbH
Europaplatz 3, 69115 Heidelberg, Germany

Printed by Libri Plureos GmbH
in Hamburg, Germany